## Praise for *Real Food / Fake Food*

A *New York Times* Bestseller

A *Washington Post* Bestseller

A *National Post* Bestseller

A Finalist, Goodreads Best Books of 2016

A *People* "The Best New Books" of 2016 Selection

"Olmsted's research is impressive, and he lets no stone go unturned. He lets the terrifying facts speak for themselves, adding just a little humor . . . With the guiding hand of a good friend and prose that keeps the reader's eye moving, Olmsted insists that readers 'shop better and cook more.'"
—*Publishers Weekly*, starred review

"Equal parts foodie chronicle and investigative exposé . . . *Real Food / Fake Food* is less treatise than guidebook, showing readers how to navigate an increasingly complex food system."
—*Outside* magazine

"Required reading for cooks who genuinely care about quality and health . . . A fascinating read that sheds light on our underregulated food industry. The book also serves as a handy guide to what items consumers should avoid, and how to find and identify the real deal."
—CookingLight.com

"Eye-opening. Olmsted's well-researched exposé reveals how often what we eat isn't what it seems. (Parmesan cheese made of wood pulp or fake lobster rolls, anyone?)"
—*People* magazine

"A striking look at the food industry. It's unnerving that so many people don't know what authentic olive oil or port wine tastes like because they've been undersold on some offshoot knockoff and no one is raising a flag—until now."

—Ming Tsai, author, chef, and host of PBS's *Simply Ming*

"Larry Olmsted makes you insanely hungry and steaming mad in this provocative account of how fraud threatens not just the world's great craft foods (think caviar, Kobe beef, and Parmigiano-Reggiano) but our everyday diet. A must-read for anyone who cares deeply about the safety of our food and the welfare of our planet."

—Steven Raichlen, author of the *Barbecue! Bible* cookbook series and host of *Project Smoke* and *Primal Grill* on PBS

"The book delivers on its main promise with no shortage of jaw-dropping accounts of international food makers seemingly going out of their way to mislead people. Olmsted also offers interesting anecdotes about the history of various foods, traveling, for instance, to Parma, Italy, where real Parmesan is made."

—PhillyVoice.com

"A page-turner, a meticulously researched, readable work full of appalling facts that beg to be read aloud to the person next to you, if only so you can share your disbelief."     —*Winnipeg Free Press*

"Do not take another bite or swallow another sip of anything, for your sake and the sake of your children, before reading *Real Food / Fake Food*. It is the health equivalent of Ralph Nader's exposé *Unsafe at Any Speed*. The content blows the doors off the kitchens."

—Michael Patrick Shiels, radio host and author of *Invite Yourself to the Party*

"Larry Olmsted's meticulously researched tour de force is chilling for what he uncovers about the food industry. At the same time his love of great food and his skill in writing about it make me want to try every one of the real foods he recommends. A must-read for anyone with an interest in, well, eating."

—Dan Dunn, author of *American Wino:*
*A Tale of Reds, Whites, and One Man's Blues*

"The world is full of delicious, lovingly crafted foods that embody the terrain, weather, and culture of their origins. Unfortunately, it's also full of brazen impostors that are hard to identify. In this entertaining and important book, Larry Olmsted helps us fall in love with the real stuff and steer clear of the fraudsters. I'll never look at a menu the same way again."

—Kirk Kardashian, author of *Milk Money:*
*Cash, Cows, and the Death of the American Dairy Farm*

"In his solidly researched new book, *USA Today* food and travel columnist Olmsted, a well-traveled and knowledgeable food writer, takes readers on an enlightening but frequently disturbing culinary journey. While providing fascinating insights into where and how some of the most delicious food products are produced, the author also reveals how often these are imitated to detrimental effect . . . A provocative yet grounded look at the U.S. food industry."  —*Kirkus Reviews*

"This is an important book to help all buyers shop prudently and with a wary eye toward the claims of food producers. Recommended for all consumers along with policymakers, those interested in food science, and marketing professionals."

—*Library Journal*

"Olmsted gives us the lay of this seedy landscape with momentum and aplomb. He demystifies the process by which fake ingredients end up in your shopping cart, explains why some of these deceitful foods could be a real threat to your health, and sheds a light on the government policies and shortsighted commercialism that landed them there." —*Mother Jones*

# REAL FOOD/FAKE FOOD

Algonquin Books

Eat Real!

Also by Larry Olmsted

*Getting into Guinness:*
*One Man's Longest, Fastest, Highest Journey inside*
*the World's Most Famous Record Book*

# REAL FOOD

## FAKE FOOD

### Why You Don't Know
### What You're Eating &
### What You Can Do About It

## Larry Olmsted

ALGONQUIN BOOKS OF CHAPEL HILL
2017

Published by
Algonquin Books of Chapel Hill
Post Office Box 2225
Chapel Hill, North Carolina 27515-2225

a division of
Workman Publishing
225 Varick Street
New York, New York 10014

Cartoon on page xviii courtesy of Harry Bliss / The New Yorker /
The Cartoon Bank. "Steven Raichlen's Best-Ever Spanish Steak Recipe,"
from *Planet Barbecue* (Workman Publishing), used by
permission of author.

Library of Congress Cataloging-in-Publication Data
Names: Olmsted, Larry, author.
Title: Real food/fake food : why you don't know what you're
eating & what you can do about it / Larry Olmsted.
Description: First edition. | Chapel Hill, North Carolina :
Algonquin Books of Chapel Hill, 2016. | "Published simultaneously
in Canada by Thomas Allen & Son Limited."
Identifiers: LCCN 2016018797 | ISBN 9781616204211 (HC)
Subjects: LCSH: Food—Quality—Popular works. | Artificial
foods—Popular works. | Food substitutes—Popular works. | Food
additives—Popular works. | Nutrition.—Popular works. | Fraud—
Popular works. | Consumer education—Popular works.
Classification: LCC TX533 .O46 2016 | DDC 641.3—dc23
LC record available at https://lccn.loc.gov/2016018797

ISBN 978-1-61620-741-0 (PB)

10 9 8 7 6 5 4 3 2 1
First Paperback Edition

*For Allison, who believed; for Alice Fixx, whose love for Parma opened my eyes to Real Food and set me on this course; for Nicholas James Peter Kau, taken before his time; and for Sundance, whose passion for Real Food—especially grass-finished, pasture-raised beef—was unrivaled.*

There's nothing more fundamental
than knowing what you are putting in your mouth.

—KELSEY TIMMERMAN, *Where Am I Eating?*

# CONTENTS

# INTRODUCTION

Food fraud, or the act of defrauding buyers of food or ingredients for economic gain . . . has vexed the food industry throughout history.

> —RENÉE JOHNSON, "Food Fraud and 'Economically
> Motivated Adulteration' of Food and Food Ingredients"

I love food.

My friends tell me I have the best job in the world, and it's hard to argue. As a journalist focused on travel and food, I've spent the last twenty-plus years visiting great hotels in some of the nicest parts of the world and eating really well. When I'm not eating out, I'm cooking at home. I have a garden, I carry back exotic ingredients from all corners of the globe, and I've traveled thousands of miles to eat at particular restaurants or taste hard to find local specialties. My work has taken me to roadside barbecue stands and clam shacks, to Michelin-starred restaurants and top celebrity chefs. It's taken me inside the James Beard house, to food laboratories and processing plants, to farms and artisanal cheese dairies. I've seen how some of the finest delicacies and specialty foods in the world are made, I've seen food infused with passion, and I've tasted dishes so good they haunt my memory. But among all these bright spots, food hides a darker side.

I've visited Japan several times in the past two decades, and while physically small, Japan packs a big culinary punch—it is one of the world's great food countries. Visitors are often surprised to learn that Japanese culture has a rich tradition of fake food, but happily it's a tradition designed to help consumers. Many restaurants in Japan display an array of replica dishes in their window so you can see what they serve, even if you can't understand the menu, and in a pinch you can always point. These replicas are works of art, elaborate and realistic despite being made of plastic. Just as New York has a garment district and jewelry district, there is an entire neighborhood in Tokyo known for its fake-food shops, where restaurant owners come to buy models. Tourists visit as well, seeking souvenirs, such as a tray of delicious-looking *nigiri* sushi that can adorn a counter at home and never go bad, or a bowl of ramen noodles topped with chopped green onions; egg; and a tempura shrimp, complete with tail. Utterly fake, the stuff is meant to be inedible.

Like Japan, the United States also has a rich tradition of faking food, but it is not quaint, helpful, or harmless. Our supermarkets and our homes are full of Fake Foods that we actually eat. At their least malicious, these are rip-offs, defrauding us economically, depriving us of quality, and literally leaving a bad taste in our mouths. At their worst, they make us sick and may even kill us. Along the way, they put farmers and food craftsmen around the globe out of work, destroy the environment, and even promote slave labor. Some of these fakeries are outright criminal, some merely immoral, and many not only legal but supported by our government. Ironically, these foods often prey most heavily on consumers who are actively trying to eat better and healthier, as well as those with more rarefied tastes. Many fakes are found in the specialty foods sector, which for the first time in 2014 topped one hundred billion dollars in the United States. This category is rife with scams, including many foods viewed as healthier choices, as well as fancy cheeses, meats, oils, and other "gourmet" items.

Whether or not you care about your health, economic justice, or the environment, if you simply care how your food tastes, this issue matters. When you've eaten something that lingers in your memory and leaves you craving more, when you've had one of those sublime meals where you lick your lips and exclaim, "Yum!," you've probably just tasted Real Food. And whenever there is a delicious Real Food, there is good chance someone is making a fake version.

When I say fake, I mean fake, as in not what you think you are buying or eating. There are a lot of problems with how food is produced in this country, and if you want to be terrified by the horrors of industrial poultry production or find out why your drive-thru meal contains so many ingredients you've never heard of, put this book down and read *Omnivore's Dilemma, Food, Inc.*, or *Fast Food Nation.* I'm talking about a massive industry of bait and switch, where you get something other than promised. I don't like industrially produced supermarket beef, but it is in fact beef, and it lives up to that billing. But when the same drug-laden, artificially fed beef is passed off as "natural," "grass fed," or "pure," then it becomes fake—it is no longer what it claims to be. Fake Foods are usually of low quality. But they are not fake because they are of low quality; they are of low quality because they are fake. The perfect example is Maine lobster, a Real Food that is delicious, coveted, and labor intensive to shell, as anyone who has eaten whole lobster knows. That's why in New England, the popular lobster roll, basically a heaping mound of lobster meat on a bun, is one of the most expensive sandwiches you can find on a menu. So how can fast-food chains sell lobster rolls for half the price or less? Simple—their lobster rolls don't contain actual lobster. And it's legal. Welcome to Fake Food.

Japan's restaurants may display fake food in windows, but inside there is plenty of Real Food to eat. On one trip years ago, I had the pleasure of tasting Kobe beef, which is perhaps the single most famous food Japan produces, one that has taken on mythical proportions. So I was perplexed when I returned to the States and found the Kobe beef on this side of the Pacific so dramatically different, lacking in both marbling and flavor, nothing like what I tasted in Japan. I decided to look into this and figure out why. It did not take me long to discover that for years the U.S. Department of Agriculture (USDA) had banned the import of all Japanese beef, without exception.

The bottom line? All of the Kobe beef sold in this country, by chefs famous and anonymous, in ten-dollar sliders or three-hundred-dollar steaks, was fake, all of it, end of story. Every single restaurant and store purporting to sell Kobe beef—or any Japanese beef—was lying, including some of the country's best-known chefs.

When I wrote about this for my online *Forbes* column, it became the most widely read of hundreds of such columns, surpassing one million readers, and several years later it still gets thousands of new reads each month. I was amazed by the interest and furious passion I aroused—on both sides of the issue. Many readers wrote in because they were outraged, justifiably, at having paid hundreds of dollars for a single steak, only to be ripped off. Others took a more xenophobic view, bashing Japan and defending the false advertising by insisting that we had no need to kowtow to other country's trademarks, and this being America, we should just do damn well as we please. Others, somewhat irrelevantly, wrote in to praise the quality of domestic beef. For me, the striking point was that almost none of the respondents had actually tasted Kobe beef.

As a matter of policy, the U.S. Food and Drug Administration (FDA) does not police most food fraud, and it hardly matters because most Kobe scams occur at restaurants, which are largely exempted from labeling laws. So they almost always get away with it.

In light of all this, I began to wonder, if Kobe's good name is so blatantly misused to defraud the public on a nationwide scale, and there are no repercussions for doing so, how many of our other foods are fake? The unfortunate answer is a lot, and these foods are often much scarier.

The seafood industry is far worse than beef, so rife with fakery, both legal and illegal, that it boggles the mind. Suffice it to say, if you think you are buying or eating red snapper—ever—you might want to think again. Several recent studies put the chances of your getting the white tuna you ordered in the typical New York sushi restaurant at zero—as in *never*. Wild-caught salmon? Wild-caught anything? Maybe not.

Every supermarket and gourmet store in the country has a cheese counter, and every one of them is chock-full of fakes. So is the wine department. And the oil aisle. It's easy to take a "so what?" attitude when you order one kind of fish and get another, until you consider that the fake is likely pumped full of drugs and antibiotics—sometimes banned and illegal—none of which would have been in the fish you actually ordered. Not all Fake Foods are harmless, and many are disgusting. If you cook, you probably have a bottle of olive oil in your cupboard. Real extra-virgin olive oil is just about the healthiest fat on the market, and studies have repeatedly shown this is the main reason Americans buy so much of it. Yet most bottles sold in this country are fake. The impostors have often been stripped of health benefits—and some might not even be made from olives. This is one of the most pervasive Fake Foods in America, reaching deep into home kitchens, restaurants, and supermarkets, and not unfamiliar to the government agencies supposedly watching over our food supply.

The Grocery Manufacturers of America estimated that about 10 percent of all commercially available food in our country is subjected to some sort of adulteration. Unless you are leaving the supermarket via the "8 Items or Less" express lane, something in your cart is likely fake. Commonly sold fake foodstuffs are not limited to exotic items like Kobe beef; they include everyday staples such as coffee, orange juice, apple juice, wine, rice, cheese, honey—and, of course, seafood.

The Centers for Disease Control and Prevention (CDC) estimates that about forty-eight million Americans suffer from some sort of food-related illness each year, and only about a fifth can be causally identified. That leaves more than thirty-eight million Americans each year sickened in unknown ways by what they ate. One of the world's leading experts believes that "food fraud probably accounts for quite a substantial proportion of that." If you've ever gotten sick after eating sushi and blamed "bad fish," you might have been only half right: it was the fish but probably not because it was spoiled. In many cases, the fake substituted for what you order is a fish that is always "bad," an inherently toxic species banned in other countries. This practice is so common it is the new normal.

As I expanded my investigation into Fake Food, I became increasingly angry. I had expected piracy, because crime thrives on profit, and if there is a buck to be made counterfeiting any valuable consumer good, someone will do it. But I wasn't prepared for the scale, with organized crime rings and infrastructure similar to large-scale drug-smuggling operations. More disturbing is our government's participation and complicity in Fake Food. At the low end of the damage curve, officials who have higher priorities or limited budgets simply look the other way and ignore what they know is widespread and often dangerous fraud. In several industries, government regulations, such as labeling laws allowing winemakers to produce domestic "Champagne," actively encourage producers to counterfeit valuable products and mislead American consumers. As I learned all this, it was hard sometimes to not just throw my hands up in bewilderment at a food world where Walmart often does a better job of protecting American consumers than does the FDA.

Michigan State University's Food Fraud Initiative (FFI) estimates fraud at nearly fifty billion dollars annually. That's twice the entire world market for coffee, the single most valuable agricultural commodity. One fake honey scam in the United States netted eighty million dollars. Michigan State's FFI is just one of several such recently opened facilities around the world. In 2013, Great Britain created a new criminal investigative division, the Food Crimes Unit—a real-life CSI devoted solely to this issue. Italy has a special police food fraud unit that *60 Minutes* called the "FBI of Food." Lots of foods we take for granted should be viewed with reasoned skepticism. Your home, from the liquor cabinet to the freezer, is full of food impostors. That's the bad news.

The good news is that there is plenty of healthful and delicious Real Food. You just have to know what to look for. When counterfeiters hawk bogus goods in the street, they are usually selling fake versions of costly brands with cachet or perceived quality, like Rolex watches or Louis Vuitton handbags. As a counterfeiter, there is little profit in faking cheap or less desirable goods. The only reason there is so much Fake Food is that there is so much Real Food.

And I love Real Food.

# REAL FOOD/FAKE FOOD

"*Not just a wheel, Trog, but a wheel of aged Parmigiano Reggiano!*"

# 1. Real Food, Perfected: A Day in the Life of Parma

This is one of the most important and influential cheeses of Italy, if not the world. Important because the genuine article is so incredibly delicious and balanced in flavor . . . influential because there are hundreds, if not thousands of imitations produced around the world, from wedges of "parmesan" to green cylindrical boxes containing a grated substance that resembles sawdust, though it still bears the name on its label.

—JOHN FISCHER, *Cheese*
(Culinary Institute of America textbook)

The Parmesan cheese you sprinkle on your penne could be wood: Some brands promising 100 percent purity contained no Parmesan at all.

—LYDIA MULVANY, "The Parmesan Cheese You Sprinkle on Your Penne Could Be Wood"

It is a typical day in Parma and time to make cheese. The first rays of the sun are just breaking through the darkness when a dairy worker—let's call him Paolo Rainieri*—is awakened by his alarm clock. It is 5:00 a.m., and to say he is used to this early hour is an understatement: Rainieri has been rising at this same

---

*"Paolo Rainieri" is an amalgam of Parma cheese makers I met, almost all male and almost all second, third, or fifth generation in their jobs. One had worked every day, save his two-day honeymoon, for thirty-five years.

time to make cheese seven days a week for the past thirty-five years. The last time he had a day off was when a scooter accident sent him to the emergency room, and the last vacation he enjoyed was his honeymoon—and even that was a short escape—twenty-seven years ago. His father was a Parma cheese maker, like his father before him, and very little has changed from generation to generation, except that Paolo has replaced the rooster's crow that woke his grandfather with an alarm clock.

The Rainieris' devotion to their endless work is hardly unusual here, more the rule than the exception among the city's cheese makers, a highly exalted bunch. After all, the cows of Parma do not have calendars, do not take vacations or observe holidays, and every single day they produce milk. Every single day the farmers who own the cows rush this white gold straight to dairies like the one Rainieri works in—because Italian law says cheese making here must commence within two hours of milking.

There are more than three hundred such dairies in a relatively confined, legally designated zone around Parma and the neighboring town of Reggio, both in Italy's Emilia-Romagna province, each of which makes one and only one product: huge wheels of Parmigiano-Reggiano cheese. Under newer EU regulations and Italian laws dating back centuries, Parmigiano-Reggiano can only be prepared in this one spot, where it has been made in the same painstaking way for more than eight hundred years. Thanks to its unrivaled quality and consistency, it enjoys a coveted nickname, "King of Cheeses," and is considered by many experts to be the finest widely available cheese. The daily transfers of ultrafresh milk from cows to farmers to cheese makers are just two small steps in an intricate dance, a complex but closed virtuous circle of life that involves grass and flowers and cows and pigs and banks and warehouses and inspectors and craftspeople, and makes Parma a near-perfect community of agricultural sustainability.

The small city of Parma is Italy's gourmet epicenter. Not too far away, Bologna proudly and loudly claims to have the best restaurants in all of Italy, a distinction the Milanese, Modenese, Florentines, Romans, and Sicilians happily and passionately argue, but no one challenges Parma for the supremacy of its products. This one small city, off the radar for most tourists, is home to the world's largest pasta maker, Barilla, which also runs a major culinary academy here. And Parma claims Italy's largest food producer of any type, agri-giant Parmalat, named for its hometown. The city produces two of the world's most recognizable and coveted foodstuffs, Parmigiano-Reggiano cheese and Prosciutto di Parma, Italy's beloved cured ham.

Less well known outside Emilia-Romagna is Parma's most elite delicacy, *culatello*, air dried eye round of pork. Because the making of a single small *culatello* loin involves cutting up the pig leg and thus rendering it unusable for prosciutto, with its much greater yield, *culatello* is expensive and rare, a cured meat specialty of Parma that is virtually impossible to find outside of, and even within much of, Italy. Commercial production is limited, so it has traditionally been a homemade "bootleg" specialty, like Ireland's famed *poitín* moonshine, easier to get from a friend in the know than a store. But with effort *culatello* can be purchased, and is worth seeking out, because it is delicious, and many fans consider it the finest of all cured pork products.

Another best-in-class food product is made just down the road in the neighboring town of Modena, equally famous for its exotic cars, as headquarters of both Ferrari and Lamborghini, and its exalted aged vinegar, Aceto Balsamico Tradizionale di Modena. This thick, powerful, complex vinegar is precious and far apart in flavor from the sad, thin, generic, and often heavily processed commodity item simply called balsamic vinegar in much of the world. Like most things in the Parma region—except the sports cars—it has been made in the same traditional craft manner, under strict quality laws, for centuries, earning it a coveted PDO (Protected Designation Origin) status from the European Union. This means that anything bearing the name Aceto Balsamico Tradizionale di Modena can only be made in Modena, just as Parmigiano-Reggiano, another PDO product, can only be made in Parma and neighboring Reggio. Regulations dictate that this real balsamic can be made only from wine-quality grapes grown within Modena, specifically of the Lambrusco or Trebbiano variety. Making balsamic vinegar from these premium grapes means not making wine from them, driving up the cost.

No other ingredients but grapes can be used. They must be crushed and then immediately cooked in an open pot over an open flame until the pressed-grape must is reduced by half. The thickened must is transferred to breathable wooden barrels, where it ages for over a decade. It ages best in nearly full barrels, so because of continuous evaporation loss—what Scotch whisky makers call the angels' share—the contents are moved every year or two to progressively smaller barrels, with six sizes in a typical set. Only after a minimum of twelve years, and often twenty-five or more, can this elixir be bottled, labeled, and sold as the famed balsamic of Modena. What remains is a tiny ultraconcentrated amount from the huge volume of high-quality grape juice that began the process well over a decade earlier.

This is why real balsamic vinegar is thick and syrupy, and why a tiny bottle can cost three figures. It is not for salad dressing—the Modenese make another excellent vinegar, *condimento*, for that, still far superior to most supermarket versions of so-called balsamic. Instead, it is used in small amounts as a super flavor booster for soups, roasts, and stews or served straight and sparingly on fresh strawberries and even vanilla gelato, an unlikely but stunning flavor combination. There is perhaps no higher calling for this fine aged vinegar than drizzled over chunks of aged Parmigiano-Reggiano cheese, a taste partnership made in heaven. In this part of Italy, the ingredients tend to speak for themselves with a divine simplicity, so a standard celebratory feast would begin with a plate of paper-thin sliced prosciutto and another of bite-sized nuggets of cheese with ancient balsamic, accompanied by good red wine. It is everything a dinner guest could hope for.

Parmigiano-Reggiano belongs to a cheese family known as hard grating cheeses, and while technically correct, this has made it widely misunderstood in the United States. It is harder than, say Brie or feta, for sure, yet hard cheese is a bit of an exaggeration. Because in the United States it tends to be kept too long, cut too small, and stored poorly at retail, it is often dried out and harder than it should be. It does make an excellent topping or recipe addition when grated and tends to be used mainly for this on our side of the Atlantic. But in Italy—and in my house—the King of Cheese is for eating first, grating second.

When fresh, Parmigiano-Reggiano has a texture just firmer than aged cheddar, sometimes called semihard, but it is filled with tiny, crunchy crystals of calcium lactate that give it a distinctive texture and mouth feel, almost an effervescence. The body of the cheese yields easily to the teeth, and starts to dissipate in a rich creaminess on the tongue right away, sort of like biting into a thick slab of chocolate, neither soft nor hard. Throw in the tiny crystalline structure and you have the cheese version of a fancy Nestle Crunch bar in terms of consistency. It's better when cut from the wheel in large slices, the size of an enormous wedge of three-layer wedding cake, and served neither sliced nor grated but broken into chunks. With the exception of near relatives like Grana Padano, there is no other cheese eaten this way.

Parmigiano-Reggiano is so special that there is a specific tool for serving it, something every household in Emilia-Romagna possesses: a teardrop-shaped knife with a gentle blade that looks like a guitar pick mounted on a handle, point down. Because of its crystallized structure, natural irregular fault lines run through the cheese, and by inserting the tip of this pick and applying a slight forward prying pressure, chunks about half the size of Ping-Pong balls easily break off.

Once you start popping them in your mouth, the nutty, buttery richness and intense flavor that come from age and concentration make it impossible to stop. When you eat a young soft cheese like mozzarella or cottage cheese, you are eating a lot of water, but Parmigiano-Reggiano is almost pure protein left after evaporation— a single two-pound wedge is four gallons of the freshest, purest milk you can imagine, compressed.

At the Parma headquarters of the quasi-governmental consortium that oversees cheese production, I participated in a structured tasting of samples from different dairies with an expert, Mario. He explained to me that the cheese is volatile, and when I broke a chunk off with my knife he advised me to smell it immediately to get the best indication. I did. I smelled cheese. Mario got hazelnuts and grass from the cow's diet. Then we tasted it. I got really delicious, creamy, nutty, slightly salty cheese. Mario got grassy, slightly salty, and fruity "but not in a sweet way, more acidic, like pineapple." Hey, at least we agreed on slightly salty. We also agreed on delicious.

But the cheese is even better with one drop per chunk of aged balsamic, so powerful it is often applied with an eyedropper. When discussing food, we use the terms *concentrated* and *intense* a lot, but there is no product I can think of, with the possible exception of saffron, that takes these properties to such an extreme as balsamic vinegar—and good balsamic is much more complex than saffron. The main quality is sweet and sour with a dense texture, but it also has berries, grapes, vanilla, and a rich earthy mustiness, in a good way. If dark was a taste, it would have that, too.

Like most foods around Parma, making balsamic vinegar takes a lot of time and a lot of help from Mother Nature, and because the start-up time frame to produce a single bottle is at least a dozen years, the small industry has what economists call a high barrier to entry. Most producers are family owned and have been for generations. The barrels themselves, usually in matched sets of five or six, can be well over a hundred years old, and in Modena it has long been tradition that such a set of well-seasoned barrels is given by the bride's family at her wedding, a priceless dowry.

It is no coincidence that so many delicious foods come from this one place, because Parma has two irreplaceable advantages: history and *terroir*. The history mirrors the Italian culture's love of regionalism, with those regions' specialties predetermined by natural resources. As a result, what is law today in Parma is nothing more than the way things have been done by custom for at least nine centuries. The high quality of Parmigiano-Reggiano cheese was famously praised by the author Boccaccio in his 1348 masterpiece *The Decameron*, but bills of sale and trade documents trace the cheese more than a century and a half earlier. Experts believe that by the thirteenth century it had achieved essentially the same form it has today. Only after being made in exactly the same way for hundreds of years, a method carefully taught to sons by their fathers, did it enter Italian legal codes.

Europeans have long embraced food purity laws, hearkening back to the world's first, the Reinheitsgebot. Variously known as the German Beer Purity Law or Bavarian Purity Law, it was enacted in 1516 by then-independent Bavaria (which not coincidentally later gave us the wonderful tradition of Oktoberfest—and to this day, only beer brewed within Munich city limits can be served at the festival) to govern production of beer. The Reinheitsgebot mandated that only three ingredients—water, barley, and hops—could go into beverages sold as "beer." Unlike some contemporary protectionist regulations drafted by lobbyists, what is thought of as a purity law was really one of the earliest forms of consumer protection, to ensure drinkers got what they thought they were buying—real beer. Over the centuries the law was modified, first to accommodate the use of yeast and later newer styles of brewing.

Other European nations have followed in the footsteps of the Reinheitsgebot for centuries, crafting similar rules governing production of wines, cheeses, and even French bread. While the term *baguette* commonly refers to a shape of loaf in the United States, in France it is such a serious legal definition that what we might think of as artistic creativity—a seeded baguette for instance—is fraud, a crime, and a Parisian baker could theoretically be punished for including anything but wheat flour, water, yeast, and salt in a *baguette de tradition française.* The purpose is not to limit the bread eating experience of the French but rather so that when consumers do decide to buy a baguette over other baked choices, they know exactly what they are getting.

Similar laws govern day-to-day life in Parma, and cheese making begins with the coming of spring and the renewed growth of the grasses and wildflowers that make up the area pastures. It is here that history intersects with that second vital part of the regional equation, *terroir.* A French word derived from *terre,* for land, it has no clear English translation, but rather a complex meaning suggesting the complexity of nature itself. In layman's terms it means that a product's specific qualities literally come with the territory. Like today's popular expression "sense of place," *terroir* is the sum of all things that give individuality to a particular region's agriculture. These can include the chemical composition of the soil, the flora, what kinds of animals, insects, and even microbes are found there, as well as weather and seasonal changes.

Proximity to the sea is a classic ingredient of a particular *terroir*, especially evident in briny, peaty, single-malt Scotch whiskies.

While *terroir* may have a notable defining factor, like the iodine in the salt air of Scotland's Speyside, it is always far more: a jigsaw puzzle of natural inputs, sometimes so unusual that they exist in only one place. This explains why it would be impossible to grow better tomatoes in a greenhouse in Alaska, despite unlimited effort and resources, than in Naples or New Jersey. It is why sweet onions grown in Vidalia, Georgia; on the Hawaiian island of Maui; or in Walla Walla, Washington, taste sweeter than the same exact onion species grown in the rest of the United States. It is why corn grows taller in Nebraska than in Vermont and why the syrup from maple trees in Vermont tastes better than that from maple trees in Indiana. There are thousands of such examples, but the bottom line is that *terroir* is so multifaceted that it can rarely be replicated intentionally.

The countryside around Parma is mountainous, with unadulterated local grasses and flowers, changing slightly in composition at various altitudes and sun exposures. By law, these pastures cannot be chemically fertilized or planted with new types of crops, thus ensuring the purity and consistency of the milk supply, and legally the cattle of Parma—some four thousand head strong and every single one numbered, monitored, and accounted for—can eat only this natural growth from spring to fall. In winter, they dine only on dried hay from the same fields. Silage, a wet feed made by the fermentation of various grasses, grains, cereals, or corns, widely used in the American cattle industry to foster fast, cheap growth, is expressly forbidden. So are all supplements, antibiotics, and bovine growth hormones—along with all hormones of any kind. If a cow becomes sick to the point where it is medically necessary for a veterinarian to administer antibiotics, it is taken out of milk production until such a time as the treatment has ended and the cow's system is clear of the drugs. This all makes the milk today largely unchanged since Benedictine monks here first invented Parmigiano-Reggiano cheese.

The Parmigiani claim it is their fields that give the cheese its taste, and that certainly makes sense, though there are many other steps in the process from field to plate, all equally adherent to strict traditions. Because the flavor and natural composition of the cows' milk varies between the first and second milking of the day, the milk used to make cheese is always a half-and-half mix of the morning milking, not more than two hours before cheese making commences, and the milking from the night before. No Parmigiano-Reggiano can ever be made with milk that has been out of the cow for over eighteen hours, but it is often far less. In Parma, mutual financial dependence, rather than fences, makes good neighbors, and the two-hour regulation guarantees not only freshness but also locality, with many farmers just a tractor ride from the cheese dairies they supply.

From the first time a calf grazes in Parma, every single step of cheese production, from temperatures to length of aging to the size of wheels to the types of round molds used, is not only set in stone but is also strictly enforced by a mini-army of inspectors. Their full-time job is to do nothing but verify—and later grade—the quality of Parmigiano-Reggiano cheese with a devotion that seeks nothing less than perfection.

When the milk arrives, our dairyman Paolo Rainieri pours it into large copper kettles, and adds a small amount of rennet, a digestive bacteria naturally occurring in cattle intestines, while the mixture is heated until curds form. These curds are broken up mechanically with a spinning blade that resembles a giant bread mixer while the liquid continues to solidify. When it reaches the desired consistency, Rainieri will shut off the heat and mixing blade and slide a muslin sheet beneath the semiformed lump, and with the help of an assistant, he will use this porous blanket to lift the ball-shaped mass. The four corners of the muslin are tied off around a metal rod from which it hangs, allowing the cheese to drain. This entire process has taken less than an hour, and since the day's milk arrives all at once, Rainieri and his assistant simultaneously manage several of these copper vats, perhaps dozens in a larger dairy, rushing from one to the next and repeating the same steps.

The leftover whey and milk from the vat is carefully put aside for another important use, and later the vats will be scrubbed clean to prepare for the next day. Since there is just one morning milking, there is just one daily production run of cheese. When it is done draining, Rainieri will unwrap the muslin and carefully cut the primordial lump in half to make two wheels, the sole yield of each copper vat and the eleven hundred liters of pure fresh milk that went into it. The size of each wheel is the same as it was a century ago, as it was when America declared its independence in 1776, as it was when Michelangelo painted the ceiling of the Sistine Chapel. Paolo Rainieri is making Parmigiano-Reggiano, the King of Cheeses, and he cannot make it in smaller or larger vats or smaller or larger wheels.

He places each freshly cut half of the ball into a round stainless-steel mold the size of a car tire, and these discs are submerged in long, open holding tanks of brine. After three weeks in this salt bath, the wheels are removed, the salt water rinsed off, and now that the rind has started to form, the cheese-making part of the process is essentially finished. But the cheese is still much too young for consumption and aging begins. Roughly two years from now the result will be a wheel of Parmigiano-Reggiano weighing eighty-six pounds.

The stainless-steel mold gives the cheese its disc shape, about ten inches thick and two feet in diameter. But the mold serves another increasingly important function, as an anticounterfeiting measure. The molds are specially produced by the Consorzio Parmigiano-Reggiano, an independent and self-regulating industry group funded by fees levied on cheese producers. Carefully tracked and numbered, molds are supplied only to licensed and inspected dairies, and each is lined with Braille-like needles that create a pinpoint pattern instantly recognizable to foodies, spelling out the name of the cheese over and over again in a pattern forever imprinted on its rind. A similar raised-pin mold made of plastic is slipped between the steel and the cheese to permanently number the rind of every lot so that any wheel can be traced back to a particular dairy and day of origin. Like a tattoo, these numbers and the words Parmigiano-Reggiano become part of the skin. Later in its life, because counterfeiting the King of Cheeses has become a global pastime, this will be augmented with security holograms.

Besides the pure milk and rennet, the only other ingredient allowed is salt, and that is added by absorption from the brine bath. This purity is one reason its health benefits are legendary: in Italy it is routinely prescribed by doctors as the first thing for babies to eat when weaned off mother's milk. Its consumption has been linked to improved bone density, and it is believed to be responsible for many other health benefits. After lengthy and sophisticated laboratory testing and analysis, it remains the only cheese approved for consumption by astronauts, chosen separately by both NASA and the Russian Federal Space Agency. It was literally the first cheese in space.

Like the grass, insects, and cows, the residents of Parma have a symbiotic relationship that keeps the circle of life very much alive. The popular business management terms *vertical integration* and *horizontal integration* are nonexistent here. Cheese makers do not own cows, and cattle farmers do not make cheese. Instead, interrelated interests bind everyone involved in the city's main industry—food production—from distributors to bankers to those who manufacture seemingly unrelated products. Without its lengthy aging, Parmigiano-Reggiano is not Parmigiano-Reggiano, and thus an entire industry exists, unique to Parma, for building and operating warehouses devoted solely to cheese aging.

Artisans like Rainieri produce hefty wheels of cheese daily, but they will not reach customers for over a year—at least—so they accumulate, hundreds upon hundreds of tons of cheese. The wheels, nearly a foot thick and weighing almost ninety pounds, are stacked by the thousands on wooden shelves lining warehouse aisles hundreds of feet long, often up to twenty-five shelves high, several stories of towering cheese, as far as the eye can see in every direction. Entering such a warehouse, it would be easy to believe that all of the world's cheese is here, like a creamy Fort Knox, but these edifices dot the Parma countryside. Each one is the size of several football fields, obsessively climate controlled with backup generators, and holds millions of dollars' worth of cheese.

The product is so valuable, with a single wheel having a "street value" of thousands of dollars, that theft has been a historical problem. Because the wheels resemble car tires in appearance, no forklifts or dollies are needed. (To the delight of thieves they also roll like tires, and burglars over the years have made use of this fact, raiding warehouses and rolling wheels to a waiting truck.) Better alarms, locks, and video surveillance have made warehouse theft largely a problem of the past. However, theft remains the number one problem for supermarkets: recent studies show it is the single most shoplifted food product in Italy, and as much as 9 percent of all the cheese displayed for retail sale is stolen annually. Apparently, in Italy even shoplifters have good taste.

The challenge to the ager is not simply storing, cooling, and guarding the cheese. Every single wheel must be flipped weekly, and before it is replaced, the wooden shelf must be wiped clean, since moisture accumulates beneath it. For hundreds of years this was done manually, with workers climbing ladders, pulling off those eighty-six-pound wheels, wiping the shelves while holding the cheese, then flipping and replacing them, one at a time, level by level, row by row, week after week—a tedious, exhausting, and dangerous job. Today, most warehouses use robotic mini-forklifts custom built to gingerly withdraw the wheels, rotate them, clean the shelves, and replace them. At all hours these robots prowl the aisles, and the design, construction, and maintenance of cheese-flipping robots is another niche local industry spun off by agriculture.

To be sold as Parmigiano-Reggiano, each wheel must be aged for a minimum of one year, but few are sold that young. To obtain the more common, desirable, and pricier Vecchio-quality designation (*vecchio* meaning "old" or, in this context, "aged"), at least eighteen months is required; a minimum of two years, and often as many as three, is needed for the most desirable Stravecchio (extra-aged) rating. Across Parma, the average age at which a wheel is sold is twenty to twenty-four months, and for this reason, warehousing is a big deal. At the same time, few cheese makers are in the financial position to wait two years to recoup their investment, having long ago paid for the milk and labor. Warehouse owners have long played the role of bankers, and lend cheese makers funds secured by their aging inventory, which is held "on deposit," while charging a fee for storage and laborious flipping. Warehouses in turn are often financed by Parma's actual bankers, an additional spoke in the wheel.

Another Parmigiani subculture created by cheese is the Consorzio Parmigiano-Reggiano, which plays a role not dissimilar to the offices of Major League Baseball or the National Football League. On one hand, the Consorzio exists to promote the greater good of all things cheese, helping to market it at the global level, including public education, special events, public relations, and litigating on behalf of its membership; on the other hand, it also tests the cheese and ensures the best quality product for consumers. Because of this duality, its relationship with its own "teams," the dairies, can be adversarial.

Like sports leagues, the Consorzio is funded by its owners yet is put in the often schizophrenic roles of booster, umpire, and jury, occasionally levying fines, mostly in the form of rejected cheese. Aging may be the last step in production, but until a final quality testing is performed, the cheese is just cheese, not Parmigiano-Reggiano. Before a grade like Vecchio or Stravecchio is assigned and the final security hologram adhered, one of the Consorzio's staff of expert tasters must personally inspect it. If flipping the aging cheeses seems daunting, consider that every single wheel must be individually inspected before it can be sold as Parmigiano-Reggiano. In 2009, there were 2,947,292 wheels made.

While the "recipe" for Parmigiano-Reggiano appears simple, the reality is anything but. Like baking or winemaking, cheese production is a funny thing, and molecules do not always behave the way we would like. Cheese is alive, and just as the most meticulously tended tomato plants do not produce identical tomatoes, every attempt at Parmigiano-Reggiano does not result in greatness. Yet the promise to the consumer is that you know exactly what you will get, and what you will get is excellence, and always the same excellence, the only variant being the three sanctioned ages. The final individual testing is a laborious but vital step.

The testers themselves, full-time employees of the Consorzio, are Old World craftsmen, arriving at the warehouses with the tools of their trade: a metal and rubber percussion hammer, a screw-like auger, and a long steel needle. They place the wheel on its side and visually inspect it for cracks, holes, or other faults. Next, they use the hammer as a doctor wields a stethoscope, tapping the wheel over and over while listening carefully, because hollow spots within suggest chemistry has failed and the proper structural crystallization has not taken place.

If a structural defect is revealed to a trained ear, the steel needle is used to test the physical structure of the interior, but only when the hammer's judging is unclear. Finally, as a last backup measure to remove any doubt, the very thin steel auger extracts a tiny cylindrical cross section of the wheel, the same way a geologist might take a core sample of the earth, allowing the Consorzio examiner to visually check the entire width of the wheel, smell it, and most important, taste it.

If the cheese passes inspection with flying colors, it is awarded a hologram and can be sold based on its final age. If it is passable but not exceptional and does not earn the higher rating, it must be sold as twelve month old, regardless of age. Sometimes the cheese is developing correctly but slowly and is sent back to the shelves for additional aging and retesting. About 8 percent, a huge volume in both weight and dollars, simply fails, and this too is part of the city's circle of life. The subpar wheel is mechanically defaced to obliterate the logo and sold as commercial grade to food manufacturers, the largest of which is the city's own Parmalat. Still far superior to most mass-produced cheeses, it is typically used as an ingredient in processed foods, often ground into powder for instant macaroni and cheese or similar products (but it cannot be called Parmigiano-Reggiano on the ingredient list).

Virtually nothing is wasted in the daily cycle of production here, from the grass in the fields to the milk of the cows to the nearly great cheese that does not quite meet lofty local standards. Even discards have value in Parma. Remember the leftover whey and milk that was removed from the copper vats and set aside from the cheese-making process? It has the same excellent nutritional, taste, and purity qualities that the raw milk had, but even more so, enhanced by the first steps of cheese production and concentration. After the wheels go into the brine, Paolo Rainieri will still be hard at work, tying up loose ends. One of those loose ends is the whey mixture, which is delivered to yet another one of his Parma neighbors, the pig farmer. This by-product is fed to what must be some of the happiest pigs on earth, at least until they meet their end in the form of Prosciutto di Parma.

Similar to its cheese cousin, Prosciutto di Parma is called "King of Ham," and has its own strict ancient rules and independent Consorzio to monitor production and quality, and to promote its cause. The Consorzio's logo is a not-subtle crown inscribed with the word *Parma*. In America, the word *prosciutto* typically refers to a particular Italian-inspired style of cured but uncooked ham, very thinly sliced. But in Italian, it simply means ham, including many types of prosciutto *cotto* (cooked) and *crudo* (raw), of which Italy's finest is Prosciutto di Parma, or Ham of Parma. It cannot legally be manufactured anywhere else in Europe.

Parma's prosciutto has an even longer history than its cheese, quite a bit longer if you subscribe to the prevailing local theory that Cato, as far back as 100 BCE, was describing a proto-Parma ham when he wrote of whole pig legs here being aged in barrels of salt and then smoked. Legend also has it that Hannibal stopped his famed road trip over the Alps to fill his stomach with Parma ham a thousand years ago. Sometime before the Renaissance, smoking was discarded in favor of air drying, using the reliable warm, dry wind that sweeps down the Po River valley. A take on Prosciutto di Parma much closer to the one we know today was produced in individual homes along the Po since at least the thirteenth century. About two centuries ago, purpose-built riverfront air drying "factories" replaced homes, and many are still in use today.

Once again, venerable traditions became law, and as in the cheese, salt is a key ingredient—the only one allowed other than the pork itself. However, the Consorzio insists that its hams actually have four ingredients: pork, salt, air, and time. Prosciutto di Parma is always totally pure and free of preservatives. Even completely natural ingredients common in ham making elsewhere—water, sugar, smoke, and spices—are banned. The twin goals of the artists who make what is known as a "sweet ham" are to use as little salt as necessary so it does not overwhelm the taste of the pork and to concentrate flavor through a slow aging process. The final product loses up to a quarter of its original weight, all through evaporation, leaving richer taste behind.

While the process begins with pigs fed tasty and nutritious whey, actual ham making begins with their slaughter at nine months old, no more, no less, and only if at that age they weigh a minimum of 340 pounds. Whole legs are delivered to the Prosciutto di Parma warehouses along the river, where they are trimmed into the familiar ham shape, not unlike a giant chicken drumstick. The ham is then salted, always by hand, by a *maestro salatore*, or master salter. The fresh ham goes into a cool climate-controlled room at 80 percent humidity for one week, then is removed, cleaned, and resalted before going back into the humidity for fifteen to eighteen more days. During this formative stage, each ham is checked daily, with salt added or removed, depending on conditions. Next, the hams move to refrigerated but much less humid rooms to age for nine to ten weeks.

The technique used to make Prosciutto di Parma is a form of what is known in meat parlance as dry curing. The two main alternatives are smoking and wet curing. The latter usually involves a bath in chemicals and is popular today because it is quick and cheap. There are natural wet cures, but they are rarer.

It is after the hams emerge from the refrigeration that Parma's *terroir* kicks into full gear. The hams are hung in long rows, one above the next, in massive aging rooms. These are usually on the upper floors of the warehouses, almost completely lined with louvered floor-to-ceiling windows. Here they hang for three months, while ham makers continuously fiddle with the louvers, opening and closing them in complicated combinations depending on the weather and breeze to continuously assure the ideal air circulation, temperature, and humidity.

After this full season of aging, the hams are spread with a paste of salt and pork lard, then moved to cool basements to sit in the darkness and further concentrate their flavors, typically for three to five months, sometimes much longer. Including all these steps, any ham that ends up labeled Prosciutto di Parma and earns the crown logo will have aged for a minimum of four hundred days, while many require as much as two and a half years. Of course, before they can be labeled, each and every ham must be individually examined by testers from the Consorzio.

Long before stainless steel, ham makers discovered that a hollow needle made of horse bone had the same neutral qualities and could be used to puncture the ham and extract a tiny cylindrical sample, about an eighth of an inch in diameter. Today, while cheese tasters use metal, the horse bone needle is still the implement of choice for ham, and inspectors test each leg in five locations for both aroma and taste. All hams sold as Prosciutto di Parma must pass this five-point test before they are given the seal of approval. Roughly 4 percent are rejected.

TO JADED CITIZENS of Parma, the miracle that turns grass and flowers into exquisite cheese and meat is an everyday occurrence. In the city's main shopping street, a pedestrian thoroughfare lined with stores specializing in lace, there is a popular pizzeria on the main piazza, with tables set out on cobblestones and a seemingly random nautical/pirate theme. Every time I have visited Parma I have come here for lunch, and while pizzas are available with a wide variety of toppings, I always choose prosciutto, which comes generously spread across every inch of the pie. It's delicious.

Like almost every restaurant in Parma, large or small, the pizzeria has a huge ornate enameled antique meat slicer proudly on display. These are almost always hand cranked, owing to a belief that the heat of a motor would harm the quality of the thin sliced, delicate ham. Whether you order a pizza topped with Prosciutto di Parma or a platter of the ham, it is sliced to order for you, carefully and lovingly, from a whole leg.

These slicers are beautiful machines, works of art themselves, and I want one. They are as ubiquitous in Parma's trattorias, osterias, and cafes as Wi-Fi is in Seattle coffee shops. I envy the locals because when they order this same pizza, they have no doubt about where it comes from, how it was made, or how delicious it is about to taste. If they grate any extra cheese onto their pizza from the huge wedge offered, they know without asking that it is Parmigiano-Reggiano, made no more than a few miles from where they sit. They do not have to be an armchair gourmand or dedicated foodie to enjoy this fine meal, made with the best ingredients available, and they do not have to read endless food blogs to learn how good the meat and cheese are—they take it for granted.

Alas, the rest of the world is not so fortunate, and ironically, the ignorance of the Parmigiani may truly equal bliss, because this is a situation where even information is not always a savior. For instance, you might go out to eat at one of the most acclaimed and expensive Italian restaurants in New York, which is to say, in the entire country, like my friend Alice Fixx did. Alice has represented the cheese makers of Parma in a public relations effort to spread their truth for two decades. She speaks fluent Italian, lives several months a year in Italy's Veneto region, and otherwise resides in New York City. She also used to do work for the Parma ham

Consorzio, and no one I know is more knowledgeable about both the King of Cheeses and Italian cuisine in general.

One night, friends came to town and invited Alice out to dinner at celebrity chef Mario Batali's vaunted flagship Italian eatery, Babbo. As Alice told me this story, at one point during their meal, the waiter displayed a grater and large wedge of cheese with great flourish, asking her if she wanted Parmigiano-Reggiano on her pasta. She did not say yes. She did not say no. Instead Alice looked at the cheese and asked, "Are you sure that's Parmigiano-Reggiano?"

He replied with certainty, "Yes."

"You're sure?"

"Yes."

She then asked to see the cheese. The waiter panicked, mumbled some excuse, and fled into the kitchen. He returned a few minutes later with a different and much smaller chunk of cheese, which he handed over for examination. The new speck was old, dry, and long past its useful shelf-life, but it was real Parmigiano-Reggiano, evidenced by the pin-dot pattern.

"The first one was Grana Padano," she explained. "I could clearly read the rind. They must have gone searching through all the drawers in the kitchen in a panic until they found this forgotten crumb of Parmigiano-Reggiano." Alice Fixx was the wrong person to try this kind of bait and switch on, but she is the exception, and I wonder how many other expense-account diners swallowed a cheaper substitute. This occurred at one of the most famous and expensive Italian eateries in the country. What do you think happens at other restaurants?

Until 2013, it was illegal to sell real Prosciutto di Parma in Canada except under the odd name "Original Ham." That is because a local meat producer, Maple Leaf Meats, trademarked the real name in 1971 and for the past forty-five years has been duping

Canadian consumers. By the time actual ham makers from Parma realized, the best available name they could secure was "Original Ham." This has been a thorn in the side of EU regulators ever since, and finally, as part of a 2013 trade agreement, they succeeded in their negotiations—sort of. Both the actual Parma producers and Maple Leaf Meats can now sell Prosciutto di Parma, real and fake, in Canada.

Americans fared better with this gourmet product, but it took the ham Consorzio ten years and over a million dollars in legal fees to get Parma ham trademarked in the United States as ham from Parma. As a result, unlike our Canadian neighbors, we weren't being routinely tricked into buying a fake version of an ultrapure ham—a fake that could be packed with chemicals and preservatives and fillers and hormones (we just call this one prosciutto). The bad news is we got duped that way on the cheese front.

Most "Parmesan" cheese is a blatant counterfeiting of Parma's product, best exemplified by the ubiquitous Kraft grated version that comes in green cardboard tubes and tastes like what you would get if you ground up green cardboard tubes. This may not be as far from reality as it sounds. In early 2016, the FDA showed that Parmesan fraud has become a very serious problem for American consumers. Its tests showed that products described as "100 percent Parmesan" are routinely cut with cheaper products, and not just less expensive cheeses but also wood pulp. Tests by Bloomberg showed that Kraft Parmesan contained almost 4 percent cellulose, a plant-derived polymer mainly used to make paper and paperboard. Other brands had cellulose content as high as 7.8 percent.

According to culinary website Grub Street, the FDA is prosecuting Castle Cheese, long a huge supplier to supermarket chains, for three decades of alleged fraud, including manufacturing three top selling brands "all of which contained no Parmesan cheese despite claiming on their labels to be 100 percent." Neal Schuman, whose family-owned New Jersey company is the nation's largest seller of hard Italian cheeses, told Bloomberg News that 40 percent of so-called grated Parmesan cheese is not even real cheese at all.

Kraft was forced by courts to stop selling this product as Parmesan cheese in Europe and renamed it Pamasello, but sells it here as "100% Grated Parmesan Cheese." My guess is that the "100%" refers to the grating, not the cheese, and in fact it is completely grated. Remember that by both EU and Italian law, the real thing is allowed to contain only three very simple ingredients: pure drug-free milk, salt, and rennet. Kraft's includes milk of unknown origin and purity, cellulose powder, potassium sorbate, and cheese cultures.

But Parmesan and Parmigiano-Reggiano are different, you might think. Except they are not. Parmesan is the direct English translation of Parmigiano-Reggiano, just as the country it comes from is not actually Italy, as we call it, but rather Italia. Italia's capital is Roma, not Rome, but to argue that by Rome, Italy, we mean something different from Roma, Italia, is pure idiocy. In Japanese, the country's name is Nippon, yet by law we insist that imported products be labeled with our version, "Made in Japan." In almost every case other than Parmesan cheese, we take the legal position that our word means the same as the word from which it is translated. In 2008, European courts correctly decreed that Parmigiano-Reggiano is the only hard cheese that can legally be called Parmesan, and with a handful of exceptions such as Argentina and New Zealand, almost all of our first world peers—not just in Europe—understand this and agree.

Furthermore, the word *Parmesan* has been used to specifically refer only to Parmigiano-Reggiano cheese since about 250 years before the United States came into existence. In the sixteenth century it was the Italians themselves, in other parts of the country, who began calling it Parmesano, which means "of or from Parma."

This was shortened to Parmesan by the French, the first foreigners to gain a deep appreciation of the cheese's virtues. The words have been precisely synonymous for five hundred years—and still are today—except to American consumers trying to buy Real Food. Today almost nothing you can buy in a store in this country labeled Parmesan resembles something "of or from Parma" in any way.

There is a museum in Parma devoted entirely to the history of Parmigiano-Reggiano cheese. To be perfectly honest, the museum is pretty hokey, and few visitors will regret having missed it—the pirate pizzeria is a far more important stop. But one display is especially humorous, though probably not to the Consorzio: it is a worldwide collection of "homages," products created to profit from an unwarranted and undeserved association with the Parmigiano-Reggiano name. These include powdered cheeselike substances, grated cheese, and macaroni-and-cheese kits, along with wheels and wedges of actual "cheese," some of which do not even meet the minimum legal standards to be called cheese of any kind. There is every imaginable variant of the word *Parmigiano*, including *Parmesan, Parmigiana, Parmesana, Parmegano, Parmesano, Parmeso, Parmetto, Parma cheese, Parma-Reggiano, Parggiano, Parmabon, Parmezan, Parmezano*, and my all-time favorite, *Permesansan* (really). From China comes *cheese Parmesan-Reggiano*, while the ultimate slap in the face is *real Parma*.

Also displayed is the short-lived Wisconsin Parveggiano, one of the very few instances in which the Consorzio actually won a U.S. trademark case. Before extending sympathies to the Wisconsin cheese factory that lost the suit, be aware that it is still able to market Parmesan, along with various other geographically designated cheeses widely protected in most of the rest of the world, including faux Asiago and Gorgonzola. The only term the Consorzio was able to legally secure in the United States is *Parmigiano*, and it can only defend this trademark against terms deemed too "similar" by

U.S. courts. Even this limited protection is thinner than it looks, because it grandfathers and exempts all previous existing copycats, such as Parmesan.

The reason *Parmesan* and similar terms cannot receive protection under U.S. trademark law is that they have been deemed generic, or common names. This first happened in 1921 in *Bayer Co. v. United Drug Co.*, the seminal case for all generic trademark issues since. At the time, aspirin was a brand name owned by the Bayer Company (as was heroin, also since deemed generic). The defendant, United Drug, asserted that the term had become the common descriptive name for the kind of drug and fallen into the public domain. United's victory cemented the notion that future courts should weigh whether a trademark has become the "common descriptive name of an article," rather than a brand. However, this overly simplistic interpretation ignores the crux of United's case—and victory—which was that Bayer's patent had expired several years earlier. The common descriptive name argument was an ancillary notion attorneys threw into the mix, but it has remained there ever since, and other famous examples of former brands names include *laundromat, escalator, kerosene, cellophane, dry ice,* and *zipper.*

On the other hand, many names just as widely used to describe common items have won their claims as distinctive brand names, including ChapStick, Crock-Pot, Dumpster, Fiberglas, Jacuzzi, Xerox, Band-Aids, and of course, Kleenex brand tissues. In many of these cases, it has been held that the real issue is not whether a name like Dumpster is widely used to commonly describe all large trash receptacles but how vehemently the company has fought to prevent this—even if unsuccessful. The Parmigiani never had their patent expire, have fought vigorously—and have still been unsuccessful.

But while most consumers may not have known who made

the original aspirin, they do know exactly what aspirin is, and FDA rules specifically prohibit using the name to describe other painkillers such as naproxen sodium (Aleve) or acetaminophen (Tylenol). Yet Parmesan can be used for any type of cheese, which contradicts the entire notion that it has a commonly recognized meaning. When I asked the legal counsel for the Consorzio about this, he said, "In most cases in the U.S., the name Parmesan is not used as a common name of a kind of cheese; it is used in a way that may mislead the public as to the geographical origin of the product. If Parmesan has become the common name of a kind of cheese in the U.S., which kind of product exactly would Parmesan designate? Hard cheese? Hard cheese with a minimum aging period? Hard cheese with a minimum aging period only made from cow's milk? Or anything else?" He's got a point—no one uses the word Kleenex to describe other members of the paper product family, like paper towels or napkins. Even generic terms mean something, but in our country, Parmesan usually only means fake.

This issue is not about splitting hairs over names, nor is it about protectionist trade policies; it is about common sense, public safety, and consumer fraud. Or as Franz Fischler, the EU's commissioner for agriculture, rural development, and fisheries, noted, "This is not about protectionism. It is about fairness." Think one last time about all the steps that go into the production of Parmigiano-Reggiano, think about the pure natural grass, the hormone-free cows, the meticulous oversight, the exacting standards to which the cheese production is held, the two-plus years of careful aging, and then the testing standards so high that they flunk nearly a tenth of the finished cheese. Then ask yourself if you believe any similar standards are being applied at any of the industrial processed cheese factories—Kraft is not the only one—around the world.

It may be fair to assume that most consumers know there is practical difference between a cardboard tube of Kraft "Parmesan" powder and twenty-dollar-per-pound wedges of the real cheese at a specialty cheese shop. But how many notice that the eighteen-dollar-per-pound Parmesan next to the twenty-dollar wedge, also hand cut and wrapped in plastic in the fancy cheese case, is from a plant in Argentina, where the only legal standard governing its import is that it not be poisonous? No, the labeling issue is not one of splitting hairs. While U.S. cheese producers would—and do—beg to differ that *Parmesan* is its own word, one that does not confuse consumers, this is simply not true.

"It's misleading to use these names, there's no question about it. The green can calls itself Parmesan but has nothing in it that I think can actually even be called cheese. Parmigiano-Reggiano is the quintessential example. It's the gold standard, but most people have never had it because everything is called Parmesan here," said Laura Werlin, a James Beard Award–winning author who has written six books on cheese and is a frequent presenter at top culinary festivals like Pebble Beach and Aspen's Food & Wine Classic. I spoke to her in 2015.

Under EU law, both Parmigiano-Reggiano and its English translation, Parmesan, are clearly protected. But when the Codex Committee on Milk and Milk Products, which sets globally accepted standards for international trade, tried extending this European protection to its entire membership, the attempt was shot down by "stiff opposition from countries such as the USA and New Zealand as well as large producers such as Kraft. One of the worries was that if the EU succeeded, it would set a precedent for other products," according to trade publication *Dairy Industries International.* It's hard to imagine how a precedent requiring accurate food labeling would be a bad thing.

Every time I've visited Parma, I've eaten my final meal of the trip at La Greppia, a classic mom-and-pop restaurant in the heart of the city, where the husband is the maître d' and his wife, a true *nonna,* or Italian grandmother, heads up an all-female kitchen (the couple just, finally, retired). La Greppia's specialty is classic local dishes, and it is wise to begin with their signature appetizer, poached pears with a thick mousse made from Parmigiano-Reggiano, milk, and cream. For sharing, nothing beats the region's most decadent starter, *gnocco fritto,* always served in family-style platters. *Gnocco fritto* consists of two parts: ultralight square pillows of fried dough, a close relative of New Orleans's beignets, served piping hot and oily, alongside a plate of Prosciutto di Parma. You grab a fritter, wrap your ham slice around it, and almost instantly the paper-thin ribbons of fat in the meat melt, creating the most delicious inside-out doughnut sandwich you can imagine. Once you start wolfing down *gnocco fritto,* it is impossible to stop until the last piece of hot dough and the last slice of ham have disappeared.

Next comes the city's legendary main course, the "Rose of Parma," a name befitting the visiting royalty for whom it was originally created. This is a whole tenderloin of beef butterflied and stuffed with layers of Parmigiano-Reggiano and Prosciutto di Parma, along with garlic, olive oil, fresh herbs, and spices, then rolled, cooked, and sliced into decadent medallions. At La Greppia, and all throughout Emilia-Romagna, the beloved local specialties even make their way into desserts, from strudels and tarts stuffed with cheese to the classic, simple, and singularly delicious combination of homemade vanilla gelato drizzled with long-aged balsamic vinegar, a match made in gastronomic heaven.

The first time I visited Parma, I was so wowed by the cheese that I brought back a dozen wedges, each weighing two to three pounds. One of the dairies had a shop that would cut wedges to order from a freshly opened wheel, then immediately vacuum seal them. Because Parmigiano-Reggiano is best enjoyed fresh, it is important to keep it from exposure to air, and even when you buy the real thing in supermarkets, it is often dried out. Vacuum sealing ensured that each time I opened a wedge, it was like cutting into a new wheel. Once opened, my wife and I took great care to meticulously double wrap it tightly in plastic between servings, and did our best to eat it as quickly as possible—we succeeded. This preserved the grainy crunch factor and underlying creaminess. I came home with over thirty pounds, enough to almost fill a suitcase to the baggage limit, which seems excessive and probably was, but nonetheless, we hoarded it greedily.

There is a famous episode of the sitcom *Seinfeld* where Elaine's favorite birth control goes off the market, and faced with a finite supply, she begins to conserve, questioning whether her suitors are "sponge-worthy." We entertain a lot and began following her lead, deeming only certain guests "cheese-worthy," despite our ample supply. As the stash dwindled, our standards went up. Only once during those months did we ever take a wedge to someone else's house, and to those friends who had us for dinner, now you know how much your invitation meant to us. It is hard to imagine thirty pounds of cheese could warrant such stinginess, but it was that good. Our worthy guests agreed wholeheartedly, and as cheese expert Werlin had suggested, many were surprised that as well-versed food fans, they had never really tasted great Parmesan before. There is a reason for that, and it is called Fake Food.

## ✱ SHOPPING TIPS

Most of the fakery surrounding the King of Cheese has to do with the misleading use of "Parmesan," not Parmigiano-Reggiano, so when you see the full Italian name and it says "Made in Italy" and has the PDO seal, it is usually the real deal. The same is true of Prosciutto di Parma. However, the cheese is made in very large wheels that begin to deteriorate once cut, so it is important to buy from retailers with a lot of volume turnover who are constantly opening new wheels and storing it right. More than many other cheeses, it's usually better to buy from a specialty cheese shop like Murray's in New York—most cities have these. If you go mail order/online, you cannot beat Zingerman's in Ann Arbor, Michigan, which buys whole wheels directly from dairies in Parma and handles them very well. This is the choice of the Consorzio itself when it needs to ship the cheese within the United States for events.

For high-quality balsamic, look for the full name Aceto Balsamico Tradizionale di Modena or Aceto Balsamico Tradizionale di Reggio Emilia. Italian law precludes the years of aging on the labels, but better retailers list it, and eight years is the minimum for the good stuff, though truly exceptional balsamic, the kind to be applied with an eyedropper to cheese and ice cream, should be at least twenty-five to fifty years and will always cost you more than a hundred dollars, sometimes much more, for a small bottle. The best are labeled by color, with silver and gold denoting the oldest. Again, Zingerman's is an excellent resource for authentic standout balsamic vinegars.

# 2. What Is Fake Food?

None of us likes being swindled, particularly when all we were trying to do was buy something nice to eat . . . Being cheated over food is one of the universal human experiences.

—BEE WILSON, *Swindled*

**B**efore we go any further down this road, let's get some paperwork out of the way. I'm planning to use the terms *Real Food* and *Fake Food* quite a bit in these pages, and since different people might interpret them differently, it is important to clarify what exactly I mean.

Real Food is straightforward—it is what it says it is. Living in New England, one of my favorite examples is the whole Maine lobster, more accurately the North Atlantic lobster, because they are exactly the same in Massachusetts, New Hampshire, Connecticut, Rhode Island, and Canada. We all know what these creatures look like, and when served whole they cannot be faked, even by relatives like the spiny Caribbean or Mediterranean lobsters. Maine lobsters are always wild caught and never farmed or artificially raised; as a result, you don't have worry about whether they were "natural," "free range," or "pasture raised." They aren't fattened with hormones and antibiotics that are hidden from consumers, and they aren't crossbred with cheaper shellfish to make hybrids. They are simply lobsters.

But most important, they are delicious, and while some lobsters taste slightly better than others, and fans passionately argue the merits of steaming versus boiling and soft shell versus hard shell (same lobster, different time of year), it is virtually impossible to get a bad whole Maine lobster—I've never had one. You crack it open, you pull out big chunks of rich, flavorful, moist meat, dip them in melted butter to make them even richer, and you have one of the world's great meals. Just writing these words makes me want one. Whether you go the lazy man's route and pay someone to break it for you in a white tablecloth restaurant, or roll up your sleeves at a beachside picnic table and dig in, it tastes equally good, and no matter which you choose, you will end up deeply satisfied and licking your lips.

Most Real Food is not so obvious. If I put a glass of actual red Burgundy on the table next to a glass of fake California "Burgundy," you'd be hard pressed to tell by looking which one was real. But if you tasted them, you could discern the imitator right away, even with little wine knowledge, because it will not come remotely close to replicating the quality of the real thing.

When you already know it is genuine, because you see the bottle of red French Burgundy, you have a different kind of Real Food example: not only is it what it says it is, but what it says is a very specific promise. If the Burgundy could talk, this is what it might say: "My name means something. It means I am made from nothing but 100 percent pinot noir, with no exceptions. This is because the place I come from is world famous for the quality of its pinot noir grapes, where vineyards have been tended for more than two thousand years. Further, my country's government assesses and rates the qualities of individual vineyards within my region, and by law I can only be made from grapes from the best ones."

Conversely, the California "Burgundy" might say, "Burgundy is a famous high-quality wine from Burgundy, which is in France, and by putting its name on my label I'm hoping to trick you into confusing me with that wine. Because I can't compete on quality, I'm not even going to bother trying to imitate real Burgundy. What is pinot noir anyway? I'm a blend made of whatever grapes were selling most cheaply this year, and next year when they make another huge batch of me in big tanks, I'll have a different recipe."

Not all Fake Food is equally fake, and throughout this discussion you'll see that there are three main ways in which food is faked.

## ❋ ILLEGAL COUNTERFEITS

This is perhaps the most understandable scam—when I say fake Nike or Gucci, you know exactly what I mean. This is the case of someone actively counterfeiting, making an unofficial or unlicensed copy of an existing individual product, usually a high-value brand. A good example happened in 2014 when Italian authorities seized thirty thousand bottles of counterfeit Brunello, Chianti Classico, and other high-end Italian DOCG (Denominazione di Origine Controllata e Garantita, or Controlled Designation of Origin Guaranteed) wines. DOCG is the highest legal classification given wine by the Italian government, "guaranteeing" quality. But these were cheaper wines put into expensively labeled bottles, complete with fake official DOCG seals. By the time police made arrests, bottles had been sold in retail stores and served in bars and restaurants. The following month six hundred bottles of similarly packaged faux high-end Barolos were seized. A year earlier, two fraudsters had netted more than two million euros—over $2,500,000—by selling just four hundred bottles of cheap wine repackaged as one of the world's most coveted and collectible French Burgundies. That's over six grand a bottle, made possible in part because the bold duo chose to also label the wines with a faux-standout vintage.

While insidious, this type of purely criminal fraud is largely skipped over in the coming pages, with a few notable exceptions such as olive oil and seafood. There are two reasons for this: First, as Fake Food issues go, it's a small one. Second, there's really nothing you can do about it, no matter how closely you read the label. These are crimes, pure and simple, akin to a pickpocketing or having your car stolen off the street, the victims being consumers in the wrong place at the wrong time. Unfortunately, crime exists, and always has, in every society on earth. But all the other types of food fraud described herein, even when also criminal, are more common and more preventable.

## ✱ UTTER IMPOSTORS

This is the worst level of common fakery, an unapologetic take-no-prisoners approach to swindling consumers, which simply substitutes an unrelated product for the thing it pretends to be. At least the illegal counterfeiters mentioned above had the "decency" to use cheap wine in place of good wine, an act known as an economic fraud, where damage is measured chiefly in dollars. But what if they never even used wine at all? What if they used something potentially lethal instead? In 1986, Italian winemakers substituted toxic methyl alcohol for grape-derived alcohol, killing more than twenty people.

These kinds of product swaps have been going on since ancient times, and in London at the turn of the eighteenth century it was commonplace for merchants to take readily available leaves, chop them up, roast them, darken them with slightly poisonous dyes and pass the mixture off as Chinese black tea. The worst version was "green tea," dyed with much more poisonous copper. A more contemporary and highly publicized example is the widespread European horsemeat scandal of the past few years, where cheaper horsemeat was found to have been widely substituted for beef, especially in processed foods.

There is no way for the average consumer to look at a bunch

of ground-up leaves in a teabag or chopped meat in frozen lasagna with the naked eye and positively identify it. This visual ignorance is a recurring Fake Food theme we will see in our restaurants and supermarkets.

This type of fraud, selling fiction, is just slightly less common today, in an era where accurately testing the contents of food is easier. But it still happens much more than you would think, and far less testing or inspection of our food supply is done than most people believe. Most of the foods we eat every day are produced or imported, labeled, and sold with almost no oversight at all. In certain food categories, this kind of utter impostor fraud is so regular as to be a public health risk. For now, let's just say that if you are drinking a cup of herb tea as you read this, you might want to put it down for another hundred pages or so. Pour yourself a Scotch whisky instead, one of the few reliably Real Foods.

While often just as criminal as illegal counterfeits, utter impostors are systemic in nature and with knowledge you can protect yourself against these fakes. The first step is to learn which foods are most at risk, and the second is to shop for these particular products from more reliable vendors or producers. In this case, our own government is also much more to blame, because perpetrators are so rarely punished. Those wine counterfeiters were arrested, but in most cases where fish, tea, cheese, or any other food is intentionally sold as something else, no matter how dangerous the deception is, the result is a slap on the wrist or warning letter—if that—which amounts to de facto decriminalization. Counterfeit wine represents a tiny fraction of the wine market, but in many cases counterfeit fish *is* the market.

## ✳ LEGAL AND GRAY-AREA COUNTERFEITS

This is where we get into a moral area on which some readers may not take my side. Earlier I defined *Real Food* as being what it says it is. By this same logic, when a manufacturer intentionally misleads the consumer into thinking she is buying something different (and usually better) than the actual product, the result is a fake, even if no law is broken. There are plenty of legal Fake Foods—like the California "Burgundy."

If you adhere to the philosophy that businesses and individuals should be able to do whatever they want and get away with whatever they can, as long as they do not break laws, even when the laws are clearly inadequate and the behavior is harmful and/or dishonest, then you probably will have trouble accepting these foods as fake. I hope to convince you otherwise.

Let's use a dramatic hypothetical example: Suppose that instead of the United States you live in Russia. Now suppose the Russian government decides to shore up the domestic auto or computer industry by making it legal for Russian companies to produce specific "American" products using the same brand names. Suddenly, you can buy a copy of Microsoft Office not made by Microsoft, but rather by some local teen, which might lack certain important components, such as Word and Excel. Likewise, you can buy a Cadillac Escalade, but instead of an SUV made in Detroit costing seventy-five thousand dollars, it might be a sedan made in Tolyatti costing seventy-five hundred dollars.

In this hypothetical new world where Russian law allowed all this, would American manufacturers like Cadillac and Microsoft become incensed? You bet. Would the U.S. government formally and vigorously protest? Uh-huh. The Russian manufacturers of these products would not be able to export them, except maybe to North Korea or China, because in most civilized countries they would be considered obvious counterfeits and banned. But the Russian and Chinese market is more than big enough to support its own domestic fakes of these well-known brands.

At the end of the day, who would be affected? First, the Russian consumer who thinks he is getting the quality, features, compatibility, and support Microsoft is known for, but is not. That is an economic fraud. On the other hand, the Russian owner of "Microsoft" is getting rich and is much better off under this arrangement, as long as he can sleep at night. The manufacturers of the real products are adversely affected because they are losing sales to the fakes, often unwittingly. Suppose a rich oligarch who knows of Cadillac's global cachet and reputation for quality and who can afford a real Escalade buys the fake, thinking he is getting the real thing. Now the damage mounts: The buyer suffers economic fraud and potentially injury or death if he has an accident in this far less safe "Cadillac." But the real Cadillac also suffers harm, as does the autoworker in Detroit who loses his job because sales are down in the Russian market. Would the respective CEOs of the affected American companies consider these Russian products real or fake? It wouldn't matter, because in Russia they'd still be legal, just like our "Burgundy" here.

This scenario brings up a key point about the Real Food, Fake Food issue. Most Real Foods are not recipes; they are executions of a process. Earlier I mentioned onions and corn, and how planting the exact same seed, kernel, or bulb in different places will yield vastly different results. You can make a 100 percent pinot noir wine in Oregon that might be as good or better than one from Burgundy, but it will never be the same, even if using identical vines and winemaking techniques, because the soil and weather are different. Burgundy is essentially a brand name for a particular style of wine. Others can make the wine in the same way, but they should not be able to call it by the brand name Burgundy. Parmigiano-Reggiano is a "brand" of cheese, with three different "models," just as Cadillac is brand of car. Cadillac can legally protect its name but cannot claim an automobile exclusive—there are lots of other brands of cars. But in all these cases, the name or brand also connotes unusually high quality. The confusing issue is that the United States has a different trademark law system from France and Italy, and ours does not allow trademarks to be collectively owned. Cadillac is one company, while Parmigiano-Reggiano is a consortium of companies.

I know the Russia example sounds farfetched, but a real version of this situation is unfolding right now on a smaller scale—with pizza. Dating back seventy-five years, Brooklyn-born Grimaldi's is one of New York's most popular and iconic pizzerias, and there is usually a long line out the door at the flagship. It is famous for using coal-fired ovens, not typical for New York–style pizza, giving it a distinctive taste. Grimaldi's has parlayed its successful original into a brand name known for both a particular style of pizza and excellence making it, and it has grown into a national chain, with nearly fifty restaurants in a dozen states. It's not quite a McDonald's or Chipotle in scope, but it is a significant food undertaking, all built on the presumption that its brand and long history of delivering a high level of product quality means something to customers—just as it does for Cadillac. Other companies can make cars, but they can't make Cadillac cars. Other companies can make pizzas, but they can't make Grimaldi's pizzas. Unless they are in China.

The owners of the real Grimaldi's woke up one morning to find their pizzeria had been carbon-copied in Shanghai, right down to signage and T-shirts identical to those their staff wears, emblazoned with the signature slogan "I'm gonna make you a pizza you can't refuse." Because the real Grimaldi's appears in every New York City travel guidebook, including those published in Chinese, and there are often many Chinese visitors waiting in the Brooklyn line, it obviously has a quality perception in Shanghai worth trying to cash in on—otherwise there would be no need to steal the name; Chinese pizzerias could just attempt to make a similar type of pizza. Many winemakers make wines in the style of Burgundy without using the name, and in fact, the only ones who do use it are selling the lowest-quality imitations. The real Grimaldi's sued a former employee involved in the "clone" for twenty-five million dollars.

Immoral? No doubt. Illegal? Well, considering the "Parmesan" standard, that depends on whether the real Grimaldi's folks had appropriately trademarked their name under Chinese law. Or maybe the Chinese government will deem the word *Grimaldi's* to be a generic term for high-quality pizza and thus incapable of trademark protection, as the United States has done with Champagne.

Regardless, Grimaldi's has spent decades building a lofty reputation for its distinctive take on pizza, and that reputation has been hijacked, known in trademark law as riding the coattails. Even if it doesn't hurt the owners economically (which of course it does), it hurts them because it is wrong, and at the end of the day, that may be enough.

Besides an attempt to mislead consumers, another reason producers usurp existing product names is to make it easier to explain what they are selling. In Switzerland, most people understand what real Gruyère cheese is without further explanation. But when a U.S. manufacturer makes a Gruyère-style cheese and doesn't want to lie and call it Gruyère, that honest cheese maker is faced with a tough choice of how to convey to the consumer what type of cheese it is—a unique name like "Joe's Great Cheese" might not do the trick. So at this point I will make an important clarification in the scheme of Real Foods and Fake Foods: I'm a big fan of using the terms *imitation* and *style* when advertising inauthentic products because they offer a transparent solution to many of these issues. Since these words clearly alert consumers that what they are buying is not the genuine article, consumers cannot accuse producers of acting in bad faith. Imitation Gruyère is not Gruyère (though it still might be real cheese). Similarly, if you see a sign for Kansas City–*style* barbecue, it's a sure indication that you're not in Kansas (or Missouri) anymore. For this reason, I heartily suggest the use of such modifiers as *imitation Kobe* or *Parmesan-style*, because no matter how good they may taste, if the Kobe isn't from Japan and if the Parmesan isn't from Parma, they are not what they purport to be.* (Interestingly, one of the largest U.S. tobacco product retailers, JR, sells "Genuine Counterfeit Cuban Cigars," which it describes as Cuban-style made in Nicaragua. Few if any consumers would confuse that with the real thing, and I can definitely live with *counterfeit* as a modifier—it is often the most accurate one!)

What I can't support, however, is the use of *domestic* and similar terms as qualifiers. While, yes, clarifying a product's origin (e.g., "domestic Kobe" or "California Champagne") will signal its inauthenticity, it also places an unfair burden on less-savvy consumers, who must now memorize the history and source of all Real Foods. The simple reality is that there can be no such thing as "California Champagne," since by definition Champagne cannot be produced there. Therefore it should not be advertised as such.

Now, what about foods labeled "natural," "pure," or "100% something or other"? This is another gray area since these terms have little or no legal definition but are often intentionally used to dupe buyers. In general, the law allows these claims to be slapped on almost anything, and manufacturers take advantage by applying them to products in confusing—and sometimes ridiculous—ways. During a court case between hot dog giants Ball Park and Oscar Meyer, in which Kraft defended its "100 percent pure beef" label

---

*It should be noted that the European Union wholly disagrees with me on the use of *imitation, style,* and similar designations. Its rules for geographic indications on foods emphatically states, "Registered names shall be protected against any misuse, imitation or evocation, even if the true origin of the products or services is indicated or if the protected name is translated or accompanied by an expression such as 'style,' 'type,' 'method,' 'as produced in,' 'imitation,' or similar" (EU Commission Regulation No. 1107/96, art. 13). These rules would ban such disclosures as "imitation Kobe beef."

on Oscar Mayer hot dogs, Stephen O'Neil, the attorney for Kraft, "told the judge that the 100 percent beef tag was never intended to suggest there weren't other ingredients." The hot dog makers later settled their lawsuits. In this case, the manufacturer apparently meant that whatever beef was in the hot dogs was in fact beef but did not clarify how much of the hot dog comprised beef. Which informs consumers not at all.

But when using such disingenuous labeling, there is a line that can be crossed, as the law also generally prohibits marketing that "misleads." In reality, misleading consumers is a far higher standard than you might think to prove, and it is resolved only through lawsuits on a case-by-case basis.

Kobe beef is solidly in this gray area. There is no doubt that almost all of what is sold in this country as Kobe beef is fake, but since there is no law specifically prohibiting it, Faux-be beef would appear to fit the bill of a legal counterfeit. Consumer lawsuits for this kind of food fraud rarely come to fruition unless they are class-action suits involving enormous numbers of transactions and deep-pocketed perpetrators. This excludes most individual restaurants, leaving them free to ride roughshod over customers with all sorts of fictional menu claims.

Masa Noda is an attorney, specializing in trademark law with the New York firm Greenberg Traurig. He has been trying to help protect Kobe beef through the legal strategy of chipping away at trademark infringement. As he told me, "I too have been bothered by the use of 'Kobe beef' on restaurant menus over the years. I took it on not for the money, but for the principle, so that people won't be deceived. When people hear 'Kobe beef,' they think, 'Oh that's something good,' so there is definitely consumer deception going on, no doubt. But once you learn that natural means nothing, organic means nothing, you learn that you need to go only with what you trust. But the more you learn, the less you trust."

# 3. Fishy Fish

Most seafood buyers . . . assume that the seafood they buy is what the seller claims it is. However, this is not always the case. Sometimes seafood products are mislabeled for financial gain—an activity called seafood fraud . . . fraud can result in food safety problems.

> —U.S. GOVERNMENT ACCOUNTABILITY OFFICE,
> "Seafood Fraud"

A civil engineer by training, my father served in the Pacific theater toward the end of World War II with the Army Corps of Engineers. He avoided ever discussing his wartime duties in detail, but from what I've read, as the fighting went island to island, one of the first tasks needed after troops seized a beachhead—and well before the place was anything close to secured—was a supply of clean drinking water. This was a job for the engineers, and the working conditions, to put it lightly, were less than ideal.

What he did like to talk about was sushi. After the war ended, my father stayed on with the Army of Occupation in a much different role, helping to rebuild the badly damaged Japanese infrastructure. It was, I imagine, a far more pleasant job, working without wondering if you'd be shot, sleeping in a bed indoors, and spending whatever leisure time the army afforded exploring a place that, as foreign as Japan can seem to visitors today, was much more foreign then. During his explorations of Tokyo and other cities, my father became enamored of the local cuisine—sushi and sashimi in particular.

Japanese food was largely lost in translation between the cultures of East and West at that time and would remain almost completely unknown in this country well into the 1970s. If you were born in the past thirty-five years it is probably impossible to fathom, but just as there was a time before smartphones and the internet, there was time before sushi. When I was growing up in the late 1960s and throughout the 1970s, if you wanted to eat Japanese and you didn't live in New York or LA you were pretty much out of luck, and even then it required some heavy lifting, on par with finding a South African eatery today. My father would pack us into the car and drive to one of the handful of small Japanese immigrant enclaves in Queens, where we would feast on sushi and tempura and sukiyaki while the other patrons stared at us, since we were typically the only "Westerners" in the place.

I've loved sushi and sashimi ever since. When it is prepared well from quality fish, it is hard to beat in terms of coaxing maximum flavor from minimal ingredients. It is all about simplicity and delicious seafood, a meal mostly prepared by Mother Nature. I've had unbelievable sushi and sashimi in Tokyo, Alaska, Chile, Australia, and memorably on a boat off the coast of Biloxi, Mississippi, where the captain carved up a wahoo we had just caught and drizzled it with soy sauce from a bottle he carried for just that reason. We ate it while the boat was still rocking. I've also had great sushi in less likely places, including Aspen, Colorado; Switzerland's Gstaad; and Las Vegas, because today, if restaurateurs care enough and spend enough, they can get excellent fresh fish flown just about anywhere. But it has been conclusively proven that most restaurants—especially sushi restaurants—really don't care at all.

Today the Big Apple rains raw fish at every turn, with sushi eateries every couple of blocks in many neighborhoods, often piggy-backed onto unrelated Asian cuisines like Chinese or Korean; sushi is also sold in supermarkets, delis, and convenience stores. But unless I'm splurging at a serious specialist like Nobu or Masa, where world-class fish comes with equally lofty prices, I simply do not eat sushi in New York anymore, and generally not in the United States at all, because ever since it became generic, it has tasted blah. This is not a coincidence, and there is a reason why most sushi is of such low quality: it's often fake.

This rampant fraud is not only a sushi problem but a seafood problem, and it is a bad one, found everywhere from coast to coast. Fake fish swim in every direction, from the sushi bar to the seafood market to the frozen-food section of the supermarket, and across restaurant menus at every price point, from fast-food eateries to five-star restaurants. Bluntly, the seafood industry is rife with fraud, substitution, and adulteration. Imagine if half the time you pulled into a gas station you were filling your tank with dirty water instead of gasoline. That's the story with seafood.

While sushi is statistically the worst offender, there is good reason to be dubious about seafood of almost every description, raw or cooked, shellfish or fin fish. While you might find fake grass-fed beef hiding in your grocer's meat case, you can still be fairly confident that the beef is beef, whatever else may be lurking in it. But this is not the case when it comes to seafood, and fake seafood can be far more dangerous than other food fakes, even poisonous.

In many major U.S. cities, your chances of getting what you ordered—and paid for—in both restaurants and stores are slim at best. Pulling no punches, Elizabeth Weise, writing for *USA Today*, unequivocally stated that "fish is the most frequently faked food Americans buy." The problem is so bad that in mid-2014 President Obama announced that he was going to clean it up and appointed a seafood task force. When was the last time a national food crisis—and it is a crisis—got so out of control that the president had to step in?

"I could talk for days about seafood fraud. It is an industry that is rife with concerns. Oh my God, seafood is just terrible," Steven Kronenberg, an attorney who specializes in food fraud cases at San Francisco's Veen Group, told me. "There's a recurring undercurrent of seafood fraud issues that surface every couple of years, and not a whole lot is ever done about it. As long as there is an economic motive for people to profit by defrauding others, it will continue. The penalties associated with seafood fraud are relatively modest compared with the money that can be made, and it's much safer, generally speaking, to perpetrate that kind of fraud than to traffic in contraband."

How terrible is it? A study of New York City seafood done by scientists at nonprofit marine conservation group Oceana found fraud in 58 percent of retail outlets and 39 percent of restaurants. The one especially scary finding that would have my father turning over in his grave was that every sushi restaurant from which samples were collected—100 percent of them—served fake fish. Obviously, researchers did not test every New York sushi restaurant, but they tested enough to make it worrisome that not even one could meet the baseline standard of serving Real Food. And the practices in New York, it would turn out, were the rule, not the exception, for the entire country.

*Species substitution* and *species adulteration* are terms for a common scam in which a much less expensive—and sometimes dangerous—fish is sold as a premium species to which it is often completely unrelated. With some of the most desirable fish, this is a frequent occurrence. Consumers ordering white tuna get a completely different animal, no kind of tuna at all, 94 percent of the time. Your odds of getting served real white tuna in a restaurant are about the same as hitting zero/double zero on a Vegas roulette wheel, which is to say, not good. Not only do you not get what you pay for, you really don't want what you do get: the single most common substitute for the tuna is escolar, one of most dangerous seafood products you can buy.

In the seafood industry, escolar is nicknamed "Ex-Lax fish," because it contains a natural wax ester that can give people digestive distress and diarrhea for days. It was responsible for a wave of six hundred illnesses in Hong Kong and has been banned completely in food-safety-obsessed Japan for nearly forty years. It was effectively banned here too by an "import bulletin" issued by the FDA in the early 1990s but then unbanned in 1998 when the bulletin was canceled. When people get sick after eating sushi or sashimi, they often blame the rawness for their stomach distress, saying something like, "I must have had bad tuna." It's more likely their problems were caused by the fact that they never had tuna at all. While no one ever orders it, escolar is one of the best-selling and most widely served fish in this country.

"You can probably go into any restaurant in most any state and not get what you ordered, particularly for grouper and red snapper," Bob Jones, who represents domestic fish suppliers, told the *St. Petersburg Times*. He was interviewed during what became known as the "Florida grouper scandal of 2006," one of the few prosecuted fake-fish incidents in this country. Grouper is a regionally beloved fish widely caught off Florida's west coast. After the paper's investigation tested fish and found pervasive substitutions in restaurants, the exposé shocked locals and the state's attorney general got involved. Ultimately a federal grand jury indicted a Panama City seafood wholesaler on charges of importing a million pounds of cheap frozen Asian catfish and passing it off as grouper, which could wholesale for more than four times as much. Florida's economic crimes division prosecuted seventeen restaurants in the Tampa area. One served an expensive "champagne braised black grouper" entrée actually made of cheaper frozen tilapia. My well-educated guess is that the Champagne was an impostor as well.

I visited the Tampa area in 2014 and made the drive up to Clearwater Beach, not to eat at the original Hooter's, a mecca for chicken wing and breast lovers that is located here and still thriving, and not to shop at the Hulk Hogan signature store in downtown Clearwater—the Hulkster is arguably the city's most famous son. Instead, I went to eat at a beloved seaside grouper spot called Frenchy's Rockaway Grill, a bustling hole in the wall where you can sit inches from the sand, the kind of open air place missing parts of the walls, with plastic sharks and Corona beer signage hung as decorations and lots of mai tais, coladas, and rum runners going by on trays carried by attractive young women. I sat under a perfect Florida sunny sky and had lunch with the owner, Michael Preston, who originally hails from Quebec of all places, hence his nickname, Frenchy. Preston had come to Clearwater Beach thirty-four years earlier to visit friends on vacation and, like so many others, was seduced by the beautiful beach. He never left and now owns a handful of restaurants and a small hotel, the Oasis. Frenchy's specialty is not *poutine* but grouper.

"The grouper has always been our signature item, it's exactly the same after thirty-four years, like a time warp," he told me. The original grouper sandwich that put Frenchy's on the map is fried in seasoned butter and served on an onion roll with cheese. I ate one with Preston, and it was delightful, the light but thick slab of fish absorbing the butter's richness and pairing perfectly with the flavor and texture of the roll, and to me, cheese improves just about any sandwich. Grouper is a meaty white fish, but light in texture and mild in taste, and its best characteristic is that it absorbs flavors very well, so it is perfect for cooking with ingredients like seasoned butter.

Throughout the decades Preston introduced several new variants of the sandwich, the two main ones being grilled and Cajun grilled, and along with the original, these three are the most popular menu items, evenly split. Since this was important research, I had another half sandwich of each style, and because seasonings and grouper go so well together, I loved the Cajun. Frenchy's grouper sandwich also comes Buffalo-style, which means batter fried and topped with hot wing sauce and bleu cheese dressing. That sounded pretty interesting, so I had one of those too—hey, it's my job. His grouper Reuben, while not as popular as the main triumvirate, has the most passionate following, with dedicated customers who never order anything else. It is grilled grouper on toasted marble rye with sauerkraut, Swiss-style cheese and Thousand Island dressing. I tried that too. My favorite was the original, which really lets the fish shine, though the Buffalo and Cajun grilled were both close seconds.

Preston won't admit a preference because "they are like children, I love them all," but he did concede that the onion roll, an innovation he brought south with him from snow country, is the key differentiator from many other grouper sandwiches served in these parts. "There have been fish sandwiches forever, and we didn't invent the grouper sandwich—we just elevated it. We do everything fresh, use good lettuce, tomato, make our own tartar sauce, and I've just always loved onion rolls and they work really well." There is one other thing that separates Frenchy's grouper sandwiches from many others, and it's the reason I visited—they are real.

Preston's claim about being frozen in time and everything being like the early 1980s is not really true. Back then it was easy to get real grouper. Now, not so much. As his local restaurant empire expanded, so did his demand for a fish that is only wild caught, never farm raised, and native to the Gulf of Mexico, about a hundred feet from me as he told his story. To ensure his supply of the real thing, he took a bold direction and launched his own seafood company. Preston hires boatmen, between eight and eleven at any time, who fish exclusively for him, though he sells off any extra, sometimes to other restaurants.

"There are certain things that don't travel well and taste better regionally. Grouper tastes better here, and we know how to handle it right. You hear all about farm to table being a hot concept, but we've been doing that forever." He described clientele who vacation once or twice a year in Clearwater Beach, and as soon as their plane hits the tarmac, they head to Frenchy's, often with luggage in hand before checking into their hotels, because they have been waiting all year long for their beloved grouper Reuben. Then they come back on the last day of their trip and do it again, so that their favorite taste is the last memory of their vacation. He can't take the chance of serving those devoted folks fake fish and letting them down. "I can trace every single fish from the moment it is caught until we serve it." That's why Frenchy's is the only place I will eat grouper.

Dr. Kimberly Warner is a scientist who coauthored six Oceana studies on seafood fraud and was living on the Gulf Coast during the 2006 grouper scandal. She explained to me that the fish most commonly used to fake grouper also plays the part of many other fishes we wrongly think we are eating, and one almost no even knows exists: the Cambodian ponga (aka pangasius), a type of Asian catfish, usually farmed. Other Florida grouper fakes included tilapia, hake, and one creepy fish that according to DNA testing belonged to an unknown species and could not even be identified. But most of the fake grouper was farmed Asian catfish, mainly ponga.

While grouper is always wild caught, ponga is almost always farmed, usually in places with dubious standards and established track records for using unapproved—or banned—antibiotics and drugs in their aquaculture. A versatile counterfeit, ponga is also routinely passed off as everything from the very different North American catfish to sole to flounder to cod. While many of us might head to the fish market with the intention of buying southern catfish, grouper, flounder, or sole to cook for dinner, I've never known a single person to voluntarily go shopping for ponga, yet according to Dr. Warner it is one of the highest-volume fishes in this country commercially, seemingly imported in vast quantities just so it can be resold as counterfeits of more valuable species.

"If you look at the top seafood items being imported, it's always in the top ten. They look amazingly like grouper, and when I was living in the Gulf in the mid-2000s, there were lots and lots of grouper being sold that wasn't grouper at all. They were mislabeling it," said Warner. The same holds true for the dangerous escolar: almost no one wants it or knowingly buys it, yet the fish is sold everywhere.

But if there is a poster child for fake fish, it's red snapper, a premium choice that is both rare and exceedingly popular at better restaurants, an apparent contradiction. Expert after expert told me to avoid buying or eating it because it is so unlikely you will ever get it. To this day, I still don't know whether I've ever actually tasted it. In the Oceana study, it did the worst, with the real thing appearing less than 6 percent of the time. Again, take your money to Vegas instead—at least you might get a free drink.

Because almost all red snapper sold in this country is fake, it has many different imitators, including mercury-rich tilefish, which is on the FDA's do-not-eat list for sensitive groups such as children and pregnant women. Tilefish is also used to fake pricy halibut. "Your Red Snapper Is Probably Fake," an article on the DailyFinance website pronounced, then laid out specific health concerns: "Eaters who are totally getting cheated: pregnant women . . . They aren't supposed to eat fish that live a long time like shark, mackerel, tilefish . . . Mercury causes birth defects. The fish industry likes to play up fish's omega-3 health benefits and say that women just have to avoid certain species. But that's impossible when so much fish is totally mislabeled."

The most common fakes for pricy red snapper were tilefish and tilapia—often farmed and drug laden—but the Oceana study found many other equally dubious swaps. When tilapia was not posing as red snapper it was often dressed up as catfish, one of the most legally protected domestic species. The high tariffs on imported catfish can be avoided through simple fakery. Undesirable farmed shrimp is routinely swapped for wild caught; steelhead trout has been a stand-in for salmon; inexpensive fish roe is used in place or to dilute expensive caviar; and in one memorable case pufferfish was illegally imported, relabeled, and sold as monkfish. Better known to exotic diners as fuju, pufferfish is the second-most poisonous vertebrate in the world, after the golden poison frog. It's a delicacy in Japan where chefs require special safety training in order to be allowed to prepare and serve it, but no one prepared the two people poisoned in Chicago when they bought, cooked, and ate "monkfish" in 2007. Real monkfish does not contain potentially deadly tetrodotoxin. They survived, but they were lucky.

Shipping and country-of-origin information is routinely—and illegally—falsified to cover up poaching and hide fish coming from dangerous farms that use unapproved chemicals and even slave labor. All the gross details you have heard about industrial cattle farming—from the widespread use of antibiotics and chemicals to animals living in their own feces and being fed parts of other animals they don't naturally consume—occurs in the seafood arena as well, only it is much better hidden.

Domestic seafood industry spokesman Bob Jones believes that from wholesalers to retailers, fish substitution is so prevalent that at this point it may well be unstoppable. I asked Dr. David Kessler, former FDA commissioner under both the George H. W. Bush and Clinton administrations, about this hot-button issue. Kessler is a medical doctor and lawyer, as well as best-selling author and public health campaigner. "If there is a fish that costs twenty cents, it's not going to have a lot of fraud. If there's fish that costs ten bucks and I can find a fish that looks like it for four bucks and sell it, there is going to be fraud," he said matter of factly. "You can almost sit back and predict, based on the underlying economics, when there is going to be fraud."

Just as the *St. Petersburg Times* had done in Florida, the *Boston Globe* investigated seafood fraud in Massachusetts and found tons of it. One local restaurant served a twenty-three-dollar "flounder" fillet made of swai, a Vietnamese fish investigators described as "nutritionally inferior and often priced under $4 a pound." The five-month *Globe* probe into the mislabeling of fish showed that "Massachusetts consumers routinely and unwittingly overpay for less desirable, sometimes undesirable, species—or buy seafood that is simply not what it is advertised to be." The study also demonstrated the prevailing attitude in an industry where even when caught, retailers and restaurants rarely get more than a slap on the wrist: "Minado, a bustling buffet restaurant off Route 9 that churns out hundreds of rolls of sushi and nigiri pieces daily, admitted it labeled tilapia as red snapper. 'Not because we are trying to trick,' said Alexa Poletti, a Minado manager. 'We're doing it how everybody does it.'"

"Consumers ask me all the time, 'What can I do?' and all I can say is just don't ever buy red snapper. Red snapper is the big one—when you buy it you almost never get it," said Dr. Mark Stoeckle, shaking his head over the breakfast we shared at a New York City coffee shop. He was shaking his head because his only concrete advice for the American consumer is to avoid a problem rather than solve it. Stoeckle echoed every expert I spoke to when he warned against ordering it, but none could suggest a way to actually get red snapper.

Stoeckle is a physician specializing in infectious diseases, a clinical associate professor of medicine at Weill Medical College, and senior research associate in the Program for the Human Environment at the Rockefeller University. In this latter role, he has spent years working on the Barcode of Life project, an international database attempting to map the DNA of practically every living thing. It was because of this that he was drawn deeply into the world of fake fish and then the larger world of Fake Food, years before the Oceana study—by his high school daughter. "In 2008, I was working on this DNA project and my daughter and her high school friend asked me whether it would be possible for me to DNA test sushi. I hadn't heard of anyone ever doing it, and I said sure. They bought all this sushi at neighborhood places and I helped them send it to the lab, and a quarter of it was mislabeled but always with a less expensive fish masquerading as a more expensive fish. It turns out this problem is not just one store or one restaurant or one city—it is widespread."

The two young women, Kate Stoeckle and Louisa Strauss, were high school seniors working on a science project, and they tested sixty New York fish samples by DNA identification. Overall, half the restaurants and more than half of the retailers sold fake fish. Besides red snapper, they found many of the other usual suspects, including tilapia widely passed off as tuna in sushi places. Their sample was small, but their study got prominent coverage in the *New York Times,* and larger studies followed, with much more statistically significant data—and these found even worse results. "Their work inspired a lot of bigger studies," said Dr. Stoeckle. "Oceana did the furthest-reaching one, which found that almost a third of all the seafood in this country was mislabeled."

Fake seafood is not a Florida problem or a Massachusetts problem or a New York City problem—it is an everywhere problem. Oceana took its study national in 2013 and found that mislabeling in violation of FDA regulations was often much worse in the biggest cities. A summary released with the report noted that "Oceana found seafood fraud everywhere it tested, including mislabeling rates of 52 percent in Southern California, 49 percent in Austin and Houston, 48 percent in Boston, 39 percent in New York City, 38 percent in Northern California and South Florida, 32 percent in Chicago, 26 percent in Washington, DC, and 18 percent in Seattle." Perhaps because of its famed Pike Place Market, teeming with gorgeous regional seafood like Alaskan salmon and fresh Dungeness crab, Seattle residents can be proud to know they did so well, with "only" one fish in five being fake.

Substitution and adulteration is easiest in products hard to differentiate with the naked eye, and therefore fish, especially fillets of white fish, are ideal. In markets, fish is often sliced so consumers never see it whole, but this practice is worse in restaurants, where you don't see anything at all until it arrives on your plate, maybe under a mound of sauce or breaded and fried. Imagine trying to ID the chunks of fish in a seafood stew like cioppino. "The National Fisheries Institute just did some research, and one of the reasons there are so many problems is that most people don't know how to pick out seafood, or even what it is supposed to look like," said TJ Tate of Gulf Wild, a marketing advocacy group for real wild-caught seafood from the Gulf of Mexico, while speaking at a Monterey Bay Aquarium conference I attended. It would be hard to sell most consumers chicken claiming it was steak, or potatoes masquerading as cucumbers, but many American shoppers have no idea what color or shape many popular fish are, let alone more subtle differences. I for one have no clue what orange roughy looks like, yet it is a popular menu item, so a restaurant could sell me pretty much any fish and tell me it is orange roughy and I wouldn't—couldn't—object. In fact, until researching this book, I assumed it was a venerable fish and not a made-up name created to better market the less tasty-sounding slime head.

WITH ALMOST NOTHING but coastline, Chile is one of the world's greatest seafood countries. The supermodel of nations, it is very tall and very thin, its widest spot barely two hundred miles across, while stretching almost twenty-seven hundred miles north to south, nearly as much coastline as the width of the United States. Almost everyone in Chile lives within an hour of the Pacific Ocean, and because the massive seaboard spans climates from subtropical to Antarctic, the breadth of creatures that come out of its waters is truly fantastic. In the heart of its capital, Santiago, there is a seafood market that resembles the classic food halls of eastern Europe, an ornate and imposing steel structure that was designed by Gustav Eiffel, of Eiffel Tower fame. If you ever have the chance to visit Santiago, one of the world's most unsung great cities, a stop at the Mercado Central is mandatory. While far smaller and less dramatic than Tokyo's famed Tsujiki Fish Market, it is still packed with eye-popping aquatic wonders. It is also unique in that it has several restaurants within the heart of the market itself, right next to the rows of varied seafood booths.

The first time I visited, I went with a friend for lunch at Donde Augusto, which had been recommended, and the menu was a who's who of the market's wet denizens. I remember that we had baby eels in garlic, served in a classic Chilean glazed terra-cotta bowl with two small handles protruding from either side that goes straight from the oven to the table. It was filled with a heap of tiny eels, each only an inch or two long, swimming in garlic and butter, delicate and delicious and clearly the real thing. But the star of the day was Patagonian king crab, a relative of the Alaskan version but from the polar opposite end of the earth. It is rare to find it anywhere but in Patagonia or Santiago. The crustacean is so imposing that before cooking the waiter presented its glory tableside, stretching its legs apart so we could marvel at its massive leg span. Wider than his shoulders, it reached from one of his outstretched hands to the other, about five feet of crabby goodness.

Once cooked, the crab was returned, now the bright red and white colors associated with king crab, this time by two waiters, each armed with gloves and an assortment of special crab scissors and tools. With great pomp and circumstance, they disjointed our friend, such a larger-than-life fish that he deserved a name, and ever since, I have called him Señor Crab. They broke each of Señor Crab's long legs down into sections about eight inches long, then snipped these shells lengthwise, until finally we were left with a pile of easy-to-eat meaty sticks of delicious crab, adorned with just a brief dip in melted butter. It was lunch as theater and I have never forgotten it, nor Señor Crab.

Two years later I returned on assignment to Santiago with my wife in tow, and having regaled her with endless stories of Señor Crab, I felt she needed to experience it for herself, so we returned to Donde Augusto for lunch. But much to my chagrin, they had no Patagonian king crab that day. I had never thought to call ahead. In retrospect, its absence on the menu is understandable: this crab is a relatively rare creature that is an expensive delicacy by Chilean standards (but still reasonable in U.S. dollars). The waiter saw my crestfallen look and inquired, and I explained that we had come a long way just for their crab. So he sent another staffer out into the market to see if any of the peddlers had any Patagonian king crab, and sure enough, a few minutes later he returned bearing the goods. My wife got the whole song and dance, from the plastic lobster bib tied graciously for her around her neck to the elaborate tableside presentation to the final lick of her lips. That is Real

Food, in a real place, and there is no mistaking the giant crab prepared in front of your eyes for the weirdly textured packaged blocks of imitation crab meat served every single day in most sushi restaurants in the United States. But to know it, you need to see it.

Historically, in zoology, species identifications were made visually, by experts looking at samples, but fish is rarely sold to most buyers whole. "If you take a fillet to the Museum of Natural History and ask them to positively ID the species, they just can't do that," Dr. Stoeckle explained. "DNA testing allows you to do something you otherwise couldn't do. What really surprised me when we did it was how many of these substitute fish were odd species that only exist in Southeast Asia. You can look at maps of fish habitats and a lot of them come from a specific area between Australia and China. I always wonder how did they get here, and who buys them? These are not fish that are ever sold as themselves in stores, and in many cases I didn't even know you could eat them."

Because he is also a physician and infectious disease specialist, this realization led Dr. Stoeckle to worry about the health risks inherent in fake seafood, especially with all the farming. "No one knows where they were raised, how they were raised, how they got here, or what kinds of antibiotics were used. There's a huge disconnect between growing consumer interest in where it's grown and how it's grown on one hand, and the fact that we are not even getting the species being advertised on the other."

From a health and environmental perspective, faking the country of origin may be a worse problem than species substitution. Much fraud revolves around what is called transshipment. This occurs when a product is exported to one or more countries between its place of origin and the United States and illegally relabeled to hide its true birthplace. Even without transshipment—which happens on a massive scale—by law, processed foods only have to indicate where they were processed, and much seafood is processed.

There is no way to know if the frozen crab cakes or breaded fillets you buy, which may have been assembled in the United States, Canada, or Europe, contain farmed fish from China—or anyplace else. And in seafood, this goes way beyond what we normally think of as "processed foods," like TV dinners. Simply shelling crab or putting tuna in cans is processing. Just as species substitution exclusively swaps cheap fish for more expensive names, transshipment is almost always done to disguise a place consumers might try to avoid, which in the case of seafood usually means China or Thailand.

Oceana's Dr. Warner told me, "There are species that harbor natural toxins and unnatural toxins—we saw high mercury fish that the FDA tells people to avoid being sold as much less dangerous fish. Other risks are allergies with seafood, which are sometimes very species specific. There are a number of other health hazards: We have ciguatera poisoning from fish in tropical and subtropical waters that are infected, and it is a very nasty poisoning with neurological symptoms that some people don't ever recover from. The tests to screen for it are not easy to perform." Such tests and safeguards are more likely to be skipped in less developed countries. "There are paralytic shellfish poisonings, viral diseases, cholera. In the U.S. we monitor our shellfish a lot more carefully, but most of it is not domestic."

Ninety-one percent of the seafood consumed in the United States is imported, and about half of this is farmed. Yet only one-thousandth of 1 percent of imports are inspected for seafood fraud. In addition, about a third of the imported seafood is poached or caught illegally, which further obfuscates any clue about its actual origins. I attended the annual Monterey Bay Aquarium Sustainable Seafood Symposium, where one of the keynote speakers was Eric Schwaab, chief conservation officer at the National Aquarium in Baltimore. Schwaab is a former assistant secretary for the

National Oceanic and Atmospheric Administration. He explained that "roughly half of the seafood we consume is the product of aquaculture, sometimes from perfectly fine operations, other times not. We have huge labeling problems. Not only do we have lots of illegally caught fish, but they make their way into our food supply with little traceability in terms of country of origin or even species. I don't think there is any bigger problem facing the industry right now."

There is nothing inherently wrong with fish farming, but there is something wrong with most fish farms in practice. Overseas aquaculture is fraught with multiple health, environmental, and social concerns. It can simultaneously destroy healthful environments and dump huge amounts of waste into the ocean. Fish are routinely fed drugs that are either outlawed or unapproved in this country, and these often remain in their systems. Adding insult to injury, the State Department released a report in mid-2014 revealing that slave labor from human trafficking is used to produce farmed shrimp in Thailand, and Thailand is—by far—the biggest producer of shrimp for the United States.

Farming is especially efficient for catfish, which is why so much of the fake fish is imported farmed catfish. The imported fish is much different from our domestically farmed catfish, which is actually one of the safest, most environmentally sound, and heavily overseen forms of food production in the nation. Aquaculture is also excellent for mollusks, which provide natural filtration to the bays and oceans. As with raising beef cattle, fish farming can be done in a healthful, responsible, sustainable way, but unfortunately it is just much cheaper to do it badly, relying on hormones and antibiotics, and dyes.

"Across the board not all aquaculture is bad," Ken Peterson, spokesman for the Monterey Bay Aquarium, the world's gold standard of expertise in seafood sustainability, production, and fisheries, explained to me over lunch. "The problem is when you have carnivores like salmon. Then you are extracting wild fish from the ocean to feed to farmed fish, so you are still taking a lot of fish out of the ocean. The conversion rates are poor: it might take 10 pounds of wild-caught fish to produce one pound of farmed salmon [three to five pounds of wild-caught feed is more typical]. It's a feedlot just like cattle and they use antibiotics. Salmon and shrimp farming are by far the worst." A 2004 study of hundreds of farmed salmon samples from five leading countries found most so polluted with dioxins and PCBs that the author suggested people not eat it more than once a month. Unlike problematic shrimp and catfish from developing nations, some of the worst salmon performers were developed countries like Scotland and Norway.

Only one salmon farm anywhere, a cutting-edge Chilean operation, gets the Monterey Bay Aquarium's seal of approval, because it uses far fewer antibiotics. Of course, in the wild salmon don't use any antibiotics. And they don't have to be artificially colored pink. Most fish-farm feeds don't include krill, a mainstay of the salmon's natural diet, which is what gives the fish its distinctive color, so farmed salmon are dyed to look like naturally occurring salmon. As a result, a *USA Today* article about the widespread substitution of farmed for supposedly wild caught fish gave one useful tip for consumers to spot the fake: "When you cook it, the wild salmon retains its color, and in the aquaculture salmon, the color tends to leak out."

A big problem is that wild-caught salmon is widely considered one of the best fish you can eat. "Alaska salmon is well managed, sustainably caught, a good source of omega-3 fatty acids, all kinds of good things," says Dr. Warner. Because salmon is so recognizable, even after it is cut into steaks or fillets, it is harder to swap it out for another species. But not impossible. In 2014, the Department of Justice charged Miami-based True Nature Seafood,

LLC, with importing nearly six tons of steelhead trout from Chile and intentionally relabeling it as salmon. True Nature was able to inflate the value of the fish by about 25 percent by reselling it to customers as "salmon." The company pleaded guilty and agreed to pay one million dollars in fines and community service fines, a rare instance of actual fake-fish punishment.

This type of salmon deception is much rarer than the more common fraud of passing off farmed as wild caught, especially farmed Atlantic salmon (the only kind of Atlantic salmon, which is extinct in the wild) for the more desirable Alaskan or Pacific salmon. Fish farming is illegal across the board in Alaska, and all actual Alaskan salmon is wild caught. Wild-caught salmon always commands a price premium, and studies have clearly shown that most consumers have a definite preference for it. When *Consumer Reports* tested twenty-three supposedly wild-caught salmon fillets bought nationwide in 2005–6, only ten were in fact wild.

If faux salmon, red snapper, and tuna sushi were our only fake fish, we'd be lucky. We are not. Shrimp is the nation's single most consumed seafood, with the average American eating four pounds each year, most of which is farmed and imported. "For a variety of reasons, imported shrimp may be one of the worst food buying decisions consumers can make," said Ken Peterson as I dug into my delicious swordfish steak at the Monterey Bay Aquarium. I could not recall the last time I had swordfish, but it had been many years, ever since it started to be widely publicized as an immoral choice, overfished to the verge of extinction and politically incorrect. That's why I was shocked to see it on the menu at Cindy's Waterfront, the seafood restaurant inside the aquarium. The aquarium is world famous for publishing its annual color-coded Seafood Watch guides, which instruct consumers on which fish they can eat without guilt and which they should avoid.

Peterson explained that the real problem with swordfish is as

bycatch, accidentally being trapped in nets intended for other species, often in other countries. The sustainable version served here
is individually harpoon caught off the California coast, which I
can see from our table. Cindy's Waterfront is run by renowned
chef Cindy Pawlcyn, a James Beard Award winner better known
for her Mustard Grill in the Napa Valley; she has been at the forefront of the farm-to-table movement for three decades. Here, she
combines great cooking with all the information of the aquarium's
science-driven research to offer what is quite possibly the most
guilt-free—and fake-free—fish-eating restaurant experience in
the country. The research has been done for diners; there is no
need to fret over menu choices; and you won't find either of the
two worst offenders, farmed salmon or shrimp.

"In many places outside of the U.S. they locate shrimp farms
in coastal areas that were mangroves. Mangrove habitat is very important to a lot of other fish species and birds, and it is also nature's buffer against tsunamis. But they clear cut the mangroves
for shrimp farms. The shrimp are raised in ponds, and their waste
has to go somewhere, so they just dump it into the ocean," said
Peterson. This environmental destruction alone would be reason
for many people to avoid imported Asian shrimp, but then there is
the matter of the slave labor used to produce it and of the antibiotics and unapproved or banned drugs in it.

While researching this book I learned a lot of shocking and
unpleasant things, and as a result there were many changes I made
in my own behavior, but few as absolute as with farmed shrimp. I
buy only truly natural grass-fed beef for cooking, but I'll eat the
occasional grain-fed steak or burger in a restaurant. I only buy real
Greek feta cheese, but I might still risk a Greek salad while out.
However, I drew a line in the sand with shrimp—I won't buy it,
ever, if it is farmed or imported. I won't eat it in restaurants unless
I'm someplace like Charleston or Hilton Head or Kennebunkport

or Biloxi or Gulfport, and only then if I am at an eatery cut from the same cloth as Frenchy's, where I have very good reason to believe they bought actual local shrimp. I will no longer eat shrimp in most Asian restaurants, period. I only buy domestic wild-caught shrimp, and only when I believe there is a strong likelihood that those two statements are not lies, which means only some of the time. That is a lot of rules, but still, my position is more flexible than that of food-fraud specialist and attorney Kronenberg, who felt compelled to give it up altogether.

"Personally I have big problems with imported shrimp, especially all the chemical residues. The working conditions are just horrible and it's a real social justice issue that consumers might not think about, because it's not like they are going to put on the front of the package, 'Made with slave labor,' but for me, I am concerned about that. They only test something like two percent of the imported shrimp, and there are any number of studies that show that the shrimp might well come from a different place than what's listed on the package. There's a lot of transshipment of shrimp with potential drug residues or illegal chemicals." He has seen so much information about it that he won't even take the chance of being duped.

According to the FDA, there are forty-one distinct species of shellfish, farmed and wild, from all over the world, which can all be simply labeled "shrimp." There are a handful of more specific shrimp names, such as "white shrimp," which can only be used for labeling one specific species, in this case typically found only in North America. Assuming the label itself is not a lie, which may be a substantial leap of faith, these specific breeds are often the most reliable "real shrimp" names from a consumer perspective. The most prized of all is Royal Red shrimp, which can also be labeled "red shrimp," with both names legally exclusive to a single rare and delicious species, *Pleoticus robustus.*

Almost mythical in status and unknown even to many dedicated foodies, the Royal Red is a coveted regional specialty on the Gulf Coast, from the panhandle of Florida to Alabama, where better local restaurants and markets specialize in them. They are found almost exclusively around Pensacola, Florida, and Gulf Shores, Alabama, and only in very deep, cold water, usually one hundred miles or more from shore, making them an expensive shrimp to catch. (Oddly, a small, commercially insignificant enclave of Royal Reds was also found in the deep waters off the coast of Stonington, Connecticut.) They are still relatively unknown in terms of scientific study, but they are delicious and live up to their billing. Silkier and richer than other shrimp, they have a distinctly lobsterlike quality to them, meaty yet tender. I ate them once in Gulfport, Mississippi, and can't wait to do it again. They are large, very rich, and delicious, and they come out of the sea unusually pink or red, looking almost cooked, hence their name. They are also soft shelled, do not travel well, are rarely shipped, and to date have not been found elsewhere in the world, so they remain one of those foods best enjoyed at its source. If you are in the neighborhood, make sure you try them, and if you see them on a menu anywhere else, well, caveat emptor.

Few of us can enjoy Royal Red shrimp, and only in a handful of places, but we can eat other wild-caught shrimp from the Gulf of Mexico, which "consistently fetch the highest prices of any commercial shrimp in the world, and are the choice of discerning four- and five-star restaurants," said Captain Mike Moore, a shrimp fisherman out of Biloxi, Mississippi, who owns his own boat, *The Sailfish*. I went out with him shrimping for the day to learn more about the industry. "Shrimp live in the mud and favor slightly warmer water, so the Mississippi sound in the Gulf is optimum. The Mississippi river carries nutrient rich soil that constantly replenishes the mud, and the average water temperature is eighty-five. Shrimp grow most rapidly when it is above seventy-two. The shrimp here are bigger, meatier, sweeter, and easier to peel. This has always been the premier fishing ground in the U.S., and seventy-five percent of the country's wild caught shrimp comes from right here in the Gulf of Mexico. Our wild caught shrimp trades internationally for the highest prices."

But while these healthy crustaceans are exported, the vast majority of the shrimp consumed in America is farmed—often under extremely dubious conditions—imported, and routinely mislabeled. In 2007, the FDA banned the import of five Chinese farmed seafood products, including shrimp, after testing revealed unapproved drugs in the shrimp, just the kind of health concerns Kronenberg and Stoeckle worry about. So Chinese shrimp farmers began illegally transshipping their shrimp through Indonesia, entering the United States with a "Product of Indonesia" label. That worked fine for the first six million dollars worth of shrimp the pirates exported, until the United States noticed a spike in the volume of cheap shrimp suddenly coming out of Indonesia and levied antidumping tariffs. Without missing a beat, the banned Chinese shrimp were next sent to Malaysia, rebranded as Malaysian, and sold to U.S. consumers. After U.S. Customs officers discovered an illegal transshipment, they began testing "Malaysian shrimp"— after it had been sold and consumed in this country—and found contamination with the same unapproved drugs that got it banned in the first place.

This incident came to light as the result of a U.S. Government Accountability Office (GAO) review of seafood fraud, a report highly critical of the FDA, which concluded that in addition to avoiding tariffs, this illegal transshipment of potentially dangerous shrimp "had a health-and-food-safety-related effect. FDA is responsible for ensuring that foods are safe, wholesome, sanitary, and properly labeled . . . FDA considers detecting violations like these a low priority and devotes minimal resources to such work, according to published program guidance and senior FDA officials . . . *no resources have been allocated for seafood fraud-related work*" (emphasis mine). As in none, zero, zilch, nada.

In the long-running hit sitcom *Cheers*, one of the main characters, Norm, favored a bargain-priced restaurant called the Hungry Heifer that served ersatz dishes such as "bef," which he described as "a Hungry Heifer trademark for a processed, synthetic . . . meatlike substance . . . What do you expect for four bucks? You see me complainin' about the 'loobster'?" Life often imitates art, and in 2005 the FDA approved the commercial use of the name "langostino lobster," at the request of Rubio's Restaurants, Inc. They also did it somewhat secretly, without adding it to the official U.S. Seafood List, the public slate of approved names under which seafood can be sold. The FDA did all this over vehement written objections from the Maine Lobster Promotion Council, which protested that the name change would allow a lower-market-value seafood, langostinos, to take advantage of the higher market value and reputation of the American lobster name. *Langostino*, meaning "prawn" in Spanish, refers to several species of shrimp and crab, none of them lobster in any remote sense. Nonetheless, a lawsuit filed in California court to try to force Rubio's, a San Diego–based chain, to stop calling its nonlobster burrito a "lobster burrito" failed.

This court decision allowed several restaurant chains watching the case, including Red Lobster and Long John Silver's, to jump in and heavily promote the term *lobster* for dishes that contained no such thing. According to a 2016 investigation by *Inside Edition*, DNA testing of the meat in lobster bisque from multiple locations of Red Lobster, the nation's largest seafood restaurant chain, came back as langostino. "Red Lobster told us that their lobster bisque *can* contain meat from Maine lobster, langostino lobster, or, in some cases, a combination of both," said *Inside Edition* reporter

Lisa Guerrero. Not surprisingly, langostino is much cheaper. Like the artificial truffle flavor that appears on the ingredient list of something called truffle oil, you might find langostino in the fine print but almost never in the name of the product, be it lobster rolls, lobster tacos, or lobster quesadillas.

*Inside Edition* tried all sorts of lobster dishes at twenty-eight restaurants across the country, from independent eateries to the biggest chains. More than a third of the dishes did not contain lobster and usually had cheaper seafood substitutes, especially whiting. The Lobster Salad Sandwich at Nathan's Famous in Coney Island, the flagship of the large national chain, was whiting, not lobster. And lobster ravioli at a restaurant in New York's Little Italy had no seafood at all, just cheese.

Some lobster deception is more subtle, such as restaurants displaying live North American lobsters but serving something else. Instantly recognizable, the iconic crustacean is most associated with Maine, and if you eat it whole or see it go from the display tank into the pot you will be okay. But in his book *Where Am I Eating?* in which author Kelsey Timmerman traces the geographic origins of many popular foodstuffs, this doesn't always happen. "There always seems to be a wait to get into Red Lobster, leaving you plenty of time to consider the bubbling tank with live lobsters staring out . . . The lobsters in the tank are North American lobsters, found mostly on the East Coast of the United States . . . But the rock lobster you order at Red Lobster aren't the poor display lobsters in the lobby. You're served a lobster that has traveled much further . . . Rock lobsters have been making the trip from warm southern waters onto U.S. plates for decades . . . Perhaps the tank in the lobby is an effort to shield patrons from the far less appetizing truth about where their meal really came from—and how it ultimately got to them."

Timmerman reports that 90 percent of Nicaragua's substantial lobster production comes to the United States, the two biggest buyers being Red Lobster's parent company and giant wholesale food distributor Sysco. You can buy these shell-on, uncooked tails (these lobsters have no claws) frozen in the supermarket. There is nothing inherently wrong with the lobster-tail meat or warm-water lobsters, except that they arrive frozen and do not taste as good. Like ponga, escolar, and langostino, many tons of it arrives on these shores to be widely sold and eaten, yet few consumers even know there is another kind of lobster. Across the globe, restaurants proudly boast of serving "live Maine lobster," but unless you go to Nicaragua, chances are good you will never see Nicaraguan lobster advertised anywhere—live or frozen.

Maine's lobster industry group estimated that langostino was costing its fishermen forty-four million dollars a year. Maine's U.S. senator, Olympia Snowe, happened to be chair of the Senate Subcommittee on Fisheries and objected vigorously to the FDA commissioner, stating that "use of this term is misleading to consumers and unfairly affiliates langostino with actual lobster . . . Langostino is not lobster, nor should it be marketed as such. The FDA will be remiss in its duties if it allows restaurants or other entities to perpetuate this hoax at the expense of Maine's lobstermen and America's seafood consumers." That's us, by the way. Nonetheless, Snowe's efforts to change FDA policy have so far been unsuccessful, and to this day, the befuddling FDA decision explains the too-good-to-be-true prices for lobster rolls and other fast-food "lobster" dishes legally sold without containing actual lobster.

It gets worse: When is "langostino lobster" not even "langostino lobster"? When it is not using langostino at all. Because freshwater crawfish from China are overabundant and subject to an antidumping duty of 223 percent, it greatly behooves Chinese exporters to transship and relabel these crustaceans as langostino. When FDA officials collected a sample of imported "langostino" meat they determined it was actually crawfish, leading to an initial investigation that indicated at least twenty-three similar imports of fake langostino meat had already occurred. Since very few American consumers buy langostino intentionally, it seems fair to hazard a guess that the fake langostino was on its way to join the cast of real langostino playing the part of fake lobster in fast-food eateries, a Fake Food twice removed from reality.

If shrimp and lobster are regularly faked, what about their near relative in price and status, the scallop? Experts say longstanding rumors of restaurants using cookie cutters to punch faux scallops out of skate or shark are largely urban myths. But the scallop industry has its own special kinds of deceit. Restaurant menus love using the term *diver scallops* on pricy entrées, referring to the best and largest specimens hand harvested by scuba divers. But according to a consumer brochure released by the Gulf of Maine Research Institute (GMRI), "Dealers often label anything that is U10 or larger a 'diver' scallop, regardless of where or how it was harvested." The shellfish numbering system for shrimp and scallops refers to the number of units per pound, so U10 are scallops so big that they come just ten or less to the pound. Weighing more than an ounce and a half each, these are routinely pawned off by retailers and restaurants as "diver caught." Further embellishing, because Maine is famous for its scallops, many advertise them as "fresh Maine diver scallops" or simply "fresh Maine scallops" at all times of the year but especially during summer, seafood's high season. But scalloping runs from just December through March—there is no such thing as fresh Maine scallops most of the year.

The more insidious way to get money out of consumer pockets is adulterating scallops (and, to a lesser degree, shrimp). This is done by adding water and phosphates, inorganic chemicals, to boost their weight, since seafood is typically sold by the pound. In addition to charging consumers fifteen or eighteen bucks a pound for water, this also lowers the quality of the scallops. The phosphates help them absorb more water than they could naturally, and as much as 25 percent of the total weight—a quarter of what you are paying for—becomes water. But you won't find phosphates, water—or any ingredients—on the label.

The practice affects most scallops sold in this country and is so common that better specialty stores often sell so-called dry scallops—meaning normal scallops—at a high premium. What makes these pricier specimens "special" is merely the fact that they haven't been doctored. Except even this is often a lie. According to GRMI, dry scallops, sold for higher prices, can still be phosphate-soaked wet scallops. As long as they remain under 82 percent total moisture, they may legally be labeled "dry." A spokesperson for GRMI told me that some suppliers intentionally add water until they get as close as possible to the legal limit while still selling dry scallops that are nearly one-fifth water at a premium price.

By choice, I shop at a fancier and more conscientious grocery store with a very good seafood counter, where dry scallops are nearly always available. When I cook them I can instantly tell the difference. In a sauté pan, they brown well, hold their shape and size, and are delicious, with perfect scallop texture and a creamy ivory interior. By comparison, when you cook wet scallops, which means most scallops, some of the extra absorbed water seeps out during cooking so the scallops can't brown properly, while the rest evaporates, shrinking your scallops and rendering them smaller, dried out, and largely tasteless. You actually see this whitish liquid, like skim milk, pool in the pan, and the scallops are uniformly white throughout.

The list of high-value seafood faked every day in this country goes on and on. In one example, Russian beluga caviar carefully smuggled in turned out to be a fake even the smugglers did not know about, not Russian at all as labeled, but rather Chinese, adulterated by mixing high-quality beluga with less valuable fish roe. Maryland is famous for its delicious blue crab from the Chesapeake Bay and especially its signature crab cakes. But even at the source, immediately around the waters the blue crab comes from, it is financially tempting for restaurants to substitute imported crab or different species, because real Maryland blue crab cakes can run over thirty dollars as a menu entrée. A 2015 study showed that four out of ten restaurants tested in Annapolis, Maryland; Washington, DC; and around Chesapeake Bay used other less expensive species as a substitute for native blue crab. Maryland's Department of Natural Resources launched the True Blue program in 2012 to certify restaurants serving the real thing. To receive certification, these restaurants agree to let the state audit their crab invoices. One participating restaurant owner described customers to the Annapolis's *Capital Gazette* this way: "They're amazed that here we are in Maryland and most places they'd go and eat don't serve Maryland crab . . . People should know what it is they're eating."

Much consumer confusion is caused by the FDA's Seafood List, a database of over one thousand acceptable names for the commercial sale of fish. This was the list that *langostino* was added to—as "lobster." The list includes both "market names," which is how the fish is usually sold, and "common names" for particular fish. So, for instance, *flounder* is the acceptable market name for labeling more than two dozen different fish, some of which are actually flounders, but also unrelated species, such as brill and a couple of types of halibut that can legally be sold as flounder. Of the thousand-plus names, there are only eight that have specific protections from misrepresentation, three of which are canned products. The most notable is catfish, which received exclusivity in order to protect domestic catfish producers. Legally, only catfish produced in the United States can be called catfish. In theory, to sell any fish by any name, that name must appear on this list, which is ostensibly accessible to consumers online. In practice, according to the GAO report, the FDA added some four hundred fish names, some real and some made up by marketers, usually at the request of the industry, over a period of sixteen years, without ever once updating the public list.

While much of the seafood business is regulated by the FDA, it is the USDA that is responsible for setting national "organic" standards in meats and produce. As we will see when it comes to pork, beef, and chicken, the newest USDA organic certifications actually provide some long-needed confidence for consumers. But not with fish: while seafood in both stores and restaurants is routinely labeled organic, it falls under the same Wild West regulations that existed in meat before the USDA created national rules. To put it simply, there are no legal organic rules for seafood at all but also no rules against using the term. Some companies claim to follow third-party "organic" standards; some, European standards. But it doesn't really matter because they don't have to follow any standards and can slap an "organic" label on any seafood, even drug-addled Thai-farmed shrimp. The USDA is considering issuing organic rules for aquaculture that would cover the farmed side of seafood, but since the department's consideration of anything important tends to take many years, the light at the end of this tunnel is dim.

The sad bottom line is that in many cases consumers cannot buy seafood knowing where it actually came from, whether or how it was farmed or caught, whether it contains potentially dangerous chemicals or natural toxins, or even what kind of fish it is, and the matter gets worse as the "quality" of the seafood goes up. As we know from other Real Foods, the problem is even worse in restaurants, which are exempt from most rules and have the added advantage of preparing food in ways that further disguises it.

Dr. Warner's most recent project for Oceana was a global "study of studies," in which she and her colleagues did a comprehensive analysis of fake fish studies conducted by many different entities in different countries, including sixty-seven peer-reviewed studies, seven government reports, and twenty-three news articles. The results are pages and pages of more disturbing fraud information, but she was able to sum up the results for me in two sentences: "All studies that have investigated seafood fraud have found it. The take-home message is that anytime someone looks for mislabeling and species substitution in the marketplace, anywhere, they find it." In case after case, when confronted, restaurateurs, chefs, retailers, and distributors caught selling fake fish almost reflexively blamed it on a mistake, labeling, or order error by a supplier further up the food chain. The convoluted nature of the seafood industry—where the average imported fish travels 5,475 miles before reaching a diner—makes substitution easy and pointing the finger hard. But the evidence indicates that this is never actually a mistake: in every study and case I found, and there are plenty, it was a cheaper fish substituted for a more expensive one and never, as an "accident" would suggest, the other way around.

All these disturbing studies seem to have pushed the government toward some action on seafood, something it is reluctant to do for many other Fake Foods. In March 2013, more than a year before Vice President Joe Biden's speech announcing the Obama administration crackdown on seafood fraud, Congressman Ed Markey (D-MA) reintroduced the SAFE Seafood Act as a new, bipartisan version of a previously introduced bill (Safety and Fraud Enforcement for Seafood Act), to combat seafood fraud "that cheats fishermen and consumers, while posing health risks to pregnant mothers and others," adding, that "fish fraud is a national problem that needs a national solution. This bill finally tells the seafood swindlers and fish fraudsters that we will protect America's fishermen and consumers from Massachusetts to Alaska." But two years later, the bill still hadn't even been vetted by committee. Until authorities take action, which may be never, seafood remains the single most confusing food to buy, but here are some tips.

## ✽ A THIRD-PARTY CERTIFICATIONS

A seal of approval from an outside auditor, usually a nonprofit, is the easiest way for consumers to shop with confidence, but the certification is only as good as the people behind it. Manufacturers and industry groups often create their own self-aggrandizing seals to make products look better. The two most respected broad certifications are those from the Marine Stewardship Council (MSC; the logo is a blue fish in the shape of a checkmark) for wild-caught fish, and Global Aquaculture Alliance's Best Aquaculture Practices (BAP) for farmed fish. The Monterey Bay Aquarium uses both in making its Seafood Watch decisions, along with another fish farming certification, from the Aquaculture Stewardship Council. A less common good one is the Blue Ocean Institute ratings by the Safina Center at Stony Brook. The Gulf Wild seal assures the authenticity of wild-caught seafood from the Gulf of Mexico and is best for shrimp. The Gulf of Maine Research Institute's Gulf of Maine Responsibly Harvested certification is excellent: not only do all products with this logo have third-party chain of custody verification that they came from the Gulf of Maine, processing must occur within the state. Most U.S. seafood is processed overseas, then reimported.

## ✽ BUY ALASKAN

Perhaps the most reliable of all seafood logos is "Alaska Seafood: Wild, Natural, Sustainable." Required sustainability, including its vast riches of seafood, was written into Alaska's state constitution in 1959, making it unique in the United States. The state also completely outlaws fish farming—there is no such thing as farmed Alaskan seafood. All is wild caught, and the state's fisheries are widely regarded as well managed against overfishing, pollution, and habitat damage. Alaska has the largest stock of wild salmon on earth and none have been classified as overfished. Wild Alaskan salmon—

which means all real Alaskan salmon—has little to no traces of contaminants, is consistently very low in levels of heavy metals and organochlorines, and is purer than fish from most parts of the world. The Alaska Seafood seal is overseen by Global Trust Certification, which earned ISO 65 accreditation (a highly respected international standard for process execution by the International Organization for Standardization), and the process requires chain of custody of the seafood from catch to retail. The seal applies specifically to Alaskan pollock, king crab, snow crab, black cod, Pacific halibut and all five species of Alaskan salmon: king (aka chinook), sockeye (aka red), coho (aka silver), keta (aka chum), and pink. If I buy salmon, it has the Alaska logo.

## ✻ BUY AMERICAN

For health, environmental, and authenticity reasons, you are usually best off buying domestic seafood. In many Fake Food cases, we have to look to other countries, especially Canada and those in the European Union, but sometimes as far flung as Uruguay or Japan, for inspiration and guidance in terms of authentic, safe, delicious, quality food and consumer protections. But that is decidedly not the case with seafood, in which the United States is far and away the world leader in fishery management, safety, sustainability, and responsible aquaculture, a model for the planet. This is true across the board, from wild-caught ocean fishing to shellfish beds to shrimp farms (of which there are very few). "Fishery management in the U.S. is the best in the world," said Michael Bell, director of the California Coastal and Marine Program for the Nature Conservancy. Domestic monitoring of the environmental factors is also better, and the supply chain is less convoluted. Alaskan fish, especially crab and salmon; Mississippi gulf fish, especially wild-caught shrimp; Maine lobster, scallops, and fish; and domestically farmed catfish are all good choices—if they are labeled honestly.

## ✳ BUY WILD CAUGHT

There are just a few exceptions to this rule, mainly domestically farmed catfish and globally farmed mussels, oysters, and clams. There are also a handful of boutique artisanal salmon farms selling name-brand fish, like Chile's Verlasso, the only farmed salmon approved by Seafood Watch, and Skuna Bay in Vancouver, which received BAP certification by the Global Aquaculture Alliance. But these are minor exceptions to the rule. Especially avoid farmed foreign shrimp.

## ✳ SEA SCALLOPS

Buy dry scallops, but not all are really dry, so avoid scallops that are frozen, cloudy, white, or translucent. Real scallops have a cream or tannish hue; treated scallops tend to be bright white.

## ✳ EATING OUT

Seventy percent of seafood consumed in this country is eaten in restaurants, which consistently perform worse than retailers, especially with sushi. Unless you eat at the nation's very best (and most expensive) sushi eateries, assume the worst and you will almost certainly be right. There's not much you can do except to avoid the most commonly substituted fish: order white tuna or red snapper, and you will almost always get something fake. Salmon and shrimp will likely be farmed. Crab will usually be imitation. At other seafood restaurants, ask very specifically about where fish comes from, be wary of grouper, and again, never get red snapper. Ordering whole fish allows you to actually see what you are eating.

## ✳ RED FLAGS

Be wary of the labels "fresh," "natural" or "organic," which have no legal meaning. Equally suspect are "sushi grade" and "sashimi grade," which are frequently used to suggest higher quality. No such grades exist.

## ✳ SHOP AT WHOLE FOODS

If pressed for one simple, nationwide solution to the fake seafood retail issue, I would say buy at Whole Foods. The chain is not perfect, has its critics, and is certainly in it for profit, but it profits by charging more for better fish by way of higher standards. If real seafood seems too expensive, eat it less often. That's what I do.

Not everything Whole Foods sells is something I would buy, like imported farmed fish, but at least you can tell it is imported and farmed, because this chain has excellent disclosure, labeling, and information practices. Signage in all seafood cases indicates whether fish has been frozen or has had color added to it. All frozen shrimp indicates both country of origin and whether it was farmed or wild. Whole Foods relies heavily on third-party certification and on audits. "Whole Foods has made a big sustainable seafood commitment," said the Monterey Bay Aquarium's Ken Peterson. For wild-caught seafood, it uses the industry's gold standard, the MSC's Certified Fisheries program. During wild salmon season in Alaska, Whole Foods also has its own port buyers who bar-code fish off the boat. It makes use of the Monterey Bay Aquarium watch list and the Blue Ocean Institute for East Coast fisheries. Whole Foods also has its own aquaculture logo, the Responsibly Farmed Seal, with very detailed standards published online, but a highlight includes "farmed seafood that's free of synthetic pigments, antibiotics, added growth hormones, added preservatives like sulfites and phosphates and animal by-products in feed."

## ✳ SHOP AT BIG-BOX STORES

While it is easy to make fun of retailers like Walmart, Costco, and BJ's, these quantity-focused companies have enormous leverage over producers and suppliers, whom they often force to adhere to higher standards. Much to my surprise while researching this book, industry expert after expert, from vegetables to fish, sang the praises of big-box stores. In the *Boston Globe* seafood study, while about half of all retail fish stores and restaurants failed, these giants did very well, sometimes perfectly: "Frozen fish at grocery stores was far less frequently misidentified, with some sellers—including Walmart, Trader Joe's, and BJ's Wholesale Club—passing muster in all instances." After the FDA's 2015 decision to approve genetically engineered salmon as the first such modified animal product allowed for sale in this country (and unlabeled as such), Costco, Whole Foods, Trader Joe's, and several other large retailers immediately announced they would not sell it. Personally, I shop at BJ's because it's my closest warehouse club and much of their seafood now has third-party certification, typically by the Sustainable Fishery Partnership and the Global Aquaculture Alliance, for wild-caught and farmed seafood, respectively. This makes Real Food much more affordable.

Brittni Furrow is the director of sustainability for Walmart Stores, Inc., the world's largest retailer, with 245 million customers in twenty-eight global markets. "When customers walk into a store," she told the audience at the Monterey Bay Aquarium conference, "they don't expect to have to pay a premium for safe food. Safety isn't a niche. The trend we see the most with food is that people want to know where their food comes from. There's a human element to it that our customers have been disconnected from. There is a rising trend toward transparency, and our seafood sourcing process was one of our first endeavors, so we made a requirement of our suppliers either having certification or actively working towards getting it. We gave them time to implement the standards and today more than ninety percent of our seafood is either certified or in a fishery improvement program."

# 4. Spoiled Oils: Olive and "Truffle"

*This* is what nearly everyone in the world thinks is extra virgin olive oil! *This* stuff is killing quality oil, and putting honest oil-makers out of business . . . *Extra virgin?* What's this oil got to do with virginity? This is a whore.

—Flavio Zaramella, quoted by Tom Mueller, *Extra Virginity*

W hat you are smelling is literally liquid sunshine expressed in fruit," says Bill Briwa, a chef-instructor—or professor—at the Culinary Institute of America (CIA). The "Harvard of Cooking," the CIA is the nation's foremost school for professional chefs.

In front of me sit three glasses full of one of the oldest and most important foods in the world, an array that would make any gourmet rapturous. They are three takes on olive oil, the lifeblood of the Mediterranean basin, the stuff of gladiators and philosophers, sultans and kings. This elixir is the secret to the longevity and health of the Mediterranean diet, the adornment that makes Tuscany's deliciously decadent *bistecca alla fiorentina*, beef steak of Florence, different from every other steak on earth, a partner in a marriage made in heaven for all kinds of seafood, vegetables, and cheeses. It is a superlative recipe ingredient, an unmatched condiment, and to the Greeks, a beverage on its own.

My samples are all ultrafresh and ultrahigh quality, representing the best of the styles of California, Spain, and Tuscany, where unlike most other parts of Europe—which prefer single varietal oils—they excel at blending. The Tuscan oil is noticeably lighter, gold and bright, almost the color of a heavily oaked California chardonnay. The California oil is darker and greener but still bright, while the Spanish version is the swamp water of the three: dark, mossy green, opaque, and mysterious. It is the color of ripeness.

Though arrayed like a wine tasting, no three wines were ever this pungent, and just a minute after Briwa sets them down, a delectable scent cloud of ripe fruit has already risen from the glasses and completely enveloped me. Soon the oil will become a part of me, but at first it feels quite the opposite, as if these glasses are sucking me in—which suddenly seems like a good way to drown. I can't wait to taste them.

Briwa oversees the new olive oil education initiative at Greystone, the CIA's Napa Valley campus. Despite rapid growth in olive oil sales for the past few years, a trend riding the twin coattails of healthier eating and interest in all things gourmet, the ancient and near-mythical substance remains largely misunderstood in this country. Many experts, including Briwa, presume that a lot of Americans, even those who love food and eat out regularly, may have never actually tasted high-quality olive oil—not once. Later, in the months after this tasting, when I start to pay attention to the oils served in "fine dining" restaurants and look at the long-expired thirty- to forty-dollar fancy bottles still for sale on the shelves of gourmet stores, I start to understand his point.

This ignorance is so pervasive that it extends to chefs, even at top restaurants, who often know much more about different types of salts than oils. Because its mission is to prepare the best professional cooks of tomorrow, the CIA recently added olive oil to its curriculum. The school also renovated a space within its impressive retail culinary equipment and cookbook store into an *oleoteca*, an oil-centric dispensary patterned after an *enoteca*, or wine bar.

It is a warm, inviting area with comfortable couches and chairs, where visitors can relax in a living room atmosphere and order a tasting flight of extra-virgin olive oil (often referred to as EVOO), along with charcuterie, cheeses, chocolates, and a glass of wine.

If you visit Napa, take advantage of this delicious opportunity, especially since the olive oil storage system here is the first of its kind in the country. I flew across the United States specifically to experience an oil tasting under Briwa's guidance because of his expertise and because this is one of the few places in the world in possession of a sophisticated OliveToLive serving system. Think of how bars handle draft beer, in temperature controlled, totally closed and pressurized systems devoid of flavor killing oxygen and light. Now substitute fresh, floral Spanish oil for Budweiser on tap and you get the idea.

Everyone who loves olive oil—and passions run very deep on the subject—has had an ah-ha moment, when the realization hits that the really good stuff exists on a higher culinary plane. Mine was more than fifteen years ago, during a visit to Masseria San Domenico, a deluxe resort in Puglia, a region of southern Italy famed for its olive oil production. More oil is produced in Puglia than any other part of Italy, and as I drove to the resort, there seemed to be nothing but olive groves as far as the eye could see. There are about sixty million olive trees locally, many of them centuries old, while some go back much further.

T. J. Robinson, aka the "Olive Oil Hunter," is one of the world's greatest oil cheerleaders, a globally acclaimed expert taster and judge who runs the mail-order Fresh Pressed Olive Oil Club. His shipments include tasting notes and a newsletter that is part sermon, part worshipful ode. Nobody captures the olive's inherent romance like Robinson, whose notes for one shipment reflect on the fact that the artisanal production of olive oil has been "a central part of the Italian culture since the days of the Roman Empire.

Olive trees can live for thousands of years . . . when Rome ruled the known world . . . or when the Empire was sacked by barbarians . . . or during the long Dark Ages, followed by the Crusades, the Renaissance, and right up to modern times. There are trees still bearing fruit today that may have supplied oil for the table of Julius Caesar or a gladiator's final meal."

It is hard to drive through Puglia and miss the evocative allure of the inland sea of olives, next to the azure waters of the actual sea, the Mediterranean. I did not pass many homes in the rural, arid, and agricultural region, but every one I did pass had its own trees—lots of them. It seems that in Puglia to be without olives is like to be in America without an internet connection. Masseria San Domenico produces its own oil, from its own trees, and serves it in the various restaurants on the property. I first tasted the oil at the open air poolside lunch spot: the elixir was generously poured over grilled baby octopus, and I still remember the moment like it was yesterday. The second the liquid hit my mouth everything changed into a world of greenness, freshness, and explosive flavor. A moment later came the finish, with a slightly hot, peppery, but altogether pleasant bite. It had a slurp-inducing thickness and viscosity that made me swirl it all around my mouth, a very pleasant silkiness that was not the slightest bit oily. It coated my tongue with its smoothness for a delightful moment, but then it was gone, not at all like the fatty residue of meat that lingers in a greasy overdose.

Olives are fruit after all, and at its best, olive oil is nothing more than fresh squeezed fruit juice, a vessel for capturing, as Briwa suggested, the brightness and energy of the sun. Another Californian, Deborah Rogers of McEvoy Ranch, arguably the finest olive oil maker in the States, describes the real thing thusly: "If you could taste and smell the color green, this would be it."

I've spent time in Italy, Spain, Portugal, Chile, Australia, South Africa, and many other top olive-producing nations since that life-changing moment, and I've had a lot more experiences with olive oil—good and bad. Excellent olive oil is certainly more widely available in Europe than in the United States, especially in restaurants, but it is far from commonplace. At its finest, olive oil is not an ingredient for salad dressing or sauce, as most people here assume—it *is* the dressing or sauce. One classic use is on fresh burrata cheese, a ball of which is punctured and filled with a generous amount of olive oil. A heavy pouring hand helps octopus, shrimp, raw and cooked vegetables, and almost every kind of fish slathered in the stuff. Actually, there aren't too many foods that real olive oil can't make better—I've even had it on ice cream.

"Aside from its intrinsic health benefits—it's the top of the heap of all fats—as an ingredient it makes other foods taste great," said Briwa. "We serve plain shredded cabbage with just a bit of salt and lemon and a *lot* of extra virgin olive oil, and it's delicious, and then you really see how important great oil is." Nowhere is this more apparent than in Tuscany's most famous regional dish, *bistecca alla fiorentina*, nothing more than a thick T-bone grilled over a live wood fire until crusty on the outside but still quite rare in the middle, then sliced and drizzled with plenty of olive oil. Meat, fire, and oil is a simple but impossibly delicious combination that depends entirely on two factors, good steak and good oil. In this country, where we'd be far more likely to drown beef in ketchup or A-1 sauce than olive oil, the wonderful concept is largely unknown. Try it on your next steak—if you can find good oil. That's the rub.

Despite being the world's third-largest market for extra-virgin olive oils, as a nation we are novices. The average person in Greece consumes twenty-three to twenty-four liters per year, or a large bottle every two weeks. In Italy and Spain, it is half that, twelve to fourteen liters, just over a bottle each month. "In the U.S., we're scaring the daylights out of a liter per year per person," said John

Akeson, CEO of Deoleo North America. Industry giant Deoleo owns the best-selling brands in Italy (Carapelli), Spain (Carbonell), the United States, and the world (Bertolli). Like wine, olive oils are made from hundreds of different fruit varietals; vary by flavor regionally; have good and bad years; and have magazines, newsletters, and critical ratings devoted to them.

Yet studies have repeatedly shown that American consumers understand only price and "Italy," and make virtually no differentiation among brands or quality of olive oils. At the opposite end of this spectrum is a typically over-the-top oil review by the obsessed T. J. Robinson: "On the nose there are ample, lovely notes of raw artichoke, green tomato, fresh-chopped parsley, baby arugula, fresh-snipped grass, fennel bulb, wild mint, and a tiny bit of rubbed sage, plus a trace of light-green vegetal sweetness, like torn butter lettuce . . . The mouth feel is round and luscious as well as bright and grassy."

For the food lover, few sights are as romantically appetizing as the olive grove, instantly recognizable thanks to its leaf shape, shimmering iridescence, and namesake color. One of the first trees cultivated by humankind, olives have excellent taste in climate, tending to grow best in beautiful places with wonderful weather, drawing mental pictures of A-list fantasy destinations like Tuscany, Provence, the Costa del Sol, and whitewashed Greek isles. Olives and olive oils are one of the fundamental backbones of Western cuisine. If you cook, you probably have a bottle in your cupboard. And it is probably fake.

"Once someone tries a real extra virgin—an adult or a child, anybody with taste buds—they'll never go back to the fake kind. It's distinctive, complex, the freshest thing you've ever eaten. It makes you realize how rotten the other stuff is, literally *rotten*. But there has to be a first time," said Grazia DeCarlo, whose artisanal olive oil farm in Puglia has been family-owned for more than four hundred years.

After my "first time," I brought back four tins from the resort, shared them, and among my friends and family, the universal experience was a paradigm shift, despite the fact that we had all consumed plenty of what we thought was extra-virgin olive oil. There was simply no comparison between the stuff in those tins from Puglia and recognizable supermarket brands.

When I tasted oil in Puglia, it left a warm tickle in the back of my throat, a sensation I would later learn is called olive sting. It is an indicator of freshness—and largely absent in oils sold in the United States. While it has become ubiquitous for American restaurants to stuff patrons with a basket of bread and a bowl of golden-colored oil for dipping, that liquid is so far removed from the real thing as to be unrecognizable. It might not even be made from the pressing of olives.

In a rarity among foods, real extra-virgin olive oil, widely considered the healthiest fat, was approved by the FDA in 2004 to bear certain health claims on its labels. Like certifying a new drug, this is a strenuous process. The cornerstone of the much-lauded Mediterranean diet, real olive oil is low in saturated fat and high in omega-3 fatty acids that reduce the risk of heart disease. Unlike vegetable oils, such as canola, olive oil also has additional beneficial properties, such as antioxidants and polyphenols (anti-inflammatory compounds that promote healthful cardiovascular function). The subject of endless studies worldwide, reputable claims include fighting some forms of cancer (including breast, colon, ovary, and prostate); assisting in the assimilating of vitamins; fostering good digestion; and lowering blood cholesterol. It is higher in oleic acid than any vegetable oil, and this monounsaturated acid helps reduce the risk of cardiovascular disease (oleic acid is found in the highest concentrations in real extra virgin). Extra-virgin olive oil also contains sterols and the liposoluble vitamins A, D, and E, to which have been attributed a protective and antioxidant action that may prevent artery-blocking deposits and cancer and slow the aging process. Antioxidants, including polyphenols, are also believed to act as direct antitumoral agents. A more recently isolated substance in olive oil, dubbed oleocanthal, was shown to reduce the adverse effects of amyloid-beta-derived diffusible ligands, suspected of contributing to Alzheimer's disease.

"Bad oil isn't just a deception, it's a crime against public health," said Flavio Zaramella, president of Milan's Corporazione Mastri Oleari, a private olive oil association. Zaramella conducted a tasting in Italy, similar to my experience at the CIA, for Tom Mueller, author of *Extra Virginity*, an informative but disturbing book about the rife industry fraud with olive oil. Unfortunately, much of the flavor and many, if not most, of the health benefits disappear in fake olive oil—and most oils sold in the United States are fake.

Like the premier cru classification of French Bordeaux, or the USDA Prime beef grading, "extra virgin" is supposed to denote the very best level of olive oil available. Starting from the legal definition that real olive oil is nothing but the juice extracted from high-quality, fresh olives, otherwise unprocessed and with its flavor and health benefits wholly intact, there are three main ways in which extra-virgin olive oil can be deemed fake. One is by diluting it with less expensive oils, usually processed seed oils, such as soybean or sunflower. Similar to drug dealers who "cut" or "step on" heroin or cocaine with other white solids like baby powder, this is a simple (and illegal) substitution of a cheap ingredient for a much more expensive one to increase profit margin. Sometimes these added oils are safe, but sometimes they are not. This has become a less common problem in recent years, simply because wholesale olive oil prices have fallen much closer to the price of less desirable substitutes. This illegal adulteration is also more easily detected with modern tests such as gas chromatography—in the rare cases when someone checks. The FDA periodically does token analyses, but most of the little testing done is by consumer groups or researchers.

The second and more common fake today is to dilute extra-virgin olive oil with lower grades of olive oil, usually ones that have been heavily refined with chemicals, which destroys the health benefits and flavor and is much harder to detect.

While both these practices are clearly illegal, the third and largest cause of extra-virgin olive oil falling short of its "real" promise is a case of what I referred to in chapter 2 as "gray area counterfeits." This involves producing extra-virgin olive oil at the very lowest end of the regulatory spectrum, typically incorporating older—and often rancid—stocks of oil held over from bumper crops of previous seasons. Because this type of poorer-quality oil deteriorates rapidly, it technically passes extra-virgin standards on the day it is blended, bottled, and labeled but often fails by the time it reaches consumers. While not illegal per se, the quick deterioration is a very predictable chemical process, often exacerbated by using stale oil in the mix, and any experienced producer knows it is going to happen.

There is a long history of olive oil fraud, and a comprehensive study in the *Journal of Food Science* showed that olive oil was the single most commonly referenced adulterated food of any type in scholarly articles from 1980 to 2010. Consumer studies by the Olive Center at the University of California–Davis and the industry's domestic trade group, the North American Olive Oil Association, both clearly found that perceived health benefits and flavor were the top two reasons Americans buy olive oil, yet they often get neither.

U.S. consumption has risen by more than 50 percent since the beginning of the twenty-first century, and by dollar volume, it is by far the most valuable oil category. We consume nearly three times as much vegetable oil, but the domestic olive oil market is worth much more. It is considerably costlier than other widely used oils, and as we will see time and time again, pricy food products are likely to be counterfeited, especially when you cannot readily discern quality with the eye. This makes our largely unregulated market attractive to shady dealers.

Fake extra-virgin olive oil does not just lack its touted health benefits; it can also include potentially toxic substances blended with counterfeit plant oils. In one notorious incident in Spain, rapeseed oil was denatured with aniline, a toxin used to make plastic. (Originally, about eight hundred deaths were attributed to consumption of this oil, but in 2012, Britain's Guardian newspaper released a report on the scientific flaws in the research, cleared olive oil of responsibility, and shifted the likely blame to tomatoes.) However, as author Tom Mueller told me, two of the more popular adulterants, peanut and soybean oil, can both cause severe allergic reactions in those who go to great lengths to avoid them and would never expect to encounter them in a product that by definition cannot contain them.

Most of our oil comes from Italy, where Italian investigators have found all sorts of other unsavory substances: hydrocarbon residues, pesticides, and pomace oil, the most common adulterant, sometimes laced with mineral oil as well as polycyclic aromatic hydrocarbons, proven carcinogens that can also damage DNA and the immune system. It is ironic that a substance that should be consumed for its anticancer properties could actually cause cancer. On the bright side, you are much more likely to buy oil that is merely rancid, spoiled, illegally processed, or what the industry calls defective than to actually be poisoned.

To be fair, some think these concerns are overblown. The FDA acknowledges widespread adulteration in olive oil dating back seventy years, and has found it every time its officials looked, but doesn't deem it a high-priority public health issue compared to foodborne illnesses such as salmonella and *E. coli* outbreaks. As an FDA official expert on the subject (who remains anonymous by request) told me, "Most of the time people who are doing economic adulteration, a cheat like this, they don't want to get caught, so they are not going to do something stupid that raises their visibility, such as putting something that's harmful in. But we can't always count on that." Reassuring.

The reality is that there can be little dispute regarding olive oil's fraudulent state of affairs: virtually every investigation, whether by universities, journalists, law enforcement, or government agencies has found an industry rife with fakery. The only remaining questions are how much extra-virgin olive oil is fake, and what can you do about it? The answer to the first question is a lot: more conservative estimates put the amount at around two-thirds, meaning one in three bottles for sale in this country delivers what it claims. That's the best-case scenario: some experts put your chances of getting the real thing at more like one in ten. One German study put it at one in thirty. Worse, the vast majority of samples in the German study weren't just not extra virgin—they were unfit for human consumption. Remember when Chef Briwa suggested that many Americans had never tasted real extra-virgin olive oil, not even once?

So what can you do about it? That requires a bit of education, including how olive oil is made, what makes oil good or bad, and how it is regulated.

The three biggest factors determining initial quality are the olives themselves, which come in hundreds of varieties; their ripeness when harvested; and the amount of elapsed time between picking and crushing. Like wine grapes, the varietal issue is subjective— if you love cabernet sauvignon, you probably won't gravitate toward Burgundies, made entirely from lighter pinot noir grapes. But olive oils are less complicated for consumers in this regard, if only because very few labels indicate varietals, so you don't have a choice.

Ripeness offers the most human control in the process. The flavor and polyphenols, responsible for both health benefits and longer shelf life, all peak relatively early. However, when these are at their maximum, the fruit is less ripe and harder to pick (thus more expensive), with lower liquid yield, meaning less oil from the same number of olives (thus more expensive). "As they get more color they get more yield but less flavor, and that is where producers struggle to get the perfect balance," said the CIA's Briwa. The easiest way to harvest cheaply and get the highest yield is to simply wait until the fruit falls off the tree on its own and then pick it up, which some producers do—even though it's rotten at this point.

Olives begin to deteriorate the minute they are picked, so time is of the essence in getting them to a mill. "Wait even twenty-four hours and you've ruined the fruit," said Bill Marsano, a James Beard–award winning journalist and expert on Italian food, speaking at a panel hosted by the Italian Trade Commission. The best oils are pressed within twelve hours and some fanatics insist on as little as one to four. Australia has become one of the most consistent producers of high-quality oil because many of their farms are designed specifically for speedy pressing (plus, Australia has the world's strictest laws governing olive oil quality).

Mike Bradley is the founder of Veronica Foods, one of the largest importers of exceptional real extra-virgin olive oils in the United States, which supplies more than five hundred specialty stores nationwide. He visits and buys from artisanal producers all over the world, in Chile, Argentina, Europe, North Africa, South Africa, and Australia. I reached him in his California office just as he was about to leave for a buying trip abroad, and he explained that by having their own mill on property and removing transit time for the fruit, artisan producers can cut the time from harvest to pressing to between four and twelve hours. But pioneering Australian farmers have gone even further: "They have a machine called the Colossus and they are able to harvest an entire tree in fifteen seconds, and it can turn at the end of each row and take the fruit right to the onsite mill. We get oil from Australia that is always crushed within two hours of picking."

Bradley then described a more romantic approach to me, used by the most famous artisanal producer in Spain, Oro Bailen. Workers form a fire brigade line with buckets, fill them, pass them down, and mill them within an hour. They also pick much earlier in the season, when the olives are at their best. "Oro Bailen picks in late October, but his next-door neighbor doesn't even go out to look at his fruit until Christmas. They pick at exactly the right time, and when you do that, it's hard to make bad olive oil. They win every contest they enter in the world. It costs three hundred percent more, but here's why—just taste it." Unfortunately, Oro Bailen is the exception, not the rule, in an industry based more on cheap oil at high volumes than quality.

Because of the timeline, olives are never shipped to make olive oil. Only oil itself is shipped. While artisanal producers bottle the product of their own estates, most olive oil is put not into bottles but rather trucks or tankers and then shipped to Italy. Here the giant factories of the world's largest oil assemblers combine shipments from places like Tunisia, Morocco, Spain, Syria, Turkey, Greece and many others. There is nothing intrinsically wrong with the oil in any of those places, but every extra grower, crusher, shipper, and broker involved in the opaque process adds another opportunity for lower-quality late-harvest oils, rotted fruit, adulteration, and addition of refined oils. This is exacerbated by the fact that oils pass through the hands of numerous shady distributors and middlemen. There are endless examples of tainted, adulterated, and illegally refined oils being delivered surreptitiously to the biggest bottlers and ending up in the products they sell.

Even if the oil delivered to blenders is good to begin with, because of a little-known but widespread industry practice called carryover, a fair amount of oil is rancid before it is even bottled.

In good years, when growers produce more oil than they can sell, they simply keep it and mix it into the next year's harvest—or the year after that. Mueller and Bradley both told me that some olive oils in the EU are stored for years before being bottled and that many supermarket "extra virgins" are a blend of fresher oil with the old stuff. Almost all these major blenders are in Italy, and studies have clearly shown that besides price, the main reason most American consumers choose a bottle is for its "Italianness"—no matter where it actually comes from.

Italy has aggressively marketed and maintained a mythical aura in the olive oil world and does produce some of the finest olive oils on earth. But it also produces many of the worst, including the supermarket brands that have routinely failed testing here, and most of the adulterated oils seized by the FDA (a token drop in the bucket) in the past decade. Despite popular belief, Italy is not the largest olive oil producer—that would be Spain. In fact, Italy struggles to meet its own domestic demand. What Italy is, however, is the world's largest olive oil importer—and exporter—buying up vast quantities of oils from all across the Mediterranean and Africa, so they can be packaged and labeled as "Bottled in Italy" or the even more misleading "Product of Italy."

"The three biggest brand names in the world are Coca-Cola, American Express, and Made in Italy," said Michele Bungaro, chief spokesman for UNAPROL, Italy's national association of olive growers, speaking at the Italian Trade Commission panel with Marsano. These are the folks actually making olive oil from Italian olives, like the stuff I tasted in both Puglia and at the CIA. They stand to lose out from the nation's declining quality image, so UNAPROL launched its own certification process, and its "100% Qualita Italiana" label has higher extra-virgin standards than those of the European Union or United States. This is a good seal to look for, but uncommon. Tom Mueller agrees: "The enormous popularity of the 'Made in Italy' label worldwide makes it an appealing target for food fraudsters, who earn an estimated €60 billion a year selling counterfeit or adulterated faux-Italian foods." These include faux Parmesan and Parma prosciutto. Just in Italy, counterfeit olive oil is estimated to cost legitimate producers more than a billion and a half dollars a year. Mob accountant Meyer Lansky, one of the most successful organized-crime figures in U.S. history, who, along with partner Charles "Lucky" Luciano, built a global criminal empire around gambling, once famously boasted of the Mafia, "We're bigger than U.S. Steel." If Mueller's estimates are correct, then just the Italian slice of the Fake Food business is bigger than Coca-Cola, Disney, or Goldman Sachs.

In 2010, the University of California–Davis Olive Center tested supermarket samples and concluded that more than two-thirds of imported oils (69 percent) and 10 percent of California oils labeled "extra virgin" were not. "These failed samples had defective flavors such as rancid, fusty, and musty . . . Chemical testing indicated that the samples failed extra virgin standards for reasons that include one or more of the following: oxidation by exposure to elevated temperatures, light, and/or aging; adulteration with cheaper refined olive oil; poor quality oil made from damaged and overripe olives, processing flaws, and/or improper oil storage." Yum.

Subsequent tests of oil for the food-service industry got similar results and also found that more than half the "extra-virgin" olive oil used in restaurants had been illegally adulterated with refined oils (cheaper, lower-grade oils that often are solvent extracted, thermally deodorized, and bleached). Rather than worrying whether we might get screwed by fake olive oil when we eat out, we should expect it.

A follow-up supermarket test in 2011 used a much larger number of samples for more consistency and found that the five top-selling imported "extra-virgin" olive oil brands in the United States failed to meet the basic legal standard 73 percent of the time. These are available in practically every supermarket coast to coast, and failure rates ranged from 56 to 94 percent by brand: Colavita performed "best" by failing just over half the time, while Pompeian took last place and almost never passed. This study used a newer high-tech test that better detects adulteration, and more than half of all samples failed one or both tests.

In November 2015, police in Turin, Italy, launched an investigation into whether seven leading producers, including Bertolli and Carapelli, had mislabeled lower quality oils as "100% extra virgin" after tested samples from all seven failed to meet EU labeling rules. Throughout the same year, Italian agricultural ministry inspectors confiscated fake oil worth ten million euros. As recently as 2016, over two thousand tons of fake Italian extra-virgin olive oil were seized in an operation that took place in the Apulia, Calabria, and Umbria regions. *Consumer Reports* magazine did its own study four years earlier, using both chemical analysis and sensory testing by a panel of tasters, the second tier of extra-virgin's legal classification, and got similar numbers, with 61 percent failing. "By definition, extra-virgin olive oil is supposed to be flawless, but only the top nine of the 23 products our experts tried were free of flaws. More than half tasted fermented or stale. Two even tasted a bit like . . . let's just say a barnyard." In Spain, an investigation by authorities in the Andalusia region found that half of fifty brands tested were inaccurately labeled extra virgin.

With little oil sold in this country qualifying as real extra virgin, that begs the question, what is real extra virgin? The main governing body for the industry is the Madrid-based International Olive Council (IOC), whose membership includes most major oil-producing countries, jointly responsible for 90 to 95 percent of global production. IOC membership most notably lacks the United States, where almost all production is in California, fast-rising

Australia, South Africa, and Chile. The IOC was established in 1959 under the auspices of the United Nations and crafted the grading rules widely used for olive oil in almost all corners of the globe.

In our country, the USDA made olive oil grades voluntary, so producers do not have to use label indications such as "extra virgin" or "virgin," but if they choose to, they must follow USDA rules, which in turn defer to the IOC. So the standards for Europe and the rest of the world (except Australia) are the de facto legal standards here as well. Many critics feel these are too permissive, a low bar that allows poorer quality oils to rate extra virgin—yet the majority still fail.

All "virgin" olive oil can by law only be extracted by physical processing, such as crushing or centrifuges, without using chemicals or heat. There are three grades of virgin olive oil: extra-virgin, virgin, and lampante, Italian for lamp oil—under both IOC and USDA standards, lampante is unfit for human consumption without further refinement. So, in theory, there are two kinds of virgin oil you can actually buy, virgin and extra virgin. Virgin is made exactly the same way but fails to pass the tests required to be ranked extra virgin. Think of extra virgin as Grade A, virgin as Grade B, and lampante as Grade F. Virgin is still available in Europe, where it is correctly understood as a lower-price, lower-quality choice often used for cooking. In this country, it has largely disappeared from shelves, not because it is no longer made, but rather because producers routinely illegally label and sell it as extra-virgin. This is fraud, plain and simple, but it is made possible by the fact that there has long been a tradition of little enforcement of olive oil laws in this country. Everyone in the industry knows there is virtually no chance of getting caught.

Under IOC rules, to be rated extra virgin, oil must pass two series of tests, laboratory and sensory. The lab analysis tests specific objective chemical standards for various components, most importantly the free fatty acidity (FFA) level (FFA of 0.8 percent or less), and peroxide value (PV, or rancidity of no more than 20 milliequivalents per kilogram). There is also an ultraviolet light test, and the oil must continuously be stored within a designated temperature range to avoid damage from heat. California, which crafted its own standards, set a stricter FFA limit (0.6 percent), though, like USDA rules, it goes largely unenforced.

It is the sensory tests that make olive oil a rarity, one of very few foodstuffs in the world whose legal definition includes a subjective taste test (along with Prosciutto di Parma and, in borderline cases, Parmigiano-Reggiano). Rules mandate that the oil have a "detectable level of olive fruitiness," and specifically bar sixteen flavor or taste defects, including rancid, musty, fusty, winey/vinegary, and grubby, among other similarly unappetizing terms. On paper, the rules have zero tolerance—oil lacking fruitiness or containing any one of the sixteen defects automatically fails and cannot be sold as extra virgin. In practice, sensory tests, while required, are conducted only sporadically and many defects are widely flouted in sales, marketing and labeling, as numerous studies have shown.

Nonetheless, these seemingly arduous regulations reflect the original intention of the extra virgin distinction—a mark of excellence, the best of the best. At an olive oil tasting class I attended in Spain, the instructor told me that "8 percent, maybe 10 percent, of the oil we produce in Spain is extra virgin." One of Mueller's European experts estimated that among the world's olive oil 2 percent is excellent, 8 percent good but not exceptional, and 90 percent so-so. Yet besides a small amount of light olive oil, a label that confuses rather than clarifies, almost every bottle for sale in the U.S. is so-called extra virgin. You would be hard pressed to buy a lower grade even if you wanted to. And you don't.

Unlike all other commercially significant oil, olive oil is not extracted from seeds, as are sunflower, soy, and rapeseed (canola) oils. Extracting seed oils generally uses industrial solvents, such as hexane, which must then be removed. To do this, seed oil is processed in a refinery, where it undergoes high-temperature de-solventization, neutralization, deodorization, bleaching, and de-gumming, which simultaneously removes any unpleasant tastes or odors. Extra-virgin olive oil does not require any of this, since it comes entirely from just crushing or spinning fruit.

So what happens to the lampante, the low-quality oil that was deemed "unfit for human consumption without further refine-ment"? What happens to the olive pomace, the remaining solids left after mechanical extraction, the skin, pits, and meat, the stuff Italian food expert Bill Marsano calls "the garbage left at the bot-tom of the press"? These are treated just like seed oils and re-fined as described by the U.S. International Trade Commission: "Both olive pomace and lampante oils are low-grade oils that . . . go through a refining process that utilizes both heat and chemicals to neutralize acidity and remove flavor defects, as well as deodor-ize and decolor the oil. This process results in a flavorless, odorless [and now edible] oil . . . This refined oil is blended with virgin oils by bottling companies to create what is commonly marketed as 'olive oil.' Olive oil products of this type typically include anywhere from 3 percent to 12 percent virgin olive oil."

As a consumer, you couldn't be blamed for rationally expect-ing bottles of extra-virgin olive oil, virgin olive oil, and olive oil to contain something from the same general family. But instead, you are expected to memorize all food-related fine print to shop safely. Because so much of it is illegally labeled "extra virgin," you probably will never see just "olive oil." But if you do, take the ad-vice Celine Beitchman, a chef-instructor at the Natural Gourmet Institute for Health and Culinary Arts in New York City gave me: "If the label just says olive oil or pure olive oil I wouldn't recom-mend using it for anything food related. Use it to oil the hinges of your door."

Bill Marsano succinctly described the refining of olive oil: "The way to make this oil is to use chemicals, crush it three or four more times, then use more chemicals to get rid of the first ones." Not coincidentally, I met Marsano when he was on a "Find the Fake" panel, sponsored by the Italian Trade Commission, in which he and his fellow experts guided us through a blind tasting of four olive oils, three real extra virgins and one impostor. While much of the fake stuff has an instantly recognizable off flavor of rotted fruit, they made it just slightly harder by choosing one that simply had no flavor at all.

Of course, you will never see anything on the supermarket shelf with a "refined olive oil" label. Some of it gets into ersatz bottles of "extra virgin," while others go into bottles labeled "light olive oil" or "pure olive oil." "Light" is another fairly flagrant marketing scam, as studies have shown that the vast majority of consumers— 84 percent—wrongly believe that a "light" product has less calories when all it has is less quality, nutrition, and taste. In the industry, this style is known as "light in flavor."

Like its legally meaningless sibling "natural," "pure" is a favorite of label pirates taking advantage of positive-sounding but unregulated terms. In a consumer perception study, the University of California–Davis found that most Americans so badly misunderstood olive oil grades that almost half think "pure" is the highest-quality grade even though it is the lowest, not virgin at all. When Australia enacted its best-in-class consumer protection regulation in 2011, it became the first country to ban misleading label terms such as "premium," "super," "light," or "pure," to provide more clarity.

While the USDA dictates rules for olive oil labels, it is the FDA that is responsible for ensuring the truthfulness of label claims. After more than seven decades of consistently finding rampant fakes and adulterated oil, the FDA gave up as a cost-cutting measure.

While budgetary limitations are very real concerns at the FDA, even if it wanted to it couldn't do much, thanks to rather circular logic that goes like this, according to an anonymous-by-request FDA official I spoke with: "In order for the FDA to do something about grades of olive oil, we would have to refer to some definition, in order to make sure it didn't conform to that definition. The FDA doesn't have such a definition. The FDA doesn't have a definition of 'extra virgin,' 'virgin,' 'pomace,' and so on, to point to and say that this is the required composition. The FDA doesn't go after those grade designations because they don't have any standards to point to." Got it? Because the USDA standard is voluntary, that doesn't count, and the FDA has repeatedly refused formal requests to define olive oil, which would in turn let officials do something about it.

The FDA has one and only one rule for the entire olive oil industry: if other oils are used, they must be indicated on the label. Every few years the agency makes a token adulteration seizure.

"I've seen oil labeled 'USDA organic,' 'extra virgin,' and 'made in Italy,' which was actually colored and flavored soybean oil," Mueller told me. "If no one is checking, that's what's going to happen—you can put whatever in hell you want on the label." Guess what? No one is checking. These problems are so widespread that while proposing new consumer protection regulations to be added to the recent Farm Bill in Congress, which were eventually shot down, California Republican representative—and farmer—Doug LaMalfa suggested that labels for imported oil should say "extra rancid" rather than "extra virgin," explaining, "It's more just the truth in advertising."

Would better enforcement actually help American consumers? Almost certainly, as demonstrated by the Canadian experience. After the Canadian Food Inspection Agency enacted a program in 2006 and began routinely analyzing product samples to check for adulteration and ensure olive oil met requirements for virgin and extra-virgin olive oil, the percentage of noncompliant samples fell dramatically in just three years, from 47 to 11 percent.

Knowing that much of what is sold in this country is spurious, it would be easy to give up and turn your back on extra-virgin olive oil altogether. But if you love food, just a sip of the real stuff will remind you why you shouldn't—because taste does matter. Bill Briwa and I tried the three samples dispensed from the CIA's *oleoteca*, all real extra virgins. The differences in weight, color, and flavor were pronounced but not nearly as dramatic as the difference between any of them—all were utterly delicious—and ordinary supermarket "extra virgin." This was the one thing on which every expert agreed and which I am very happy to confirm: once you taste the real thing, you know it, and then you'll also know the fake. Briwa laid out an impressive spread of cheese, charcuterie, and bread crisps with our oils, but like wine, we could have just sipped them straight and still enjoyed them.

Briwa was once a student at the very institution he now works for, the CIA, but back in 1980 when he graduated, the professional perspective on olive oil in this country was a tad different. "I remember very clearly, the chef-instructor for Italian cuisine back then told us to be very careful using it because no one in the U.S. likes olive oil. He also told us it's very expensive, so we should cut it with neutral oil to save money. They kept a three-gallon tin on the top of the stove, exposed to heat all day long, and it was rancid. That was our entire education about olive oil. Flash-forward three decades and there's a lot more attention being given to it, but there's still a lot of misperception. Unfortunately, adulteration and mislabeling are reality. It's part of our mission to educate, and the only reason olive oil can so easily be adulterated is because people are uneducated."

Fortunately, there is a lot of great real extra-virgin olive oil in the world, and plenty of people who make it exceedingly well. (Briwa became enamored of olive oil not merely as a chef, food lover, and renowned culinary instructor, but by making his own. "My real conversion came when I decide to make my own. It took me ten years but now I say that I like olive oil on toast more than butter—I had it this morning for breakfast.") I now get most of my oil from T. J. Robinson's Fresh Pressed Olive Oil Club, and every time I open a bottle, my kitchen literally fills up with the smell of fresh crushed olives—the scent explodes out of the bottle. Just breaking the seal transports me to Italy or Spain or Chile. With knowledge and the shopping tips at the end of this chapter, you can enjoy nothing but true extra-virgin olive oil going forward, and both your body and taste buds will be better off for it.

AS SINISTER AS the olive oil landscape is, it is not the worst "gourmet" oil duping American consumers on a regular basis. That dubious honor goes to so-called truffle oil, which has quickly and quietly burrowed deep into our culinary landscape, infecting menus at neighborhood taverns and fine dining eateries, especially in the already passé dish of truffle fries. Almost no truffle oil is real. The fakeness runs so deep that truffle oil sets itself apart even in the crowded world of ersatz edibles by virtue of not really being counterfeit—there is so little actual truffle oil that the fake stuff is more a made up artificial food than a copy of something real.

Like lobsters or caviar, truffles are one of the most well-known names in luxury foodstuffs, synonymous with high cost and perceived quality. But what restaurants tell you they are serving and what you get are two very different things. The common clue is often, but not always, price: there would be an economic prohibition to serving truffled popcorn as a bar snack if it actually included truffles. It does not. Of course, expensive dishes aren't any safer; the rip-off is just bigger. It would be hard to argue with a straight face that a food sold as including truffle oil wouldn't contain any truffle at all, but that is almost always the case. And unlike the ignorance surrounding extra-virgin olive oil in the restaurant business, most chefs are fully aware that what they are selling is not a valuable fungi harvested by pigs in Alba but rather a cheap chemical cocktail from a laboratory. The truth about truffle oil, while kept from consumers, is well known in the restaurant business.

In 2007, acclaimed Bay Area chef and cookbook author Daniel Patterson, whose Coi restaurant earned a vaunted two Michelin stars, went public about truffle oil in his widely read *New York Times* story, "Hocus Pocus, and a Beaker of Truffles." He noted that "all across the country, in restaurants great and small, the 'truffle' flavor advertised on menus is increasingly being supplied by truffle oil. What those menus don't say is that, unlike real truffles, the aroma of truffle oil is not born in the earth. Most commercial truffle oils are concocted by mixing olive oil with one or more compounds, like 2,4-dithiapentane, that have been created in a laboratory; their one-dimensional flavor is also changing common understanding of how a truffle should taste." And this base, olive oil, is the stuff for oiling door hinges.

He goes on to personally confess to having somewhat blindly overlooked compelling evidentiary weaknesses in the very notion of truffle oil: "I suppose I could have given some thought to how an ingredient that cost $60 an ounce or more could be captured so expressively in an oil that sold for a dollar an ounce." Finally, Patterson asked the big question that remains largely unanswered nearly a decade later: "Why are so many chefs at all price points—who wouldn't dream of using vanillin instead of vanilla bean and who source their organic baby vegetables and humanely raised meats with exquisite care—using a synthetic flavoring agent?"

Not all chefs embrace this particular truffle-seeming chemical concoction. Jean-Georges Vongerichten, a renowned celebrity chef awash in Michelin stars and other accolades, told the *Wall Street Journal*, "The most overrated ingredient is truffle oil. It's like gasoline. I never use it in my restaurants." Equally high-profile celebrity chef Gordon Ramsay, who has ranked as highly as second in the world in total number of Michelin stars, went on one of his famous tirades—this time aimed at truffle oil—while judging Season 2 of the cooking competition show *MasterChef* with fellow judge Joe Bastianich, a restaurateur involved in numerous high-profile eateries in New York, Las Vegas, Los Angeles, and overseas. When one of the contestants added truffle oil to a dish, Ramsay commented that the liquid was "one of the most pungent, ridiculous ingredients ever known to chefs. I can't believe you've just done that. I think you just put your apron up in flames." Bastianich added that using the oil was "a sure sign of someone who doesn't know what they're doing . . . Do you know that truffle oils are made by perfumists that have no white truffles in them? Generally if you go to a restaurant and you see white truffle oil on the menu, it's a good reason to run away." Do the same if it says "black truffle oil" or simply "truffle oil."

In a self-proclaimed rant on the culinary website Serious Eats, the site's managing culinary director, J. Kenji López-Alt, who is also the author of the James Beard Award–nominated column The Food Lab, ponders the circumstances by which "for some reason, back in the '90s, truffle oil became an acceptable—even desirable—ingredient for chefs to use . . . Problem is, truffle oil isn't even made from truffles . . . using truffle oil is the culinary equivalent of . . . making soup from a chicken bouillon cube—worse, even. At least bouillon cubes usually start with real chicken." He notes that it is the only ingredient renowned Boston chef Ken Oringer of Clio and Toro fame has banned completely in his kitchens, for tasting synthetic and too artificial. He ends by dropping Serious Eats founder Ed Levine's truffle oil punch line: "Comparing truffle oil to real truffles is like comparing sniffing dirty underwear to having sex."

The CIA's Briwa was more direct: "There's nothing even remotely natural about it. Truffle oil is all manufactured. Truffles are one of those one-percenter foods that very few people get to ever taste, so it's easy to pawn off manufactured oil . . . if you overuse it your food tastes artificial."

Like so many Fake Food issues, this one comes down to labeling regulations and their general laxity. Pricier bottlers love to use those familiar but meaningless labels "natural," "pure" and "100%." A quick online shopping trip finds gourmet store Williams-Sonoma hawking an Italianate "100% organic white truffle extra virgin olive oil" called Tartufi di Fassia. What the 100%, which by definition means all, refers to is anyone's guess, and despite its name the ingredient list has no white truffles, organic or otherwise. It does have truffle flavoring, but "flavoring" is to FDA label regulations what "New York–style" is to pizza, code for something other than the actual thing. One of the most widely available brands, Roland, contains "white truffle aroma," another labeling loophole that allows for a variety of natural or synthetic definitions.

The genuine article is almost nonexistent, in part because of cost, but mainly because many experts believe real truffles don't infuse flavor into oil well. If you do find it, the ingredient list should contain just two entries, extra-virgin olive oil and truffles. What you more commonly see is lower-grade olive oil labeled with "natural truffle flavoring," "artificial flavoring," and "truffle aroma," all synonyms for synthesized additives. The "natural" in natural truffle flavoring typically refers not to actual fungi but rather to the process by which the imitation flavor compound is derived.

Fortunately, the truffle oil solution is easy—just avoid it altogether. The best use of truffle oil is as a warning, a red flag indicating restaurants to avoid. It is the only Fake Food in this book that I cannot think of a good reason to bother seeking a real alternative to. On the other hand, real extra-virgin olive oil is well worth the trouble to hunt down. Here are some tips on how to buy the real thing.

## ✳ RELIABLE PRODUCERS

California's McEvoy Ranch makes high-quality real extra-virgin olive oil, available by mail order and at gourmet stores. McEvoy's acclaimed oil maker, Deborah Rodgers, also recommends Australia's Boulder Bend, sold under its Cobram Estate label in the United States. Cobram is Australia's most-awarded olive oil, winning more than 150 medals in competitions. Their top-shelf ultrapremium collection is guaranteed milled within four hours of harvest and is sold online, as is Spain's vaunted Oro Bailen.

## ✳ RETAILERS

Michael Bradley created the specialty olive oil shop model, where hand-selected oil is stored in bulk metal tanks and bottled from taps on demand—olive oil is best purchased frequently in small quantities. The stores have tastings of up to forty extra-virgin olive oils available and post detailed information on each, including producer, country, harvest date, chemical stats, and olive varietals. There are hundreds of these nearly identical shops with different names across the country, in most midsized and large cities, and tourist towns. Once you go into one you will recognize the format. T. J. Robinson's Fresh Pressed Olive Oil Club sources exquisite small batch oils—even from the producer that supplies the Vatican. His club sends quarterly shipments of three oils—mild, moderate, and strong—always new and fresh, alternating seasonally from the Northern and Southern Hemispheres. It's fantastic but pricy. Famed mail-order and brick-and-mortar gourmet retailer Zingerman's, in Ann Arbor, Michigan, has one of the biggest and best arrays you can taste under one roof. But even ordering blindly is reliable, as they stock carefully curated oils. French specialty olive oil retailer Oliviers & Co. offers mail order and has retail boutiques with tasting in New York, New Jersey, and eighteen countries. Last, but hardly least, author Tom Mueller's site, www.extravirginity.com, has a frequently updated list of his recommended olive oil buying resources.

## ✣ LABELS, PART 1

Taste is the absolute best indicator of olive oil quality and it is always best to try before buying, but only a handful of retailers allow this. If you need to buy oil "blindly," using only the label, as a general rule, the more information it contains the better, if only because producers most concerned with quality tend to include more detail than they have to. Unlike wine, olive oil is never going to be better than on the day it was bottled, but it will get worse. The most important thing you can find is the harvest date, which few bottles carry but should be no more than a year earlier. Ignore meaningless "best by" or "bottled on" dates. "Extra virgin" is no guarantee, but its absence on a bottle is a guarantee of inferiority. Don't ever buy anything labeled "virgin," "pure," "light," "extra light," "olive oil blend," "Mediterranean blend," or simply "olive oil." Very few labels include chemical composition, but if they do, Michael Bradley recommends looking for FFA of 0.3 percent or less and PV of 8 or less. European oils, especially from Italy, may also have DOP, DOC, or similar geographic indications (GIs). While not foolproof solutions, these improve your chances, theoretically ensuring the olives were grown in a designated quality zone and produced with more oversight.

## ✳ LABELS, PART 2

Commonly misunderstood label terms are "first pressed," "cold pressed," and "first cold pressed," none of which have any regulatory meaning or contemporary significance, since most oil today is not pressed at all but rather spun out of olives using centrifuges (both are legal), and *extra virgin* by definition cannot come from secondary extraction. Mueller told me that "first cold pressed" is his favorite misleading descriptor, "basically three lies in one, a highly anachronistic term that no longer has any relation to reality, a classic example of wholly useless marketing speak."

## ✳ LABELS, PART 3

There are several third-party certifications that promise higher standards and enforcement than the IOC and USDA rules. McEvoy's Rogers told me that "here in California you can look for a seal of certification from the new California Olive Oil Council. It should also say 'certified extra virgin,' which means [under California law] it has been laboratory tested and sensory tested." The actual label she describes reads "COOC Certified Extra Virgin." There's also EVA, the Extra Virgin Alliance, an excellent global organization and label. UNAPROL, the association of actual Italian olive growers, has its 100% Qualita Italiana. Any of these are excellent signs. On the other hand, every expert I spoke to put little stock in the USDA's organic certification for olive oil, from here or abroad. In early 2016, Italy's National Association of Olive Growers, in partnership with the country's State Mint, announced the planned rollout of a new antifraud labeling mark, similar to that now used for wine, only for bottles of 100 percent extra-virgin olive oil. The Mint's yet unnamed label will include a scannable QR code linked to traceability information on the oil's distribution channels.

## ✤ GEOGRAPHY

There are good and bad producers everywhere, and country of origin is no guarantee of quality. But if you have to purchase blindly with no other clue besides where it was made, choose Chile or Australia. Neither practices the carryover of old oils common in Europe, and Australia has the strictest standards and is the only country using advanced tests to detect adulteration with refined oils. The impartial U.S. International Trade Commission report looked at each nation's average quality of extra-virgin olive oil across the board and gave its highest marks only to Australia and Chile—followed by the United States.

## ✤ SEASONALITY

European oils are extracted in late fall or early winter and rarely begin arriving in the States before late winter. The end of the year is the worst time to buy any Northern Hemisphere oil because it is already nearing the end of its useful life—in a best case scenario. Buy European oils in the spring and summer; Chilean, Australian, and South African oils, in the fall and winter. Newer is always better.

## ✤ STORAGE

Many consumers buy a large can of olive oil at a big-box store and keep it in their home for far too long, because one of the most misunderstood things about olive oil is that it is highly perishable—remember, it is fresh-squeezed fruit juice. "The notion that it is a perishable commodity needs to be better understood by both consumers and retailers," said the CIA's Briwa. "I've seen fancy gourmet stores displaying clear bottles in the window, breaking two rules at once, exposing it to heat and light." Olive oil hates both and should be stored out of sight, ideally in a cool, dark cabinet. Most bottles are opaque glass and some come wrapped in foil, but many experts prefer tins because they block all light. Oxygen is the third enemy, and shelf life is far longer unopened—

after you introduce air, even once, oil heads downhill fast. Specialty stores fill small bottles from large tanks for this reason, so buy no more than you will use in six weeks. Likewise, it is better to buy two small cans than one bigger one, because they can last six to 12 months unopened. "In our house we throw it out three weeks after opening—but it rarely lasts that long," said Bradley.

## BISTECCA ALLA FIORENTINA

A classic Tuscan dish, this is perhaps the most famous use of olive oil as a main ingredient in an entrée. Florentines will insist the dish requires the local Chianina breed of beef, but any good beef will go with any great olive oil. Serves 2 to 4.

> 1 good-quality (at least USDA Prime) bone-in porterhouse
>    or T-bone steak (2 to 3 pounds), cut 2 inches thick
> Coarse sea salt
> Freshly ground pepper
> Extra-virgin olive oil

### DIRECTIONS

– Let the steak come to room temperature for 45 to 60 minutes.
– Preheat the grill to high. (A grill using wood or natural charcoal is best, but gas is okay.)
– Season the steak with salt and pepper. Cook the steak 5 minutes on each side for rare (the Tuscan way!) or 2 to 3 minutes longer per side for medium-rare to medium. The outside should be well crusted.
– Slice both sides of the steak off the center bone, then carve these into perpendicular slices about ½ inch thick. Generously drizzle extra-virgin olive oil over the slices. *Mangia!*

# 5. What's in a Name? Real Foods Come from Real Places

This can't be repeated enough: these foods gain their character from the earth they grow in, the climate that nurtures them and the skills of the people who make them . . . I used to fool myself that prosciutto di St. Louis, Missouri was just as good. But it isn't.
—ARTHUR SCHWARTZ, "Italian Food Labels"

The Fairmont Kea Lani is a luxury waterfront resort on Maui, twenty-two acres of manicured paradise and sandy Pacific Ocean beaches, and popular with honeymooners, as many such Hawaiian resorts are. But the Fairmont is also a favorite of locals, an impressive and far less common accomplishment on the island, thanks largely to its award-winning Kō Restaurant, where more than 90 percent of the produce is locally sourced from Hawaiian farmers. Under the capable hands of Hawaii chef Tylun Pang, Kō was voted Maui Restaurant of the Year in 2013, no small feat on an island with a vast hospitality infrastructure and more than eight hundred eateries.

Kō's website claims the restaurant is "the only fine dining restaurant on Maui to offer cuisine inspired by Hawaii's sugarcane plantation era," and in this vein, Chef Pang features second-generation recipes taught to him by his father. "A recipe I like to prepare is Ginger Steamed Kumu with Asian sausage and scallions. It's light and lets you taste the flavor of the fresh fish. This recipe was my dad's. He would serve fish whole for special occasions at family gatherings, so it's special to me."

I had never heard of kumu, so I called my brother-in-law, who was born and raised in Honolulu in the 1950s and asked him if he knew what it was. He hadn't tasted the now-rare fish in decades but assured me it was delicious and fondly remembered his mother serving it. He lamented its current scarcity, limited mainly to spear fisherman, but considered himself lucky to have tasted it at all. The delicious red nocturnal member of the goatfish family is considered such a delicacy that in ancient times it was used as an offering to the gods. Eating it was considered *kapu*, or forbidden, for everyone except the ruling class of chiefs, who alone feasted on tasty kumu. In modern times, before it was overfished, kumu became so popular that it was featured as a breakfast item, broiled in butter, Hawaii's answer to smoked salmon, but today it is uncommon there and unheard of "off island."

Hawaii boasts a staggering amount of endemic fish, plants, insects, and even mammals found no place else on earth, but it is hardly alone. The coco-de-mer (sea coconut), was once nicknamed "billionaire's fruit," something wealthy gourmands went to great lengths to eat. But today it is so rare and protected you cannot buy it even with a fortune, and the fruit, containing the largest seed on earth, grows only on two Indian Ocean islands in the Seychelles.

Less scarce, but still valued highly, the American breakfast indulgence maple syrup comes from maple trees, mostly sugar maples, found only in colder climate regions of North America. While we take maple syrup more or less for granted, especially in Vermont where I live, as a strictly New World product, it is still foreign and exotic to Europeans, Asians, Africans, South Americans, Australians, and pretty much the rest of the world. The rare Royal Red shrimp, arguably the best-tasting shrimp in existence, has been found in only two locations worldwide, both deep water pockets off the eastern coast of the United States. The most valuable honey in the world is manuka honey, so named because the bees that make it pollinate the manuka tree, a kind of myrtle found only in New Zealand and southeastern Australia. You may not be eager to put kangaroo on your menu, but plenty of people do, and this is perhaps the most famously endemic of all meat sources, limited to Australia. There are plenty of examples of creatures we don't eat, such as lemurs, found only in Madagascar; gorillas, which live only in very particular ecosystems within Central Africa; and the fierce Komodo dragon, the world's largest lizard, found on just five Indonesian islands, most notably its namesake Komodo.

Such plants and animals are Mother Nature's way of reminding us that the world is varied and that not all places are the same. Ecosystems are amazingly complex, from climate, geography, and geology down to the insect and microbial level. This makes particular places better or worse than others at growing particular things. There are forests in Europe that look just like the forests in Vermont yet don't support maple trees. Parts of the Australian Outback look just like parts of southwestern Utah, but Utah has never had kangaroos (and Australia has no rattlesnakes, endemic to North America, while Utah has at least six distinct species). On the surface, little appears to differentiate the two spots where coco-de-mer is found from thousands of similarly tropical islands around the world.

The concepts of *terroir* and places being suited for different purposes translate to nonendemic foods as well—coffee is grown across great swaths of the planet, but a handful of select spots, such as the Blue Mountains of Jamaica, are prized above all others. Basil can be grown in just about any garden, or even on windowsills, yet it almost never rivals that of Italy's Ligurian coast, where pesto was born.

"Terroir has no direct English translation, but the notion behind the Latinate word is simple: the product's qualities 'come
with the territory.' To put it less poetically, terroir is the idea of an
'essential land/qualities nexus.' This is the idea of terroir: that the
particular geography produces particular product characteristics
that cannot be imitated by other regions," wrote Justin Hughes,
associate professor and director of the Intellectual Property Law
Program at New York's Cardozo School of Law.

Usually there is one obvious *terroir* feature, such as the famously
chalky seventy-million-year-old substructure the Champagne region
sits on. It is hard to read any primer about Champagne without
encountering the word *chalky*. But in each *terroir* there is also much
more than this one glaring factor, an intricate system that resists
duplication. It is not enough to add chalk to your soil to re-create
Reims or Epernay, because Champagne is much more: it also gets
a lot of rain and sits at an unusually high latitude. The world's
northernmost premier wine growing district, it is far cooler, wetter,
and more seasonally affected than Napa, Tuscany, or Burgundy.

*Terroir* is almost always a combination of the land itself, the
shape of that land in the form of mountains, hills, and valleys, plus
the abundance or absence of water, fresh or salt; the temperature,
day and night; the seasons; the sun; the wind; and the inhabitants,
including birds, bugs, animals, plants, and bacteria—and, important, people. With kumu, you also have the depth, temperature,
and cleanliness of the ocean; the health and abundance of coral
reefs; predators; and the suitability of the food supply, from fish
to microscopic plankton. Places like Hawaii even have their *terroir*
uniquely shaped simply by remoteness from other places. *Terroir*
has an enormous number of variables, even before you add in the
human factor.

• • •

THE SOUTH OF France is dotted with small towns similar in style and appearance, narrow streets lined with brightly colored houses bedecked with flowers, which grow wonderfully in the warm and fertile region. But one of these towns is not like all the others, although it looks the same above the surface. Below ground is an odd subterranean world riddled with caves, which are completely free of light, and regardless of what happens in the outside world, in these tunnels the weather forecast is always exactly the same: dark and fifty degrees Fahrenheit with 95 percent humidity. It is a climate far from ideal for most things, but excellent for one very particular task: aging moldy cheese.

This town is named Roquefort, and it was the first place in France ever to be recognized and afforded legal protection for the food it specializes in producing, a crumbly, tangy, moist sheep's milk cheese dotted with distinctive green mold, also named Roquefort. It is believed that the cheese has been made in the area, long popular with shepherds, since at least the first century CE. As with so many place-specific products there is more to the Roquefort story than just the amazingly consistent climate of the caves. There would be no cheese if the caves were not also home to an endemic natural mold spore, *Penicillium roqueforti,* which creates those signature green veins.

The caves and mold are essential, but still there would be no such cheese if the surrounding land did not also produce grasses and plants superb for grazing sheep, and if actual human shepherds did not choose to graze their sheep right here and, at the same time, look for ways to preserve milk. All the perfect natural conditions could not produce Roquefort cheese without a human element, an element that has been part of the *terroir* of this one and only town for two thousand years.

This natural and human environment is so special that in 1411 King Charles VI created France's first "appellation" by his royal decree that Roquefort cheese could only be produced in Roquefort.

It is among the most famous of cheeses, and the second most popular in France, but all of it is made here. Six hundred years after
it became protected, there are still only seven producers allowed
to make all of the real Roquefort cheese. Today, the mold can be
manufactured in a laboratory, but under French law, only mold
produced from the naturally occurring spore in these caves can
be used, and there are many other requirements too. The milk
can only come from three specific breeds of sheep, all of which
have to be ranged in this area, where what they eat is natural and
regulated. In addition, the time from milking to cheese making is
tightly controlled. Every other step of the process, from matura-
tion to cutting to packaging, must also occur here.

The French have historically been the most ardent *terroir* en-
thusiasts, long at the forefront of the effort to codify and legally
define the notion and its resulting impact on the quality of foods.
To do this, they created laws governing the Appellation d'Origine
Contrôlée (AOC), or Controlled Designation of Origin, the places
where outstanding foods can legally be made owing to reasons of
*terroir.* This process began to develop in Roquefort but was formal-
ized in a modern sense in 1919, when the Law for the Protection
of the Place of Origin was enacted, specifying regions or towns in
which certain named products of significance must be manufactured. In 1935, a special branch of the agricultural ministry was
created to delineate these AOC designations, and the very first
label based on its regional *terroir* was proclaimed in 1937 for the
Rhone wine "Côtes du Rhône." According to Professor Hughes,
"French law defines . . . a product of that origin whose qualities or
characteristics are due to the geographic milieu, which includes
natural and human elements."

The concept is best represented by the interconnected circle
of life we saw in Italy's Parma, which operates on multiple human and natural levels simultaneously, none of which can be sep-
arated from the others. As Hughes notes, "Appellation laws are

traditionally justified by the idea of terroir . . . The local producers
are entitled to exclusive use of a product name because no one
outside the locale can truly make the same product."

The French AOC system was created specifically for wine but
later expanded to foods, and it became the progenitor of many
similar geographically based quality designations in other countries, most notably Italy's three-tiered system, DO (Designation
of Origin), DOC (Controlled Designation of Origin), and the
highest-quality DOCG (Controlled Designation of Origin Guaranteed). Portugal, Switzerland, and Austria all adopted similar
regulatory structures, and while Spain's Denominación de Origen
is technically Europe's oldest such wine law, starting with Rioja in
1925, the French system had been in informal development for
centuries. Even the United States, which has generally been un-
supportive of the philosophical concept of connecting geography
with quality, adapted the AOC framework to its own wine appellation system, American Viticultural Areas. All such laws, whether
national or international in scope, and whether they refer to wines
or foods or spirits, are collectively known as geographic indications, or GIs, the key being where something is produced.

To be fair, these designations are not a panacea, and not all
products with colorful histories and AOC protections are top shelf.
I've had plenty of wines authentically labeled AOC or DOCG that
were subpar—not every Rioja is great. There are many foodstuffs
that I have traveled hundreds or even thousands of miles to taste,
and most memorable to me is my long but ultimately disappoint-
ing pursuit of the "legendary" Bresse chicken, aka "the Queen of
Poultry, the Poultry of Kings." The first livestock of any kind to be
granted AOC protection (1957), production of the famed Poulet
de Bresse is so small and demand so high that very little leaves
France. In the domestic market, it commands at least five times
the price of other chickens. Under French law, each free-ranging

bird must have more than one hundred square feet to itself, essentially a studio apartment in New York, along with lots of other rules. The pampered poultry has been praised by everyone from star chef Heston Blumenthal to the *Guardian* newspaper, which smartly called it "the top of the pecking order."

For years, I'd wanted to try the legendary Bresse chicken, but its home is near Lyon, and it is hard to find elsewhere, even in Paris, where it shows up on menus at Michelin-starred eateries sporadically, usually as a special. It's not like going out for pizza. I'd been back and forth to France several times without luck when on a trip to Burgundy I found one restaurant in Beaune that featured a whole Bresse chicken for two as a regular menu item. Thanking my lucky stars, I made a reservation, weeks in advance. My wife and I visited and eagerly anticipated the bird, which was ceremoniously paraded out of the kitchen on a large wheeled cutting board and carved for us tableside by a stately waiter. He even proudly displayed the metal ID tag affixed to the leg to prove its Bresse roots. The 2011 price for a small whole roast chicken, served with nothing but a side of *pomme frites*, was $125. We dug in. It tasted exactly like the $8 rotisserie chickens at my local supermarket. The fries were just okay. As the old adage goes, tastes like chicken.

But Bresse chicken is an anomaly, and many of Europe's geographically indicated products are truly best in class. After the advent of the European Union, a new legal framework for certifying and protecting geographic indications was created in 1992 (and extensively revised in late 2012). The European Union takes a three-tiered approach, the lowest level of protection being Traditional Specialties Guaranteed (TGI), which is not based on a legally defined place but rather a way of making a food, which to be considered "traditional" must have been made and sold in this way for a minimum of thirty years.

Next is Protected Geographic Indication (PGI), which does

guarantee that product was made in a particular place known for producing it in a notable way.

The highest designation is Protected Designation of Origin (PDO). which combines a particular place with an exceptional level of quality, or as EU law states, "designation of origin is a name which identifies a product originating in a specific place, region or, in exceptional cases, a country; whose quality or characteristics are essentially or exclusively due to a particular geographical environment with its inherent natural and human factors; and the production steps of which all take place in the defined geographical area."

All three levels of certification are backed by detailed regulations governing production, and awarded to products in the form of a distinctive symbol developed by the European Union. While France and Italy still also use their overlapping AOC and DOCG schemes, today the PDO designation is by far the widest-reaching and most important mark of Real Foods that are real based on where and how they are made. In this confusing world of food acronyms, it is the one most worth remembering.

PDO status can be awarded to geographically based products from any country, even if it is not an EU member, and places as varied as China and the Dominican Republic have successfully obtained PDO or PGI status for signature products, as have India, Sri Lanka, Norway, Thailand, Turkey, and Vietnam. In 2007, the European Union even granted its first-ever GI to an American product—Napa Valley wines—protecting them in the European market. This is the exact opposite of how the United States has handled EU wines such as Champagne, Burgundy, Chianti, and so on. Colombian coffee was one of the highest-profile outsiders to ask for and be awarded PDO status. It is important to remember that this does not in any way suggest that coffee cannot or should not be grown elsewhere, just that coffee from outside Colombia should not be sold as Colombian coffee, a concept so obvious it seems hard to imagine anyone would oppose it. Yet lots of people oppose PDO designation, especially U.S. producers that make knockoffs (think Kraft "Parmesan").

Compared to Europe, the United States has very few GIs, but we do have some. However, the significant difference is that our legal system views these more as trademarks and less as regulations that govern methods of production or quality. The most widely cited examples of protected domestic GIs are Florida oranges, Napa Valley wines, and Idaho potatoes, all globally protected through registration with the World Trade Organization. In the case of Florida and Idaho, both names associate a large family of products with equally large and very varied regions known for generally high quality production, but neither specifies what kinds of potatoes or oranges, where or how they are grown within the state, and there is no quality assurance oversight.

There are five main varieties of oranges grown in Florida, each different, and the original region selected for commercial growing owing to its environmental qualities, or *terroir*, in the eighteenth century has dramatically expanded statewide. From the consumer perspective, buying an Idaho potato tells you nothing useful except that it is some kind of potato from somewhere in Idaho, not how it was grown, whether it is good, or whether it is fresh. The Napa Valley is a highly respected viticultural area and on paper very similar to regions like Burgundy. The chief difference is that all grapes used to make wine in places like Burgundy must be grown in Burgundy, since that *terroir* is the implied reason for quality, while the Napa Valley GI allows a substantial amount, 25 percent, to be grown elsewhere and imported. While high-quality producers typically use 100 percent local grapes, it is very difficult for the consumer to differentiate among "Napa" wines.

Because of examples like these, it is easy to overlook that in most geographically indicated cases the *where* also means the *how*. What the sheep can eat, and not just where it eats, is part of the legal GI for Roquefort, as are the sizes of the wheels. In sharp contrast to Idaho, when a consumer in the United Kingdom buys Royal Jersey potatoes, which carry a PDO designation, they know exactly what they are getting. For more than a century this unique, elongated, greenish, early potato has been grown exclusively on the British Isle of Jersey in the middle of the English Channel. There are some four hundred farmers, but all the potatoes are believed to come from a single tuber in 1880 related to a potato variety clone known as International Kidney, and technically the Jersey Royal is classified as "*Solanum tuberosum* cv International Kidney cl Jersey Royal."

It is grown nowhere else in the world, and the farmers are responsible for growing their own seed stock for the next season. The potatoes, traditionally fertilized with nutrient-rich seaweed, are the earliest of the season to ripen in the British Isles, thanks to Jersey's southern latitude and many sunny south-facing slopes. Because they are fragile, there are specific rules for how they are harvested and inspected for quality, with the Department of Agriculture and Fisheries going so far as to plant "electronic potatoes" with sensors among the real ones to monitor the sensitivity of harvesting. Four packing cooperatives are responsible for handling and packaging all the potatoes that leave the island. The Royal Jersey has its own entry on English commodity trading lists and commands a higher price than all other potatoes, and much like fresh asparagus in parts of the United States denotes the coming of spring, the Royal Jersey receives mentions in the press along the lines of "The First Royal Jerseys Have Arrived!"

The product is so intertwined with its homeland that while farmers on Jersey grow other types of potatoes, none of those are allowed to be shipped off island for fear of consumer confusion.

So unlike the vague potatoes from Idaho, which can be excellent or mediocre, and any one of more than two dozen very different varieties ranging from russets and Yukon Gold to red fingerlings and blue potatoes, when someone buys a Royal Jersey potato, which are only sold seasonally, they know exactly what they are getting in terms of potato variety, where it was grown, how it was picked and packaged, and that it is fresh. It is the combination of geography and the skills of the people producing the product, plus the regulations and oversight guiding them, that make Real Food so real.

When Americans come back from a vacation in Italy and wonder—as they inevitably do—why even the simplest dishes taste so much better there than at Italian restaurants here, it is because they have just eaten Real Food—often for the first time. Take the simplest tomato sauce, which can be stunning in Italy. The country is justifiably famous for its tomatoes, especially the legendary San Marzano, grown in rich volcanic soil and so special it has been awarded a PDO (Pomodoro S. Marzano dell'Agro Sarnese-Nocerino). The San Marzano is not a salad or eating tomato. While there are very few things everyone agrees on, the San Marzano is widely believed by chefs—and not just in Italy—to be the best sauce tomato on earth, a status reinforced by how widely it has been imitated. The Real Neapolitan Pizza Association mandates PDO San Marzano tomatoes as the only ones that can be used for sauce on true Neapolitan pizzas—the original pizza.

The San Marzano is an illuminating example of what an appellation or PDO designation really means to consumers. Regulations cite several factors making this a superb place to grow the notoriously delicate fruits: the volcanic soil, rich in organic matter, phosphorus and exchangeable potassium; the climate; large amounts of quality groundwater; the influence of the nearby Mediterranean; even lack of damaging hail.

But the rules go far beyond designating geographic borders. They also define in extreme specificity the characteristics of the plants and fruit that qualify for the PDO mark, with minimums or maximums for size, shape, color, pH, refractometric residue, axes ratio, presence of peduncles, and lactic acid. They regulate the quality of the taste and odor, how closely together plants can be planted, how the fruit must be picked by hand to protect it from damage, what type and size of containers the tomatoes can be transported in, what type of jars or cans they can be put into, and in the case of canned sauce, what else can be added (salt and basil, yes; artificial ingredients, colors, or flavors, no).

The idea is not that we as consumers need to know what pH to look for in tomatoes but rather that the heavy lifting is done for us already by these regulations and by the fact that the Italian government spot-checks the authenticity of San Marzano tomatoes with DNA testing. There are those who scoff at the many different European appellations as protectionist or marketing gimmicks meant to drive up the price of a particular product, but you have to remember that there are lots of other tomatoes grown in Italy, far more than in this PDO region, all of which are hurt more by the San Marzano's lofty status than American-grown tomatoes, which can simply steal whatever names or reputations they like. Yes, PDO designations add value to products and often raise their prices, but usually the effect is felt mainly in their own country—and usually because they really are better.

You can buy "San Marzano" tomatoes in the States, often with Italian-looking labels and names, but they are usually copycats, not from volcanic soil, not from Italy, and often not even the same kind of tomato. Fortunately, if you try hard enough, you can also buy real PDO San Marzano tomatoes here.

Consider pesto, a famously regional dish of Italy's Ligurian coast. Pesto does not originate in Liguria by accident but rather because the area is famous for the quality of all three main ingredients: *pignolia* (pine nuts), basil, and olive oil. In comparison, most of the pine nuts sold in the United States, around 80 percent, are a different type grown in China, which neither look nor taste like those found in Europe and North America. As the *Telegraph* reported, China is now the world's leading exporter of pine nuts—and has been caught exporting cheaper species "deemed unfit for human consumption by food safety experts at the European Commission." The pesto in Liguria tastes better for exactly the same reason lobsters taste better in Maine and salmon tastes better in Alaska.

Italy's two greatest food towns are Parma and Bologna, longtime rivals for the title of the nation's epicurean epicenter, and each has a namesake food, respectively, Parmigiano-Reggiano cheese and bologna, a type of salami. Bologna can only be made in this region, under strict methods and from very particular ingredients. In Italy, bologna is rightly considered a delicacy, while in the United States it's almost a punishment. I can remember my elementary school lunches in the 1970s and the kids who brought Oscar Mayer bologna sandwiches did so presumably because their parents couldn't afford roast beef, turkey, or ham. As a nation, our entire perspective of bologna is skewed against the real thing because we only eat the fake. As a result, our taste buds suffer, our health suffers (real bologna can't legally have all the preservatives and artificial chemicals), and the artisans around the world who make these products suffer. Would farmers and their families across the globe be better off if we as a nation didn't counterfeit so much food? Absolutely.

Perhaps the clearest example is Chianti, one of the world's great wines but one that still hasn't fully recovered in the market from the stigma of the fake, low-quality, ersatz Chianti that proliferated in this country in the 1960s and '70s. Real DOCG Chianti is one of most reliably delicious and high-quality wines on earth, while our fake version has given the wine an image here akin to pink zinfandel—if you grew up in that era you might well think Chianti bottles are better emptied and turned into candle holders than poured for enjoyment. Do the winemakers suffer as a result? Yes, because Chianti could command higher prices if its reputation had not been so widely slandered. And it's not just Chianti we've hijacked; it's Burgundy and Chablis and port and yes, Champagne, perhaps the most widely known luxury brand name on earth, routinely faked here. My favorite description of the practice comes from the blog *Box Wines*, which not surprisingly is devoted to all things boxed wine. It calls wines using elsewhere-protected names "terroir poachers."

There are many who look at this geographic fraud through the "so what?" lens, deeming it okay for the cheese makers of Parma and the winemakers of France to suffer financial losses at the hands of Kraft's "Parmesan" powder or jugs of "Burgundy" from upstate New York, because, well, because this is America. But at the same time, our government considers it a high priority to protect our music, film, technology, and software industries from just the kinds of international "piracy" we widely condone when it comes to food. This is not exactly practicing what we preach, and whether you are buying a copy of Microsoft Office or a slice of Gruyère cheese or a quart of Florida orange juice, it benefits everyone in the chain to buy the real thing—everyone, that is, except the counterfeiter.

But even if our own government is not looking out for us in terms of Real Food, which it largely is not, as we will see again and again, at least the European Union is, for products from all over the world, and in many cases these EU protections make our shopping and eating experience better and easier.

Since the formation of the European Union, the confusing

universe of acronyms like AOC and DOC has been greatly simpli-
fied for food (not so much for wine) into three tiers designating
standout quality, PDO, PGI, and TGI. To receive the highest tier,
PDO, "exceptional quality" is an intrinsic requirement for taste,
allowable ingredients, and methods of production. As a general
rule, PDO products are not what we'd consider processed foods.
The online DOOR (Database of Origin and Registration) is a
compilation of more than fourteen hundred products currently
awarded or under review for PDO, PGI, and TGI status.

American manufacturers rip off protected names, but they
do not rip off the EU seals. Forget "Bottled in Italy," and look
for the PDO, PGI, or TGI seal—I won't buy canned San Marzano
tomatoes or many other products without it. Period. While not
foolproof, it is much harder to go wrong when buying anything
bearing one of these three logos:

# 6.  Q: Where's the Kobe Beef?
A: Not on Your Plate

Restaurants across America claim to sell Kobe beef on their upper-class menus, charging customers hundreds of dollars for the delicacy. However these so-called Japanese Kobe meat products are fakes.

—OLIVIA FLEMING, "$40 for a Burger
and $100 for a Steak . . ."

This is bullshit." The exclamation was a mix of awe and mounting anger, as my friend Pat used both hands to push himself away from the table. He was shaking his head slowly back and forth, with a look of confused disbelief plastered across his face. "I just don't understand—how can this taste so good? It doesn't make any sense . . ." He stumbled for the right words. "It's like steak married foie gras and had a bastard child," he concluded, licking his lips. That might be a biological impossibility, but he's right about one thing—it is all because of breeding. Pat has just tasted Kobe beef for the first time, and that's where his awe comes from. The mounting anger is because it is dawning on him that all the other so-called Kobe beef he thought he had eaten before was fake.

What makes traditional Japanese beef so special is its marbling, not just the amount of fat, but the fineness and perfect dispersion. It can almost look as much like raw sushi salmon as beef, a creamy pink rather than red. There are no white bands or streaks or veins, just tiny dots so thoroughly integrated into every inch of the meat that I always describe the appearance as if it had been hit with a shotgun shell of fat.

In his book *Steak*, food writer Mark Schatzker recounts traveling the world seeking the single best piece of beef (spoiler alert, the winner is not Kobe). Early in his trip to Japan, after hunting down the finest beef in the United States, Scotland, France, and Italy, he stares wondrously into a fridge of steaks "so fatty that 'meat' may no longer be the correct term for it. We were gazing at a loin of beef ornamented with wisps of fat that looked like crochet work, a pervasive filigree that reached into every nook of red muscle. It was the most marbled steak I had ever seen." It turns out Schatzker has yet to actually see his first piece of Kobe beef: the steak he was so wowed by was a lesser type of Japanese beef scoring only A3 on a marbling scale that runs from 1 to 5. All Kobe score A4 or A5 (more on the lettering system below).

The Japanese are fat obsessed, and at their famous tuna auctions, fattier fish equal much higher prices. But in Japan, both fatty tuna and Kobe beef are culturally eaten in small quantities, and through my travels there, the beef was repeatedly compared not to other meat but rather to butter. Over and over I was warned not to eat too much of it, and a Kobe rancher who owns one of the largest herds in existence told me he never eats the stuff more than twice a month. I quickly found out why.

I've now tried real Kobe beef and other highly touted regional wagyu (Japanese steer) several times in Japan, and all these experiences were similar to my first: overwhelming. The Japanese don't serve you a steak per se in the sense we are used to—you are never going to be presented with a Kobe T-bone and rarely with any whole slab of beef at all. A meager three- to four-ounce portion is considered generous. American steakhouses routinely

plate a single cut four to eight times that size. Every Kobe steak I
saw on my trips to Japan, whether strip, rib eye, or tenderloin, was
boneless and thin.

When I sat down at a restaurant in Kobe City that cooked on a
*teppanyaki* grill, the big flat metal griddle used at places like Beni-
hana, the chef first displayed the raw strip steak on a plate with a
flourish. It was an oval barely bigger than a pack of playing cards
and just as thick. With rapid motions and a sharp knife, he sliced
this into symmetrical rectangles about a half inch across. The comparison to fish continued, because now my still-raw steak looked
just like blocks of sashimi, only beefier. I was tempted to just dig
in and eat them uncooked. Each slice was seared quickly on the
hot grill but only for about sixty seconds before the flip, browned
and caramelized on both sides but still quite rare and served in
bite-sized pieces.

The meat was the textbook definition of tender, with absolutely no chew, graininess, or gristle and a rich, beefy flavor that
is almost overwhelmed by its creaminess. Unlike most beef, the
fats in true wagyu have a liquefying point well below 98.6 degrees,
and thus all those tiny shotgun pellets of fat melted in my mouth.
Later, I would see a meat inspector dramatically demonstrate this
by trimming a piece of fat from a Kobe carcass and placing it in
the palm of his hand, where it melted into a pool like a chip of
ice would, right before my eyes. You can't do that with your steak
back home.

For most who try Kobe beef, the first bite is delicious and decadent, a delicate balance of flavor and succulence, so packed with
meatiness, so rich, and so juicy it is hard to imagine anything better. But each subsequent bite is a little less thrilling, because the
fat quickly starts to build up on your tongue. By the end of my four
ounces, it was almost too much, the last piece like taking a bite off
a stick of butter.

I agree with Schatzker—and almost every chef I've discussed this subject with. Kobe beef is not necessarily better or best, but it is definitely one of a kind. It's like single-malt Scotch: some people love the powerful seaside malts full of smoke, peat, and iodine, and others do not. Whichever camp you fall into, these Laphroaigs and Lagavulins of the world are an easily identifiable subcategory of whiskies, and one every whisky lover should try but also one that only die-hard fans will want to drink every day.

Pat is a frequent traveler and easily the biggest meat lover I know. For more than two decades his job in finance has included a lot of time spent entertaining colleagues, often with a Wall Street–sized expense account. He eats at my favorite New York steakhouse, Keens, more in a month than I do in a year. He's had the finest dry-aged beef at the nation's top steakhouses from coast to coast, and he has dry-aged his own meat at home. He's downed the best grass-fed beef in Buenos Aires, the original Aberdeen Angus in Edinburgh, and the decadent *bistecca alla fiorentina* in Tuscany. He was the one who convinced me to make the not-insignificant pilgrimage to Casa Julian, an off-the-beaten path temple of beef in Spain's Basque country, which since 1951 has offered just one entrée, a once-in-a-lifetime, fire-charred, Flintstone-sized bone-in rib steak for two. In short, Pat really, really loves steak, and he knows beef. But he's never been to Japan, and until recently, that meant he could not try real Kobe. Since 2001, it's been banned in this country for far more time than it has been available. Yet after years of eating out at fancy New York restaurants, he thought he had—several times. He had certainly wasted a lot of money trying, and he was far from alone. As was noted in the *Wall Street Journal*, "With so-called 'Kobe beef' appearing on U.S. menus in recent years, many Americans may have thought they had already tasted one of the prized cuts. But that would have been simply impossible."

Precisely because I wanted to see Pat's reaction when he lost his Kobe virginity, I invited him to be my dinner guest at 212 Steakhouse in midtown Manhattan, which since the ban was lifted in late 2012, had become one of only two restaurants in the entire United States at the time officially approved by Japan's Kobe Beef Association to import and serve its legendary meat. (The other is the Wynn Resort in Las Vegas, and just since mid-2015 there is a third, Teppanyaki Ginza Sumikawa in Honolulu.) He was so impressed with dinner that when he went back to work the next day, he visited his boss, the head of his firm, and flatly insisted that he and his wife eat at 212 Steakhouse—that night. They did, and they too concluded that they had never tried real Kobe beef before.

A little background: In 2001, the USDA banned the importation of Japanese beef after discovering cases of bovine spongiform encephalopathy (BSE), better known as mad cow disease. The USDA sometimes restricts only industry segments rather than entire countries, but in this case the prohibition was total, and it did not matter whether the beef was from Kobe or elsewhere, whether it was fresh or frozen, processed or whole, on the bone or off. This ban remained in place until 2006 and was reinstated in 2010, again owing to BSE concerns. The most recent embargo was lifted at the end of 2012, so for most of the twenty-first century, the history of the food supply in this country was characterized by the complete absence of anything resembling Kobe or Japanese beef.

Nonetheless, the decade in question was a boom time for "Kobe beef," a veritable gold rush of never before seen menu items like the quickly ubiquitous "Kobe sliders" and even "Kobe hot dogs." Before the ban, only a tiny handful of pricy specialty steakhouses, a niche within the luxury red meat niche, imported the very expensive product, and these were typically the only places with the word *Kobe* on the menu. But the USDA sanctions removed competition from the real thing and opened the floodgates for everyone in the restaurant business, which responded by throwing *Kobe* onto their menus in every way imaginable. It started with very expensive three-digit Faux-be steaks, like the hundred-dollar "Kobe beef filet mignon" on the menu at Uncle Jack's Steakhouse in New York City during the ban, which caused *Wall Street Journal* writer Katy McLaughlin to note, "The USDA currently bans imports of Japanese meat because of a mad-cow outbreak there. The result: That Kobe beef you're eating may well hail from Boise, Idaho." She rounded up other examples of high-priced dishes claiming to use the banned beef from New Orleans to Washington, DC.

In January 2003—more than a year after the ban—New York's Old Homestead Steakhouse made headlines when it rolled out a forty-one-dollar "Kobe burger" that weighed a whopping twenty ounces, a pound and quarter, yet sold for far less than this much Kobe beef costs in Japan at wholesale. One New York City Japanese restaurant, Shaburi, even had the gall to put another prized—and banned—Japanese beef, Matsuzaka, on its menu and claimed it was "even better than Kobe" when it was equally fake. Japanese beef became such a wannabe foodstuff that even Burger King—yes, that second-rate fast-food chain best known for making McDonald's look good—created a $170 wagyu burger for its UK outlets, topped with foie gras and blue cheese instead of ketchup and yellow cheese slices. Kobe beef was not available in the United Kingdom either.

The Faux-be phenomenon was quickly accelerated by the gourmet burger craze, trickling down from fake steaks to very expensive Faux-be burgers, and before long it was routinely appearing in bars as bargain priced "Kobe sliders." In a very short time, Kobe beef went from an inaccessible luxury item to a cheap menu staple—even at fast-food chains. You can even order frozen "Kobe beef" burger patties on Amazon.com—even though Kobe beef is never, ever frozen.

In the world of Fake Food, Kobe is the new black. As a reporter
for London's *Daily Mail* explained, "Restaurants and butchers are
using the label's longstanding reputation for excellence to deceive
customers who think they are paying more money for a specific
product, when they are not. Real Kobe beef is produced under
some of the world's strictest legal food standards." She cited an example of a New York City butcher charging $120 a pound for fake
Kobe porterhouse steak, nearly three times the shop's $44 price
for U.S. porterhouse, which was likely the same meat. To add insult
to injury, even when it isn't banned, there is never such a thing as
a Kobe porterhouse—only boneless cuts can be imported.

With fake seafood, chefs and restaurant owners routinely pass
the buck and blame their suppliers, claiming they'd been duped,
but they can't make that argument about something that was illegal to order in the first place. Yet these lies have long been widely
endorsed by our foodie pundits in the atmosphere of culinary wor-
ship we've created, without a single editor at a top food magazine
or renowned restaurant critic stopping to ask how they could be
singing the virtues of this nonexistent product.

"Kobe beef, it seems, is everywhere these days; it's the luxury
ingredient of the moment . . . Kobe hamburgers are now so ubiquitous that they're close to becoming a cliché . . . A quick check
of *Los Angeles Times* restaurant reviews shows that Kobe beef has
been mentioned 45 times in the last two years—and only 11 in the
two years before that. What gives? How did Kobe beef become so
ubiquitous? Well, the short answer is: because it's not really Kobe
beef," wrote *Los Angeles Times* reporter Russ Parsons. While Parsons
grasps the fallacy at play, what he fails to mention is that in almost
all those reviews by his colleagues, "Kobe beef" was never ques-
tioned but rather presented by the newspaper's food critics as if it
were possibly a real thing, reinforcing the public stereotype.

As Olivia Fleming of the *Daily Mail* wryly noted, "Restaurant reviews in the *New York Times* also repeatedly praise the Kobe beef served at high-end Manhattan restaurants. However it is illegal to import, or hand carry for personal consumption, any Japanese beef in the U.S." As recently as 2010, the *Wall Street Journal* published a flawed story about the meteoric rise of the high-priced celebrity chef burger, wrongly describing the claims made about Kobe burgers on American menus: "Most menus specify that the beef used comes from American wagyu cattle, a breed famous for its highly-marbled meat.'" Not only do many menus not make this claim, even if they did, it is erroneous: Kobe beef is simply not American wagyu. In turn, American wagyu is neither famous nor a breed.

FOR A FAKE Food slap in the face, consider the "Glamburger," rolled out in 2014 by a London chef and quickly awarded a Guinness World Record thanks to its nearly eighteen-hundred-dollar price tag. Yes, that's almost two grand for a hamburger, which of course claims to be made from Kobe beef. The Glamburger has plenty of other rare ingredients cited, from Iranian saffron to Canadian lobster, but I won't list them here—given the restaurant's lack of credibility, there's no reason to believe any of them are real. The story got lots of media pickup worldwide, but none of the many outlets that reported it, nor the folks at Guinness World Records, ever paused to consider the fact that even one Glamburger patty would represent more than the total amount of Kobe beef imported into the United Kingdom, or all of Europe, which is none at all. As the Kobe Beef Marketing and Distribution Promotion Association assured me, not one ounce of its precious beef goes to Europe.

So many people in the United States, the United Kingdom, and the rest of Europe are easily duped by fake Kobe beef because most of us don't know what the real stuff is. So I went to Kobe to learn more. It turns out we are not the only ones who are ignorant about it.

"Even here in Japan people don't really know what Kobe beef is—they believe all the myths, that the cows get massages and listen to music," said Tatsuya Sakai, an account executive with the marketing firm for the Japanese agricultural ministry and the translator for my visit. Kobe is the sixth-largest city in Japan, located in the Hyogo Prefecture, where by law all Kobe beef originates. The rules are very strict, as they are for Parmigiano-Reggiano and other geographically indicated products: Kobe beef can only come from Tajima cattle and only from those born, raised, and slaughtered in the prefecture. Their feed is free from the growth hormones, animal by-products, steroids, and most of the antibiotics widely used to produce beef in the States, but while ideal for promoting marbling, it has some downsides. Kobe cattle consume far more grain than grass, a naturally unbalanced diet, and much of it dried, but it all must be grown in the prefecture. Every step of the process is closely regulated, from their age to the very high standards for grading, far above the benchmarks for our highest grade, USDA Prime. But the strictest rule about Kobe beef is its genetics, and this is a case where the *terroir* is not so much something the region has as something it historically lacks—other cattle. The Hyogo area is mountainous, remote, and was long secluded, which for centuries served as a natural deterrent to animal migrations.

The word *wagyu* could be interpreted to mean all cattle in Japan but traditionally has been used to specifically refer to the four historically Japanese breeds, excluding imports like Holsteins, which are now widely found throughout the country. These four types are brown, polled, shorthorn, and black, but 85 to 90 percent of Japan's wagyu is black. Tajima is a strain of 100 percent genetically pure Japanese black cattle, which by law has to have been born in Hyogo Prefecture and whose parents, grandparents, and every known ancestor were also born here, without exception: an entire family tree of nothing but pure Hyogo Tajima. On the walls of the Hyogo Prefectural Technology Center for Agriculture there are drawings of Tajima cattle dating back to 1310.

"The Tajima region is a valley surrounded by steep mountains, nature's way of preserving the integrity of the breed, creating barriers against crossbreeding. Today they still retain all these characteristics from seven hundred years ago," explained Dr. Eiji Iwamoto, a veterinary researcher with the agriculture center. In the United States, it has long been customary to crossbreed cattle with the goal of better adapting animals to their particular environment for yields and survival rates. They do the same thing in parts of Japan, but in Hyogo they make a niche product, and the focus is entirely on the best-quality beef. "The big difference is that here the single most important thing is the bloodline, and it is managed very precisely," said Iwamoto. He is not kidding: in the entire prefecture there are only sixty-nine hundred head of Tajima cattle and only twelve bulls. When one passes his prime, a carefully picked replacement with the best characteristics in all of Hyogo takes his place. The farmers buy the sperm and all real Kobe is fathered by one of those twelve.

These dozen genetically perfect monuments to marbling and flavor are kept in two government facilities, six and six, to protect against disease, and just to enter the agricultural campus I had to disinfect my shoes—even though I was not permitted anywhere near the buildings the bulls occupy. Despite the strict breeding and all the rules, of the sixty-nine hundred pure Tajima cattle, only about half will be superb enough to qualify as Kobe beef, just three thousand or four thousand head per year. This is the total world production of the real thing, and it is smaller than one mid-sized U.S. cattle ranch. Annual production is less than, often much less than, three million pounds, 90 percent of which never leaves

Japan. To put this in perspective, on top of our own huge domestic cattle industry, the United States imports more than three billion pounds of beef each year, and just these imports equal more than a thousand times the entire Kobe supply.

"When we talk about Japanese wagyu there are five main quality regions for black cattle, Kobe, Matsuzaka, Ohmi, Yonezawa, and Sendai, plus one notable exception, Hokkaido beef, which comes from brown wagyu. But the quality they have on Kobe beef is the best and it always translates to great flavor, while that consistency cannot be said for the other regions. They can be very good, but it's not guaranteed like it is with Kobe beef," explained Takuya Ozawa, sous-chef at the upscale New York Grill restaurant in the luxury Park Hyatt Tokyo hotel. (Movie buffs will recall the New York Grill's fame as the frequent cocktail and live-jazz setting in the Bill Murray film *Lost in Translation*.)

When I spoke with Ozawa in 2013, he oversaw the restaurant's extensive international steak program, which includes wagyu from several different regions. He has since changed jobs, but told me then that "it's something you need to experience once in your life but it is expensive—it's double what the others cost. When people come from America and ask what they should try I always suggest the Kobe because I know it is new for them. But I get people here all the time from America who say they have had Kobe beef, and then ninety-nine percent of the time they say they can't understand why it tastes nothing like this at home." Just ask my friend Pat.

In beef, the higher the level of saturated fatty acids, the tougher and chewier the meat is. Kobe is famously tender, and the reason is that it is unusually high in the healthier, melt-on-your-tongue unsaturated fatty acids, especially oleic acid, responsible for flavor. All real wagyu has this trait, but according to Dr. Iwamoto, in a comparison of monounsaturated fats between the five major Japanese beef producing prefectures, the cattle in Hyogo had the highest levels. He also insists that Japan has the toughest grading regulations for beef cattle of any country in the world, and I believe it. I've seen USDA-style grading, based almost entirely on the amount of marbling, and the Japanese process is far more discriminating.

A letter, *A*, *B*, or *C*, denotes yield percentage, or the amount of the cow that is edible. From a buyer and seller profit perspective, A is best, but despite what many restaurants purport, from a consumer perspective it doesn't taste any better. Each carcass is scored for four different properties, color and brightness, firmness and texture, fat coloring/luster, and most important, the beef marbling standard (BMS). All four scores use different scales and are converted into ratings from 1 to 5, with the final tally reflecting the lowest/worst score, not an average. The highest possible grade is A5, which means top rankings in every category, and only those scored in the upper range of 4 or 5 can qualify as Kobe beef. I watched inspectors go through this process, and it is as strict as you could imagine. Remember that the "most marbled steak ever" that Mark Schatzker saw upon arriving in Japan was just a 3.

BMS uses a scale of 1 to 12, with 1 being pure red and 12 being completely and evenly dotted white throughout. In the United States, we use names instead of numbers, and USDA Prime, our highest marbling grade—representing the upper 2 percent of American beef—would equate to about 4 or 5 on Japan's scale. The *Los Angeles Times* estimated that most domestically raised wagyu-breed beef here would rate between 6 and 9, while real Kobe usually scores 10 or higher.

Only 10 percent of the tiny Kobe production leaves Japan, exported to just seven sovereign regions. Most are in Asia, including Singapore, Hong Kong, Macau, and Thailand. Outside the Pacific Rim, Kobe goes only to the United Arab Emirates, Canada, and since November 2012, the United States again. Hong Kong buys by far the most, about 40 percent of the total, followed by Macau. The amount that reaches the United States is so miniscule that in many months the total number of pounds imported has been zero. In the first eight months after legalizing import, meat actually arrived only twice, with three month gaps between these tiny shipments. Over one four-month span, the delivery for the entire country was 27.5 pounds—enough for about a hundred small steaks. This perennial shortage is exacerbated by the fact that Kobe beef is never frozen and has an expiration date forty-five days after slaughter.

Once the legal importation of trace amounts of Kobe resumed in our country, you might think fraud would dissipate. Instead, since the ban was lifted, the Faux-be problem has gotten worse, because it gives chefs a highly implausible but theoretically possible leg to stand on. Now, rather than a certain lie, it is almost certainly a lie. But restaurants get away with it because it is at least partly legal, for the same twisted reasons we make "Champagne" in California and "Parmesan" cheese in New Jersey. We are a nation of laws, but when it comes to the concept of trademarks and protection of intellectual property, our system is philosophically at odds with most of the rest of the world.

Under U.S. law, a trademark is sort of a monopolistic license belonging to an individual or company that grants its owner a degree of exclusivity. As such, trademarks can be sold or transferred. Most GIs, such as Champagne or Kobe beef, on the other hand, are available to all regional producers who qualify under the terms of production and therefore essentially belong to the *terroir* and cannot be sold or transferred. This is a fundamental disagreement in legal structure that for well over a century has led the United States to actively refuse participation in numerous international agreements to protect intellectual property and brands, often at the expense of our closest allies. And our taste buds. And our health.

The underpinnings of our trademark system make sense and are a fundamental part of our capitalist economy: they are supposed to encourage invention and innovation, rewarding someone who comes up with a better way to do something by granting them exclusivity to profit from their creativity. But in reality, U.S. trademarks are often available to whichever company gets to the trademark office first, whether or not that company actually created anything. So while Kobe beef has long been a patented trademark in Japan, along with Kobe meat and Kobe cattle, these Japanese trademarks, and indeed the entire Japanese trademark system, is neither recognized nor protected by U.S. law. Nor could the Japanese at this point obtain a trademark here under our system, because after more than a century of worldwide fame, the term *Kobe beef* would likely be deemed generic by U.S. regulators, who have applied the same "logic" in denying protection to hundreds of other products. For example, the term *Champagne* has been so widely used that it no longer refers to a particular product, but if you ask virtually any American consumer what they think the word means, as I have repeatedly done, they will answer very differently from the imaginary regulatory version. Ditto for Kobe beef—people buying it think they are buying something exclusive and Japanese, not a generic lower-quality version of something exclusive and Japanese, but of course they are wrong. In the case of Fake Foods, our trademark system is frequently used to protect copycat manufacturers and as a bludgeon against American consumers.

To a small degree, we reap what we sow: much to the chagrin of Idaho potato producers, one of the few well-recognized U.S. GIs, someone else beat them to the local trademark offices, and registered the term *Idaho* for potatoes—in Turkey, Mexico, Argentina, and Germany. A more glaring example is the legal usage of the valuable term *Napa Valley wines* for wines from anyplace, which is allowed in much of the world. The Napa Valley Vintners only just recently gained protection in the world's biggest consumer market, China, but still lack it elsewhere. Many of these protections are negotiated individually in international treaties, and it does not help the bargaining position of U.S. producers seeking foreign protection that our government routinely turns down almost all such requests from other countries.

So the rightful owners of the Kobe beef brand can get little protection for it here, but on the other hand, what is protected by our laws (and tax dollars) is an entire line of "Kobe-Crafted" meat products made by a U.S. company called Steakhouse Elite, which was first to the trademark office and registered the name Kobe-Crafted for its packaged burger patties, ground beef, and hot dogs. In the typical subterfuge associated with such products, Steakhouse Elite variously claims that it uses only "100% American raised Wagyu," which is markedly different from "American raised 100% Wagyu." It means only that the cattle were entirely raised in America, not in any way that they are pure wagyu cattle. In fact, its press release clearly states that its products use a mix of wagyu and "traditional" (i.e., non-wagyu) beef. Steakhouse Elite further says its hot dogs are "100% Kobe-Crafted beef," which doesn't even mean they are 100 percent beef of any kind—there are many other ingredients on the label—but rather that the beef the company does use is what it has trademarked as "Kobe-Crafted," which in turn means nothing. The company is so obsessed with plugging in the lofty 100 percent terminology over and over that it even describes the hot dogs as "100% skinless." This is probably the truest of its many assertions.

"What's this 'American' Kobe beef I've seen in the States?" asked intellectual property attorney Michael Atkins in his blog about trademarks. His Seattle-based firm, Atkins Intellectual Property, specializes in federal trademark issues, and Atkins also teaches trademark law at the University of Washington School of

Law. "I know that menu item got a hearty laugh from two intellectual property lawyers from Japan I lunched with a while back. Judging by U.S. trademark registrations, use of the phrase seems like a free-for-all." Atkins examined three different trademark registrations using variations of the phrase in this country, including American Certified Kobe Beef, which begs the obvious questions, certified by whom and for what?; Premier American Kobe Beef; and my favorite for extreme repetitive hyperbole, Mishima Ranch Exclusive Extraordinary Distinct Wagyu Beef American Style Kobe Beef. Try saying that five times fast. Atkins, who presumably understands the issue far better than the average American consumer, comes away as confused as I am, wondering "what 'American Kobe Beef' really is— and whether it even exists."

It is the ultimate case of "let the diner beware." Under USDA regulations, the only legal requirement for calling something Kobe beef is that it qualifies as beef. Kobe is a completely unregulated term, and in any case, no agency—not the USDA, the FDA, or any other—regulates restaurant menu claims. Any restaurant in this country can, at any time, claim that any piece of meat it serves is Kobe beef, Kobe chicken, Kobe pork, Kobe goat, or even Kobe lobster (I've seen chicken and pork) without breaking any specific law, which as a consumer, I find sort of scary. When it comes to outright menu lies, Kobe beef is hardly alone: restaurants can claim beef is dry-aged twenty-eight days, natural, cruelty-free, organic, and grass fed—all higher quality traits associated with lofty price tags—without any of it being true.

"Many a pork cutlet has headed to a table disguised as veal, and many an organic salad is not . . . Unscrupulous chefs can falsely claim that a steak is Kobe beef or say a chicken was humanely treated without penalty," the *New York Times* reported. Celebrity chef, restaurateur, cookbook author, and television personality Tom Colicchio, well known for serving well-sourced naturally raised, antibiotic-free meats, which costs him 30 percent more, agreed: "This has been going on for as long as I've been cooking. When you start really getting into this stuff, there's so many things people mislabel. I have a restaurant down the street that says they have organic chicken when they don't, and they charge less money for it [than I do]. It's all part of mislabeling and duping the public." And hurting the honest restaurateurs.

The only legal protection the American consumer has is the general prohibition against "misleading" marketing practices, and even then, damages are limited and hard to collect. Pay $300 for a Kobe steak that is actually a $20 North Dakota steak, as is often the case, and your theoretical damage is the difference, or $280. So if an expensive steakhouse does this two thousand times a year and nets itself a cool half-million dollars in ill-gotten gains, its windfall is still much too meager for most lawyers to pursue.

But fake Kobe beef has become so ubiquitous that it crossed the line to large-dollar volume/fakery. Steakhouse and seafood chain McCormick & Schmick's, with more than five dozen locations nationwide, served enough Faux-be steaks over the years to cross the tipping point and attract a class-action suit. Attorneys representing the injured class of deceived diners rightly pointed out that Kobe beef imports had been totally banned by the USDA over a roughly two-year period during which the chain had advertised and sold "Kobe beef." Despite the impossibility of serving real Kobe, the company denied the allegations but did agree to settle the suit, issuing refunds.

Perhaps emboldened by his success, Kevin Shenkman, the attorney who led the suit, next turned to the SBE Group, which operates a number of high-profile restaurants and nightclubs in Los Angeles and Las Vegas. As Shenkman said, "These businesses are passing off their beef as being Kobe beef when it is anything but Kobe beef and they're charging premium prices to consumers who are paying those prices because they think that it is in fact Kobe beef and it's not." Again, the company settled without admitting wrongdoing, offering compensation to diners misled over a five-year period and agreeing to no longer use the term *Kobe beef.* A similar Faux-be suit against the Sushi Roku and Boa Steakhouse chains was settled, and suits were filed against Marriott International and other operators as well.

But despite Shenkman's impressive success, Fake Food purveyors still hold the upper hand: SBE can now instead use the illogical term *American Kobe beef* and still trade on the reputation of a Real Food. Since volume seems to matter, class-action attorneys might want to next turn their attention to BurgerFi, a national chain that every day dispenses "100% Wagyu Kobe Beef Hot Dogs" in large numbers—despite selling them for far less than what the Kobe beef required to make such hot dogs would cost.

Those suits against large restaurant groups for selling overpriced fake Kobe beef are encouraging but still barely offer any safety net at all. It puts the onus on the consumer and only makes the largest retailers accountable, those with deep pockets and a large enough volume of deceit to justify a class-action suit. Famed New York and DC gourmet store Balducci's, a longtime institution where you might expect to find Real Food, offers a (not real) Kobe roast beef sandwich and tried to sell me, I kid you not, "Kobe pastrami" on rye.

The only reason to put a Kobe burger on the menu versus, say, a Robe burger, is because real Kobe beef is famous and commands a high price. To me, the vast majority of current uses of the words *Kobe* and *wagyu* in this country blatantly fail the smell test, and there is no question that calling anything that is not actual Japanese Kobe beef by the Kobe name is misleading, and intentionally so.

That said, the wagyu issue is far more confusing, especially since as the public becomes more and more aware of the Kobe lie, many restaurants and chefs have switched their deceptive marketing claims to wagyu, another popular menu term for Japanese-style beef, which is even more enigmatic and imprecise to consumers. Wagyu can be completely real, somewhat real, arguably real, or totally phony, and there is almost no way for the consumer to know which. The word has almost no legal meaning, and even its actual meaning is debatable. With so many people using and misusing the terms *Kobe* and *wagyu*, an important question to ask is, what do they really mean? What are these things, and what are they not? I returned to Japan to answer these questions.

"Japan has a lot of really great beef, like Matsuzaka, but outside of Japan only Kobe is known," said Troy Lee, an Australian who is the head chef at the Oak Door steakhouse at the Grand Hyatt Tokyo. There are a lot of great steakhouses around the world, from my beloved Keens in New York to Spain's Casa Julian, but there is a good argument to be made that the Oak Door is the greatest of them all, if only because of its menu. Attached to the restaurant, in plain view, is a glassed-in meat storage locker, displaying in butcher shop fashion a wide variety of the different beef offered to diners. These range from Kobe to all the other major regional wagyu styles of Japan, plus imported wagyu hybrids, and even good old dry-aged USDA Prime American meat—our beef is a popular import in Japan. I have never seen this breadth of selection under one roof, and the steak smorgasbord allows travelers from all over the world to try and compare different styles of beef.

Chef Lee and I did a four-meat tasting of an A5 Kobe; A5 Matsuzaka; premium Australian F1 wagyu hybrid; and a Hokkaido F1 hybrid, a Japanese bred mix of brown wagyu and Holstein. F1 means a first-generation offspring from breeding a purebred wagyu with a less expensive animal to produce something with 50 percent wagyu genetics. In parts of Japan and Australia, the biggest artisanal wagyu producer outside Japan, the cattle are often crossed with Holstein, traditionally a dairy breed, because they hold fat better. In this country, Holsteins are typically used for milk (at least until they get old and dried out and are thrown into ground beef). "The hybrid produces a meat that is less fatty, a lot redder, and considerably less expensive. I'm from Australia and they produce a lot of what they call wagyu, but it's really not, because it's not Japan," Lee said.

Since the ban was repealed, but still with far too little real Kobe to go around, some restaurants have begun importing other regional purebred Japanese wagyu, which while not as well known, are similar. To be honest, if the first time I had tasted Kobe, I had Matsuzaka instead, the experience would not have been any different, and even side by side I could just barely tell them apart. If I had taken Pat out for A5 Miyazaki beef, he still would have pushed his chair back and exclaimed, "This is bullshit." So foodies who really want to try the true Kobe beef–like experience at least once—and they should—can now get it more broadly. Most importers bothering to buy the real thing are insisting on the highest-graded beef, and at the top end, the regions become nearly indistinguishable.

"When you start talking about real A4 or A5 wagyu beef from Japan, whether it's from Kobe, Sendai, Miyazaki, you're splitting hairs. It's all good, and like two similar wines, few people can tell the difference in a blind tasting," said George Faison, co-owner of DeBragga meats. Nicknamed "New York's Butcher," DeBragga is a legendary restaurant meat supplier and retailer famous for its in-house dry-aging program and specialty products, from venison to heritage breed pork. Faison's customers include vaunted fine dining spots like the Four Seasons and Le Bernardin. After the ban was lifted, he traveled to Japan and set up an exclusive agreement to import wagyu from the Miyazaki region, making DeBragga a retail rarity, selling real Japanese wagyu directly to consumers. In sharp contrast, according to the Kobe Beef Association, what little Kobe comes to the States goes only to restaurants, and as my agricultural ambassador Tatsuya Sakai said definitively, "There is no way for a consumer to buy any Kobe at retail in the U.S." Faison concurred, adding, "Sure, I'd love to be able to also offer Kobe and Sendai beef, but it can't all be Château Latour. Sometimes we have to drink Château Margaux," he joked, comparing two of the world's most renowned wines.

Celebrity chef Michael Mina has two steakhouse brands, Bourbon Steak and Stripsteak, in several U.S. cities. He was among the very first to begin importing Japanese beef after the ban was lifted, and he traveled to Japan for red meat research. The James Beard award–winning chef told me about this, "Last year we went to Japan and met the butchers, the distributors, the ranchers and saw what we wanted. Some of the beef, like the Matsuzaka, is just out of this world, and it's easier to get regularly than Kobe. It's not about trying to give someone the most expensive thing they can eat; it's about giving them an experience. Since they lifted the ban, it's going to give more people the chance to try this great product— people who have never tried it before."

While more and more restaurants are coming cleaner and listing "American wagyu," "American Kobe," "domestic wagyu," and so on, the only real clarification this provides is that the product is not Japanese—it doesn't say anything about what it actually is. To its credit, the American Wagyu Association urges its breeder members not to use the word *Kobe* out of respect for Kobe's being a place name—like Champagne. But it can't stop them, and the issue is further complicated by not having members differentiate among "100% wagyu," "high percent wagyu," or "wagyu-influenced beef," all very different products marketed to consumers exactly the same way—as wagyu.

Interestingly, more and more U.S. purveyors are trying to have it both ways, such as the bizarre "Wagyu Kobe Burger" at the Tender Restaurant in Las Vegas or the "American Style Wagyu Kobe Beef" supplied to many top restaurants and chefs by leading "gourmet" meat producer Snake River Farms. My suggestion to these companies is that if they want to stop being taken for scammers, drop the "Kobe." Celebrity chef Hubert Keller takes a catch-all approach at his Vegas Burger Bar restaurant with a sixty-five-dollar "Kobe-Style Wagyu from Australia" burger. As names go, it's pretty awkward, but at least it actually tells the customer what they are not getting.

In a similar vein, there are many in the food industry like Chef Lee who argue that wagyu is equally place sensitive, and by definition wagyu cattle cannot exist outside of Japan. I've been on the fence on this issue, but because wagyu are several different breeds, and indigenous to all of Japan, not to a specific area. I'm willing to accept that it is the cattle themselves, not where they live, that make them wagyu, just as my golden retriever was a purebred even though he did not live in Scotland, where the breed originated. However, if I crossed my dog with another breed, the offspring would no longer be golden retrievers but rather mutts or hybrids or, if I were trendier, maybe Goldendoodles. The same is true with wagyu— once you start crossbreeding you get something different, potentially even better, or maybe worse, but either way no longer wagyu.

The USDA disagrees with me, and its "Specification for Characteristics of Cattle Eligible for Approved Branded Beef Programs Claiming Wagyu Influence," used to approve labeling claims, is very straightforward: either the mother or father must be at least 93.75% wagyu, which means the finished product you buy could be somewhere between 46.9 and 100 percent wagyu, which is a pretty big range of varied quality, with no way to tell. As butcher Faison explained: "People go to the supermarket here and see 'American wagyu' or, even worse, 'American Kobe,' and it's got less marbling than the USDA Choice steak sitting next to it." That's not an especially favorable comparison, given that Choice, typical of "supermarket steak," falls below the more desirable Prime and would be lucky to receive a score of 2 on the 12-point wagyu scale. The vague USDA wagyu rules don't govern restaurants, where the promised wagyu might not even be 46.9 percent pure—it might well be zero.

There are two primary reasons why ranchers crossbreed wagyu. The first is that it is less expensive and results in cheaper meat. The second is to intentionally change the taste of the meat to be more like other domestic beef. This is often done with the argument that "American palates are different" or that "Americans prefer our style of beef and find Japanese wagyu too rich and fatty," which could well be true for some folks, and personally I think a toned-down version of pure Japanese wagyu is better for regular consumption. On the other hand, it is very hard for producers to make this claim considering how few people have ever tasted the real thing.

"Dear Larry, I enjoyed reading your article last year on Forbes .com about Kobe beef and Wagyu cattle. As a farmer and restaurateur who raises Wagyu cattle, let me take this opportunity to say that you got it right. Many in the media, as well as a number of chefs and foodies, are often misled about Kobe and Wagyu beef . . . I am part of a group of Wagyu farmers who are dedicated to raising Wagyu as close as possible to the Japanese way without being in Japan. As you stated in this most recent article, not all farmers are raising Wagyu equally. We are trying to set the standard." Pete Eshelman, who wrote those words, is not just a rancher (and former professional baseball draft pick of the New York Yankees) and restaurant owner, but he is also the author of a beautiful coffee table book, *America's Wagyu Trail.* In it he profiles several like-minded, authenticity-driven, family-owned wagyu ranches around the country, and this is a great resource for anyone trying to find a trustworthy supply source. But you can't order Eshelman's own meticulously raised beef, which is only available at his retail store and adjacent fine-dining restaurant, Joseph Decuis—the only eatery I know of in the world raising its own wagyu—in Roanoke, Indiana.

Not everyone reacted to my article as politely as Eshelman did, and I received a few angry responses arguing that there are passionate, considerate, and honest ranchers raising undiluted herds of 100 percent pure wagyu that can trace their family tree directly to cattle or semen legally imported from Japan. So as I move into the discussion of domestic wagyu, I want to be as clear about this as possible. Despite these letters, many, if not most, producers of so-called domestic wagyu do not take this enlightened approach, and most of what is sold as wagyu in this country is actually a diluted hybrid, some good, a lot not so good. Nonetheless, it is entirely possible to raise 100 percent pure wagyu with identical or very similar genetics to those in Japan right here in the States, and there are several great ranches that do just that.

Still, much of the best-intentioned 100 percent pure wagyu raised in this country simply does not match up with the Japanese version, for several reasons. For Kobe beef, in particular, the twelve most perfectly suited fathers are chosen from many thousands, something individual ranchers with much smaller pools of animals can't match. Some other regional Japanese wagyu have even bigger pools to select genetics from. Then there is diet, and while it is possible to replicate the Kobe diet—Eshelman does—most of the responsible wagyu farmers here don't, because, ironically, they tend to go more natural than the Japanese. I'm normally a huge fan of grass-fed, pastured beef, which is healthier, and it is virtually all I eat at home. However, this is one case where it doesn't always work out, and in Japan it is believed that vitamin A, abundant in fresh grass, adversely affects the marbling, so great pains are taken to avoid it, substituting grain for grass. In Kobe, cattle spend almost their entire lives inside, albeit with more space than typical feedlot raised U.S. animals. Yet most of the top-shelf wagyu operations I have seen in the U.S. range their cattle freely on natural grass.

I've repeatedly tried purebred domestic wagyu from artisanal producers, and while it can be delicious, I've yet to taste one that truly equals the Japanese version. The closest I've found so far is from Colorado's 7X, with a 100 percent pure herd of Japanese-descent wagyu, raised naturally outdoors on grass (and which they adamantly market as *not* being Kobe beef). It is becoming widely available as a bragged-about menu item at finer Colorado restaurants and is sold online. It is a great compromise for those of us who favor the natural wholesomeness of grass-fed meat but also like abundant marbling and fatty richness.

Every expert I spoke with, though, including Michael Mina and George Faison, both fans of domestic wagyu, agreed that it is noticeably different from the Japanese version, even at its best. Shea Gallante, chef at Cru, told *New York* magazine that "you can't compare the real thing to the American product." In *Gourmet*, Barry Estabrook did a side-by-side taste test and wrote, "The evening I sampled Japanese Kobe, I also tucked into a slice of Wagyu from the States, garnished with, yes, a tiny paper facsimile of the Stars and Stripes. It has the same over-the-top beefy flavor, but lacked the melt-in-your mouth sensuality and tenderness of Kobe." Longtime *New York Times* food critic Florence Fabricant described the American wagyu in glowing terms, but also as redder, "beefier-tasting, more like a super tender, classic American steak." DeBragga's Faison said, "American ranchers typically do a wagyu/Angus cross, and you can really taste the difference from the Japanese meat. Australians do wagyu and Holstein crosses, and have had better results than Americans in getting the high marbling. The Australian wagyu definitely tastes more like the Japanese in general." You can get Australia's version of wagyu in this country.

Mina poaches his domestic wagyu steaks in butter for added richness, a step he doesn't need when he serves the real Matsuzaka version. "You can't just buy 'wagyu' and expect it to be good; you have to know the ranch," he warns. "It always varies, and it comes down to the individual ranch, because people are trying to commoditize it, but you can't. As a consumer, it comes down to the chef and the restaurant—you have to go somewhere reliable." Unfortunately, that's easier said than done, since the fake Kobe/wagyu scam has involved some of the highest end steakhouses and most famous chefs in America, just the kind of places you'd expect to be beyond reproach.

To the naked eye, all real Japanese wagyu looks just as radically different from western breeds as Kobe does. So when I was served a pricy "American Kobe" steak at celebrity chef Charlie Palmer's Dry Creek Kitchen restaurant in Healdsburg, California, I didn't even need to taste it to know it wasn't real. It wasn't a bad steak, if you were looking for traditional American beef, uniformly red except for the outer band of white, without a single drop of wagyu's signature interior fat dispersion.

At the end of the day, eating a great steak—and knowing what steak you are eating—is far more complicated in our country than it should be. But there are solutions.

## ❋ KOBE BEEF IN JAPAN

The Kobe Beef Association maintains a list of restaurants worldwide officially approved to buy and serve its beef, most of which are in Japan. This list is not exclusive and other eateries, such as the Oak Door Steakhouse and New York Grill, still serve Kobe. However, there is no more classic and trustworthy place on the planet to try the fabled meat than at the Kobe Plaisir restaurant in Kobe City: it is owned and managed by Japan's department of agriculture, sort of the flagship Kobe beef eatery for the world.

## ✻ KOBE BEEF OUTSIDE JAPAN

This is much trickier, and the only three places in the United States I consider reliable are the restaurants in the Wynn Las Vegas casino resort, 212 Steakhouse in New York City, and Hawaii's Teppanyaki Ginza Sumikawa, the sole spots in this country certified by the Kobe Beef Association. In 2015, renowned Montreal chef Antonio Park got Canada's first license, covering both the Park and Lavanderia restaurants. Kobe beef is exported only to Hong Kong, Macau, Thailand, Singapore, and the United Arab Emirates, and everywhere else, including all of Europe, it is fake.

## ✻ PAPERS

Pundits will tell you to ask for documentation about your meat, and it's true that every Japanese carcass is accompanied by extensive paperwork including its lineage, slaughter info, unique nose print, and ten-digit identification number. However, unless you speak and read Japanese and really know cattle, it is impossible to correlate the paperwork with what is on your plate. All the impressive but unintelligible document proves is that the restaurant once got its hands on a copy, and given the elaborate cheats in the world of food piracy, that is about the easiest counterfeit going. I have a Kobe certificate on my desk I could show you over dinner while telling you the supermarket steak I'm serving is from Japan.

## ✻ KOBE GENERAL TIPS

Real Kobe beef is never frozen; never on the bone; never sold at retail; and never, ever cheap. Steak on the bone here is a telltale sign of fraud—any Kobe porterhouse is a fake Kobe porterhouse. According to the Kobe Beef Association, every ounce of imported Kobe goes through one of four approved distributors and all of it goes to restaurants, none to retail. There is no "bargain" Kobe: at the source in Hyogo it is $120 to $200 a pound, and this is as cheap as you can find it in the world.

### ❋ KOBE BURGERS, SLIDERS, DOGS, AND SO ON

In recent years, the ideal meat-to-fat ratio for the perfect burger has been a passionately debated topic, but just about everyone agrees the target is somewhere around 70 to 80 percent lean. Real Kobe beef is simply too fatty to make a good burger, and even when using leaner domestic wagyu, many restaurants blend in leaner non-wagyu meats. A cheap Kobe burger can't be real, and an expensive one should not be real, because it would be gross. A Kobe hot dog? Fuggedaboutit.

### ❋ BONUS ANECDOTE—KOBE BRYANT

"How many people in your country know that Kobe Bryant is named for Kobe beef? His father came to Japan and liked the Kobe beef so much, he never forgot the taste, and he named his son Kobe after it," said Iyori Takayoshi, one of the Kobe cattle farmers I met. I heard the story, which is apparently true based on myriad news reports here, many times in Japan, where they are justly proud that their famous beef had such a flavorful impact on the visiting American. Can you imagine being so wowed by a cheese or pasta that you named your children Manchego or Bucatini? The talents of both NBA star Kobe Bryant and Kobe beef speak for themselves.

### ❋ JAPANESE WAGYU BEEF

In theory almost any restaurant can now import real wagyu, but very few do. The handful I'd feel confident spending my money at are Red the Steakhouse, Stripsteak, Bourbon Steak, and Wolfgang Puck's CUT, all with two or more locations; the restaurants in the

Wynn Las Vegas; and Empire Steak and 212 Steakhouse in New York. That's it. There are certainly other places importing wagyu, but I'm very cynical and don't trust them. DeBragga butcher shop, which has a direct supplier in the Miyazaki prefecture, sells wagyu online and is the only retailer I would order from. To a large degree, I'd also trust the restaurants DeBragga supplies, so don't hesitate to ask waiters where they get their wagyu from—there are not many sources. Like Kobe, real Japanese wagyu is never cheap, and to try it, you will pay dearly: When I ate at Stripsteak, the Japanese Matsuzaka beef cost about twenty times as much as the most expensive steak at Whole Foods.

## ✳ AMERICAN KOBE
No such thing, skip it. Even if it happens to be excellent domestic wagyu, the use of the word is an obvious attempt to deceive you and you shouldn't pay anyone to do so.

## ✳ DOMESTIC/AUSTRALIAN WAGYU
Like the Clint Eastwood classic *The Good, the Bad and the Ugly*, this can include almost anything, especially in restaurants. Lots of people like "wangus," the wagyu/Angus crosses, essentially a fattier, more marbled version of typical domestic steak. If this is what you are after, it's easy—look for Snake River Farms meats on menus, as it is commonly found at fine dining restaurants, or mail-order it, but don't fool yourself into thinking you are trying true wagyu. The only domestic 100 percent wagyu I've mail-ordered and cooked at home is from Colorado's 7X Beef, and it is very good, as well as grass fed and pasture raised without antibiotics and hormones. In general, Australian wagyu tends to taste more like the Japanese style than our domestic wagyu, but just because a menu says "Australian wagyu" doesn't mean the steak is either.

## ✳ FINAL THOUGHT

Not everyone loves real wagyu, and even if you do, this is not steak for everyday eating—after I had it three times in three days, I started thinking about gout. Hybrids produce a steak most find superior to conventional American beef, which you could eat every day, at least to the degree that you could eat any steak every day. I'm not suggesting less than pure wagyu breeds are inferior, as taste is an individual thing, I'm trying to cut through a sea of false and misleading claims and make clear what these hybrids are not, which is the famous Japanese wagyu beef.

# 7. Champagne and Scotch: The Sincerest Form of Flattery

Generic? Really? Saying Champagne means any sparkling wine is like saying Rolls Royce means any car. You have to be an idiot to believe that.

—DAN DUNN, *The Imbiber*
(personal communication, summer 2005)

Easy travel by high-speed train is one of the many advantages of a European vacation, and in Paris that convenience begins almost the moment you step off the plane. France's bullet train, the TGV, is among the fastest on earth with routine speeds of two hundred miles per hour, and there is a station right in Charles de Gaulle airport. After disembarking my transatlantic flight, I cleared customs, followed the signs downstairs, boarded the train, and just thirty-five minutes later—less time than it takes to get from the airport into central Paris—I was in Reims.

The short ride has no stops, but despite the high-tech train, it is very much a journey back in time. The airport's concrete jungle gives way to the warehouse-laden industrialized area around it, then to a suburban stretch running parallel to a major motorway, and then, about twenty minutes out, modernity yields to thick wooded forest, broken only by the occasional farmer's field and white stands of birch. This in turn soon opens into hillier agricultural terrain, and as the miles roll by, these hillsides become increasingly dotted with vineyards, the landscape that surrounds Reims.

Founded in 80 BCE, the city has had more than its fair share of ups and downs, and in pure richness of French history, is second only to Paris. In 496 CE, Clovis, leader of the Franks and progenitor of the royal rulers of France, converted to Christianity and was baptized in the cathedral here, giving birth to the concept of French kings ruling by divine right. Right up until the French Revolution, nearly thirteen centuries later, every future king of France would travel to the cathedral in Reims for his coronation. The arrival of democracy curbed the city's historical importance, but certainly did not end it—it was in a schoolroom in Reims that the Germans unconditionally surrendered to General Dwight Eisenhower on May 7, 1945, effectively ending World War II in Europe.

History aside, Reims is a charming small city, and when I gazed at the elaborate stained glass in the cathedral, sipped coffee in one of its many splendid cafes, and strolled the lively downtown area, lined with hotels, shops, outdoor cafes, and even an ornate antique carousel, it felt unchanged and frozen in time. But this is an illusion, because much of what I saw is relatively new. The entire city center was destroyed by heavy German bombing and artillery fire in World War I, including the cathedral, and pieces of the original structure now occupy a museum next door. The current version, impressive in its Gothic grandeur and seemingly straight out of the Middle Ages, is as much a re-creation as a renovation of its predecessor, in turn a 1218 reconstruction of the badly fire damaged original. The current cathedral took more than two decades to complete, finally reopening in 1938—just in time for another world war. Virtually every building in downtown Reims has been damaged or leveled at one point or another, but the people of Reims have always stubbornly rebuilt, and today, most of what can be seen above ground is twentieth-century work. Below ground is a much older and different story.

Virtually anywhere you go in Reims, whether you are walking, sitting, sleeping, eating, or shopping, you are right on top of an elaborate subterranean network of caves and tunnels, carved though the region's famous limestone bedrock. They stretch back and forth, running more than 120 miles beneath the city and were largely undamaged by the wars and bombing, making them a historical treasure trove. The tunnels contain the remnants of wartime hospitals, a thirteenth-century crypt, ancient chapels and even third-century Roman ruins. It is from these tunnels that Reims's lifeblood flows, and almost everything above ground is powered by the magical but silent process continually occurring down here—the slow transformation of still wine into bubbly Champagne. The same alchemy occurs in tunnels under Épernay and, on smaller scales, in cellars all throughout Champagne.

If you have ever tasted a glass from one of Reims's famous producers like Taittinger, G.H. Mumm, Veuve Clicquot, or Pommery, it came from these tunnels, still home to unpopped bottles from the 1800s. The city is built on Champagne, literally and figuratively, and it flows freely aboveground as well: bars and restaurants here all feature long lists, store windows are full of magnums and labels from little-known boutique producers, and the Holiday Inn I stayed in may well be the only one in the global chain with an entire lobby wall of Champagne bottles for sale, including pricy prestige cuvées. But the action takes place underground, where hungry yeast devours sugar and converts it into delicate, tiny bubbles of gaseous carbon dioxide, creating the world's most famous wine. Per the ancient and ultrastrict French laws governing its production, this process cannot take place in tanks or barrels, but only in each individual bottle—at any given time, an estimated *one billion* bottles of Champagne are aging below the streets.

Reims has been invaded, conquered, and reconquered, by the Romans, Napoleon, the Huns, the Vandals, and the Germans, and repeatedly destroyed. Throughout all of this, the wine industry has survived and thrived, with the cultivation of vines here dating back to at least the fifth century, and the actual bubbly for about five hundred years, ever since the process for making sparkling wine was invented in these parts. Today, Reims is under assault yet again, but the barbarians at the gate are not soldiers but rather U.S. winemakers.

Along with Épernay, Reims is one of two major production cities in Champagne-Ardennes, the Champagne region, but before aging most of the labor-intensive process goes on in the surrounding countryside. The Champagne region is small to begin with, but when you look at a map highlighting its vineyards, the scarcity of grapes here is astonishing—all the growing occurs in just three little clusters on the map, occupying a tiny fraction of the region—less than 1.5 percent. There are more potatoes—and even beets—grown in Champagne than grapes. While this is the single most expensive vineyard real estate in the world, over a million bucks an acre, it is not the cost that prohibits more growing—after all, grapes sell for a lot more than potatoes. Rather, it's the regulations that dictate in painstaking detail exactly where grapes deemed worthy for Champagne production can be grown.

The best-known characteristic of the *terroir* in Champagne is the chalk and limestone in the ground where the vineyards are located. Mostly composed of ancient marine shells from the microorganisms that lived here when the area was under the ocean eons ago, it absorbs incredible amounts of water relative to rock or soil, preventing an excess of groundwater in the frequent rainy seasons and then acting as reservoir to feed the vine roots during dry spells.

Back in 1927, the Institut National des Appellations d'Origin carefully delineated exactly what parts of the region produced the best-quality grapes, and this totals just eighty-four thousand acres, an area not much bigger than New York City's largest borough,

Queens. Because of the strict quality control and the long history of Champagne making, the vast majority of vineyards are tiny and family owned—by some seventy thousand families in more than three hundred small, approved "Champagne villages." Many are pure farmers, selling all their grapes to winemakers. While the famous houses like Moët & Chandon and Perrier Jouet are based in embassy-like gleaming white marble structures lining the Avenue de Champagne in Épernay, much production is a actually conducted by, well, moms and pops. Most Americans, even wine fans, would be very hard pressed to name a dozen Champagne producers, yet there are about four thousand. Most of these labels never leave France, and many vintners sell only from their garage-like home cellars.

Other than a small sign in the front yard, there is little to indicate that the nondescript one-level suburban house in tiny Montgueux is also the world headquarters of Champagne Corniot. The home of Alexis St. Jude and her husband is also their tasting room, retail store, and office. The actual winery is in a garage/warehouse just down the street. Her husband's grandfather started the family down the Champagne path, and now her daughter—the fourth generation—has dropped out of law school to return home and learn the ropes to take the reins.

"We've got chalk here, and we own seven hectares [seventeen acres] of grapes," said St. Jude. "We are making our own Champagne with our own grapes and that's what everyone in Montgueux does. Every single family has its own unique characteristics and flavors." About half of their grape harvest gets sold to Veuve Cliquot, and the rest gets made into their house labels, most important a blanc de blanc, one of the less common Champagne styles known as mono-cru because it contains only one grape variety, in this case chardonnay. "Our older vineyards now only produce about half as many grapes as the younger ones," she lamented. In most wine regions around the world, they would simply be torn out and replanted for productivity gains. "We can't replant because this particular strain of chardonnay grape doesn't exist anymore. It's so delicate no one wants to grow it, but the flavor is very nice and it's the choice of our family." Corniot makes between twenty-five thousand and thirty thousand bottles a year, and its flagship, a nonvintage bubbly aged a generous four to five years—more than three times the legal requirement—costs about half the price of the cheapest bottle of real Champagne in the States.

There is no such thing as an assembly line or industrial production in towns like Montgueux, which are scattered across Champagne-Ardennes. At Corniot, the bottling machine fills just three bottles at a time and the labeling machine would fit comfortably on most kitchen counters. In all the smaller family-owned houses I visited—which means most of the Champagne houses—it was common to see several generations working together, with mothers and fathers, sons and daughters, grandchildren and grandparents all picking grapes together—by hand, of course. It is illegal here to do it any other way. And while shorter aging would increase output and quite possibly return on investment, every single place I visited waited two to three years, considerably more than required. Why? As Alexis St. Jude, who ages all of her wines at least three years, said matter of factly, "A winemaker shouldn't be in a hurry." Alison Napjus, senior editor at *Wine Spectator* magazine and the publication's Champagne expert, told me that "in Champagne, the regulations are just a starting point. Many producers age well beyond the minimums."

Just outside Épernay, on a hillside overlooking the city, sits the tiny hamlet of Hautvillers, where you can visit the abbey that was long home to one of history's most famous monks, Dom (Father)

Perignon. A small medieval village, the cobblestone streets of Haut-villers, more like alleys, are still lined with family-owned Champagne houses, set in family homes. Many of the colorful stories surrounding Dom Perignon are fanciful embellishments, including his mythical quote to fellow monks upon first "discovering" Champagne, "Come quickly, I am drinking the stars!" He did not invent Champagne at all, as he is often credited with, but he did make many important contributions to its current quality—and to winemaking in general—from the perfection of blending still wines to the introduction of the cork.

Champagne was born here, perfected here, and based on consumer demand, market prices, and critical reviews, it has always been the world's best sparkling wine. In some other chapters, I've noted that not all famous products are necessarily best in class, but in this case, it is a simple truth that across the board, Champagne is the best. You can get fine sparkling wines from many regions, but in each of these you can also get bad sparkling wines. Because of the incredible quality control, you just can't buy a bad bottle of real Champagne.

"It is so consistently high quality that consumers recognize that virtue without even thinking about it," said *Wine Spectator's* Napjus. "It starts on the micro level with the *terroir* . . . It's one of the most technically demanding and detailed versions of winemaking in the world."

Dozens of producers, large and small, in Épernay, Reims, and throughout the countryside offer winery tours to learn how Champagne is made and usually to enjoy a tasting. These are the most popular experiences for visitors to the region, typically conducted in several languages. While some Champagne houses also have art collections, antiquities in their cellars, restaurants, museums or much more elaborate facilities than others, the winemaking process you view is always pretty much the same, because there is only one way Champagne can be made, with some minor variations in style. When you sign up for one of these tours, this is what you will learn, just as I did.

- Only seven varieties of grapes are allowed in the production of Champagne, in any combination from just one to all of them. However, almost all Champagne uses a combination of three: chardonnay, pinot noir, and pinot meunier. The other four—pinot blanc, pinot gris, arbane, and petit meslier—are historical oddities and rare—there are less than four acres of arbane grapes in the entire region and out of thousands of labels, the number that use it can be counted on your fingers.
- Grapes for making sparkling wine grow better here than elsewhere, owing to *terroir*. This is the world's northernmost prestigious vineyard region, much wetter and colder than others, with two hundred days of rain a year. This is not well suited to producing fruit for many styles of wine, but it is unrivaled for making bubbly. However, without the limestone and chalk it would be too wet and at times in summer too dry. You can see these famous geologic layers during underground tours of the aging caves.
- One hundred percent of the grapes used must be grown in designated AOC vineyards within Champagne-Ardennes. Exacting rules govern how these grapes can be grown, and while more is better in much modern agriculture, here there is a maximum yield per acre to prevent dilution of flavor and quality. Even how vines are pruned is regulated, and because mechanical harvesting might damage grapes and reduce quality, every grape used for Champagne must be picked by hand.
- Grapes are first made into still wines. To produce the most

common nonvintage Champagne, these wines, including barrels from previous years, are blended (called assemblage), a complicated process to balance the flavors of each grape and individual vineyard. Some houses blend hundreds of different wines: Moët & Chandon's "entry level" Brut Imperial contains more than one hundred. More exclusive vintage Champagne, made only in years of exceptionally high-quality harvests, are also blended only from still wines using grapes picked in a single season.

- After blending, the wines are put into bottles with yeast and sugar, then placed in caves or cellars to age. As the yeast eats sugar, it converts it to carbon dioxide, which is where the bubbles come from. Smaller, finer bubbles are a sign of higher quality. For the last six to seven weeks of aging, the bottles are "riddled," a process by which the bottles must be regularly rotated one quarter turn at a time while lying on their sides during secondary fermentation so the solid sediment from the spent yeast (lees) collects in the neck of the bottle.

- After aging, the necks of the bottles are flash frozen, which turns the sediment into a solid icy plug. The bottles are then opened and pressure ejects the solid plug, leaving only wine behind. The bottles are then recorked and ready for sale. This process is called disgorgement.

- Unlike some still wines, which get better with age at home, Champagne improves far more before disgorgement, a period called resting on the lees. For this reason, the initial aging period is crucial: nonvintage Champagne must be aged at least fifteen months and vintage versions at least three years, but these are just minimums: Moët & Chandon typically does between twenty-four and thirty months on its nonvintage and seven years on vintage bottles. Its flagship

Dom Perignon is sometimes more than twice that, and in 2014 the producer disgorged and sold a 1998 vintage.

"There is probably no other product in all of France that is more heavily regulated than Champagne," said Barbara, my tour guide of Moët & Chandon's seventeen miles of private caves below Épernay. "Everything about the grapes is precise—where you can plant, what you can plant, the density. You need a special diploma just to be allowed to prune these vines. Then every step of the wine making and the aging is also regulated."

This entire process is known as the *méthode champenoise*, or the way to make champagne. It is time consuming and expensive. Just imagine if you were a Champagne maker and suddenly you didn't have to use the designated varietals, did not have to source grapes from the most expensive vineyards on earth, and instead you could get them from anywhere at the lowest market cost regardless of quality. Imagine you didn't have to do secondary fermentation in the bottle but instead could create the bubbles by making your sparkling wine in industrial-sized batches in big steel tanks. Imagine you could sell it as soon as you wanted. If you could take all the regulatory quality controls, lengthy aging, better grapes, and crafts-manship out of the process, you'd have a much cheaper product that almost no one would pay a premium for if they knew what it actually was. But if you could circumvent this perception of lower quality by labeling and selling it as "Champagne," riding the coat-tails and hard-earned reputations of Dom Perignon and company, you could make a profit. That's what they do at places like Andre and Cook's, two of our biggest domestic "Champagne" producers.

There are three ways to make wine sparkle. One is traditional Champagne production, with fermentation in the bottle. This style is also used to make Spain's cava (by law), South Africa's cap classique (by law), other French sparklers (known as crémant) from outside the Champagne region, and premium American sparkling wines like Schramsberg, Gruet, and French-owned California houses Domaine Chandon (Moët & Chandon), Domaine Carneros (Taittinger), Mumm Napa (G.H. Mumm) and Roederer Estate (Louis Roederer).

An alternative is the Charmat method, with fermentation from yeast in large tanks rather than in bottles. This more cost-efficient process is used for most Italian proseccos and some low-priced, high-volume American so-called Champagne. The third and cheapest way is to do what Coca-Cola does with Coke and carbonate it by injecting carbon dioxide, skipping secondary fermentation altogether, with no yeast at all.

Only one of these methods, the first, can be used to make real Champagne. Which can be used to make "Champagne" in America? All of the above. The world's most famous wine, at least in name, can legally be made in the United States in just two easy steps. Make wine with grapes you've grown or bought, of any quality from any place. Inject carbon dioxide. Done. Ship it. This may explain why there are so few good sparkling winery tours in this country and so many in France.

Domestic "Champagne" does have to include the place of origin, so if you read the label closely enough you will see it didn't come from France, and thus cannot be real Champagne. The problem is the notion that real Champagne can only come from France is so deeply ingrained in consumers that once they see the word Champagne, they rarely look for more information, and they should not have to. If you buy a Rolex, Omega, Longines, or any Swiss watch—even a Swatch—in a jewelry store, you don't have to turn it over to see if it says "Made in Switzerland," because all real Swiss watches are. The Fake Food bottom line in this case is whether or not American consumers are confused by domestic "Champagne" that's not from Champagne?

The answer is, they are absolutely mystified. "If you gave a hundred people on the street a bottle, at least ninety-five would think it is Champagne," said *Wine Spectator*'s Napjus. "They have no idea. You can make sparkling wine by injecting it with gas like soda, and that is definitely done here . . . it's completely different and it tastes completely different."

When I wrote about this topic for my column at Forbes.com, countless readers wrote in to tell me I must be wrong, that it would be impossible to sell Champagne labeled Champagne made in this country, that it can only come from France. I got comments telling me that domestic wines can't be labeled Champagne but rather might say *méthode champenoise*. The truth is that some do say this, although the term is also France-specific and under EU law banned on sparklers from every place else but Champagne, including the rest of France, no matter how they are made. Some U.S. labels use the term, and some might actually use the method, but they don't have to.

The whole reason this particular Fake Food scam works so well is because so many people rely on the perceived French exclusivity for Champagne. Champagne is a victim of its own successful reputation for coming from only one area. There is no other food or drink product as synonymous with a particular place as Champagne: the connection is so obvious that it is the only AOC product not required to display the AOC symbol on its label, because the very reasonable assumption is that buyers understand its place of origin.

So when people here see "Champagne" and think it is a legally protected term, they in turn automatically assume they are getting real Champagne. This is not a small problem: Cook's, made in steel tanks in California and sold for about seven bucks a bottle, until recently proudly boasted on its website of being the "best-selling champagne in America." While not a true statement from my perspective, it is true that it outsells any real Champagne. The price is certainly attractive: just the grapes required to make one bottle of real Champagne cost more than a finished bottle of Cook's. By some estimates, more than half of the wine labeled "Champagne" sold in this country is not the real deal, and there are many producers, from Long Island to the Finger Lakes to California, with the biggest being Cook's, André, Great Western, and Korbel. Great Western, made by Pleasant Valley Wines in New York's Finger Lakes, uses numerous grape varieties prohibited in real Champagne and sells its stuff for about eight bucks a bottle, yet many stores that carry it sell it as just Champagne, with no mention of where it is made.

This is especially problematic online, where more and more people shop and where you don't actually get to see the bottle identifying it as made in New York. The company's own website doesn't help much either, claiming, "The winery is the largest producer of bottle-fermented champagnes in the eastern United States and for over a century Great Western Champagnes have been the most-honored American Champagnes," as if there was such a thing. But to me, among many bad players, California's Korbel is the worst offender, taking a high-and-mighty position and seeming to believe they are entitled to the word rather than just using it as legal dodge.

For a disconnect from reality and logic, I visited the Korbel facility in Napa, where the tour guide answered my question about the use of the Champagne name by claiming that the company, due to its long history, had a special agreement with France to use the term. It doesn't. Korbel also routinely claims to use the *méthode champenoise*. It doesn't. While secondary fermentation is done in the bottle, like real Champagne, this is hardly the only requirement of *méthode champenoise*. Korbel routinely uses grape varietals not permitted in Champagne, including riesling, chenin blanc, muscat, colombard, gamay, sangiovese, and even zinfandel. It specifically markets its "Riesling California Champagne" as being made with the *méthode champenoise,* despite the impossibility of this. Similarly, on its website, the company boasts that all of its "California champagnes are made according to the traditional *méthode champenoise* . . . This time-honored process takes almost a year to complete." Except that the actual process to which they erroneously refer never, ever takes less than year.

Since the term *méthode champenoise* implies making actual Champagne, the use of these words has been banned in most of the world, along with "Champagne-style." None of that matters here.

In the tasting room, I sampled Korbel Rouge, made with merlot, another prohibited varietal. As the woman conducting the tasting explained to me, it was special because "you'll probably only find it here. Not many places make a red Champagne." In fact, none do because there is no such thing. Adding insult to injury, she gleefully added, "Most people don't realize we make fifteen styles of Champagne because we only distribute six outside the winery. We also make sherry and port." Add Spain and Portugal to the list of Real Food places where centuries of winemakers are rolling over in their graves.

Under ATF regulations, the word *Champagne* on domestic products must be accompanied by the place of origin, so Korbel labels its bottles "California Champagne," an oxymoron. But on much of the company's collateral marketing materials, which do not include the regulated label, "California" is dropped and only "champagne" is used. For example, the company refers to its winemaker as the "champagne master" and its mail-order business is a "champagne and wine club." Korbel's online store describes Le Premier as "Korbel's ultimate reserve champagne," and the Korbel Brut as "our most popular champagne." At a high-profile golf tournament of which Korbel was a sponsor, I was invited to its "celebrity champagne spray off." "California" is noticeably absent from all the company's "Champagne" descriptors.

In an interview with National Public Radio, Gary Heck, the owner of F. Korbel & Bros., defended his company's practices by saying: "You go into other parts of the United States, you ask somebody what sparkling wine is and they're going to tell you it's wine with club soda added to it. It would be very detrimental to our brand to put sparkling wine on there." Seriously? That is about as lame an excuse as I can imagine. I've been all over this country and have never heard of anyone thinking that was the definition of sparkling wine. It certainly doesn't jive with the fact that all of the considerably more expensive, high-quality California sparkling wines are successfully sold as just that, sparkling wines, and have been for many years.

Acclaimed wine journalist Lettie Teague did a taste test of California sparkling wines, which she wrote about in the *Wall Street Journal.* "We started with the Korbel Brut, whose producers have the temerity—or the history, depending on your perspective—to call their wine 'California Champagne' . . . (The European Union, on behalf of French Champagne producers, has convinced sparkling-wine producers world-wide to stop using the region's name on their labels—except Korbel). The Korbel was pretty much an insult to the name—soft and flabby, and a bit sour. We quickly moved on." And Korbel is probably near the top of the quality heap of low-priced ersatz Champagnes.

As a rule, the best domestic sparkling wines producers don't use the word *Champagne,* and I'm very happy to drink one of these bottles from Gruet, Domaine Chandon, and others. This makes the shopping much easier than for other Real Foods. All real Champagne is labeled "Product of France," without exception.

Or as longtime *New York Times* wine critic Eric Asimov succinctly put it, "I'm always happy with a bottle of Schramsberg,

Iron Horse or Roederer Estate from California . . . But when talking about sparkling wine, let's be honest: There is Champagne and there is everything else. The others are good, but they're not Champagne."

In 1891, the nations of the world, including the United States, gathered for the first major international negotiations on trademarks, the Madrid Agreement Concerning the Registration of Marks. The following year, the Madrid Convention laid out the first rules for protecting Champagne, already an AOC within France, in other countries. But the United States did a last-minute about-face and refused to join the agreement. For the next hundred-plus years, we would stubbornly refuse to sign the updated Madrid protocols. Champagne got a second chance at the end of World War I, when its legal protection in Europe was reinforced as part of the Treaty of Versailles. This time the United States signed the treaty, but it was never ratified in the Senate. Had it been, we might today be protected from much Fake Food. French Champagne producers suffered another blow in 1934, when the United States deemed the term generic. Today, there are at least 163 different domestically legal uses of "Champagne" registered under U.S. trademarks.

In 2006, for the first time, the United States made concessions on protected wines when we signed the Agreement on Trade in Wine with the European Union. This was the result of more than a century of complaints and negotiations by foreign producers whose brand names had been hijacked, and in the deal the United States committed to restrict the use of sixteen protected names solely to wines originating in the applicable member nation. This should have effectively ended the reign of terror of domestic "Champagne," "port," "Burgundy," "Chablis," "sherry," "sauternes," "Madeira" and several others—all GIs—except for one significant exception. The agreement included a grandfather provision under which all domestic producers who had been making these wines before March 10, 2006, could keep doing so. So while a new "Champagne" maker cannot start up today, Korbel—and dozens of other existing domestic "Champagne," "port," and "sherry" houses—can keep doing just what they have been doing.

BECAUSE REAL CHAMPAGNE is so unfailingly good and delicate, with its lighter-than-air effervescence, more like a stream of tiny dots than individual, identifiable bubbles, it has taken on a lofty reputation as a luxury item, and in turn, celebratory status. It is served at weddings, used for ship christenings, and enjoyed on Valentine's Day and New Year's Eve. But it is almost always consumed as a toast or aperitif. It is easy to be awed by how good real Champagne is and equally easy to forget that it is wine, after all. As such, it goes wonderfully with many foods, and I have increasingly become a fan of and cheerleader for Champagne with dinner. When Champagne is served with a meal here, it has traditionally been brunch, and this makes sense, because eggs remain one of a handful of ingredients, like artichokes, that befuddle sommeliers and do not go well with most still wines. But because Champagne and eggs are a classic pairing, and it also goes very well with mushrooms, another brunch staple, it has gotten pigeonholed. It is a great breakfast choice, but you might be surprised how well Champagne can perform at lunch or dinner, especially with some favorite comfort foods that might not seem "Champagne worthy."

It is Champagne's high level of acidity that makes it a great food wine, but interestingly, the one pairing many people do opt for is the worst choice possible—dessert. There seems to be an association between a flute after dinner and the final course, but Champagne typically performs worst with sweet foods, and as Elise Losfelt, winemaker for Moët & Chandon, told me, "The acidity of the wine and sweetness of the dish will not work together. Imagine pairing a glass of lemon juice with chocolate cake—it's the same principle."

What do go great with Champagnes are rich, intense foods like risotto, a classic match for the wine's acidity, almost all medium weight proteins, including fish, poultry, pork, and veal, and anything with mushrooms or truffles (but please, no fake truffle oil). Other time-honored combinations for sparkling wine include caviar, aged cheeses like Parmigiano-Reggiano or older Gouda, foie gras, and anything creamy or in cream sauce. Avoid tomatoes because of their high acidity, so no spaghetti and meatballs, but Champagne and fettuccine alfredo are a match made in heaven. Perhaps most surprising, Champagne, especially the slightly sweeter sec or demi-sec varieties rather than the more common brut, are fabulous with spicy foods, like Thai, Indian, and even Cajun. A lot of people would pop a bottle of crisp white, like a New Zealand sauvignon blanc with take-in spicy Asian food, but if you try dry Champagne you won't go back.

At Champagne-and-food-pairing meals, I have asked many industry experts, including the winemakers at Moët & Chandon, Nicholas Feuillatte, Dom Perignon, as well as Devon Broglie, the associate global beverage buyer for Whole Foods Market and one of the nation's few certified master sommeliers, for a perfect Champagne pairing, and much to my surprise they all said the same thing—fried chicken. Moët's Losfelt told me that "oily and salty foods bring out the fruitiness and freshness of Champagne, which pairs wonderfully with really fun, salty foods like fried chicken." Other similar comfort food suggestions were french fries and salted buttered popcorn.

I love fried chicken and have made pilgrimages around the country to eat it at the most famous purveyors, places like Willie Mae's Scotch House in New Orleans, Mary Mac's in Atlanta, Gus's Famous Fried Chicken in Memphis, and even Joe's Stone Crab in Miami Beach, where it is a secret local favorite hiding behind the more famous namesake crustacean. While researching Champagne I became so fascinated with the repeated suggestion that I finally broke down, and ran out one night to bring back the merely average fried chicken from my local gas station, which I ate with a bottle of Nicholas Feuillatte brut. It was everything promised, the Champagne taming the grease while amplifying the salty, rich flavor, and it made even this run of the mill fried chicken much better. It was so good I don't know how I'll ever go back to beer. I can't endorse KFC, but if you have a Popeye's near you, I suggest putting down this book, taking a break, making a fried chicken-and-Champagne run, and then picking up where you left off, decadently satisfied. Just don't buy Korbel or Cook's.

IN SHARP CONTRAST, Scotch whisky is not a great food pairing, except for dessert—especially with dark chocolate—which can go surprisingly well with a peaty seaside malt like Bowmore or Talisker. In another sharp contrast, there is no Fake Food version of Scotch whisky in the United States, which is a refreshing exception to all the other high-value product names routinely counterfeited in this country. In fact, there is no geographically indicated product on earth better (or more aggressively) protected than Scotch, a great example of a label or name that consistently delivers its promise to consumers.

There are two reasons for the unusual security of Scotland's namesake product. Unlike regional names such as Kobe beef, Parmigiano-Reggiano cheese, or Champagne, Scotch has an actual national name built in, and our laws offer stronger protections for country of origin claims. If a distiller here were to start selling domestic "Scotch," the argument could be made that they were fraudulently identifying it as a product of Scotland. However, like Champagne, producers might circumvent this issue with

"California Scotch." The more important protection the Scottish enjoy is a specific entry under U.S. law, a safety net afforded to very few other high quality, instantly recognizable, geographically designated products. The *Code of Federal Regulations* states simply that: "Scotch Whisky is whisky which is a distinctive product of Scotland, manufactured in Scotland in compliance with the laws of the United Kingdom regulating the manufacture of Scotch Whisky for consumption in the United Kingdom." Amen.

Scotland is also adamant about protecting the good name of Scotch. Because the European Union has a generic standard for whiskey (only the Scots, Canadians, and Japanese spell it without the *e*), under EU law a Scottish manufacturer could theoretically make a cheaper spirit and sell it as a "whisky product of Scotland," creating consumer confusion. To avoid this, the Parliament of the United Kingdom took a fairly drastic and unusual step with the Scotch Whisky Act of 1988, reinforced in the Scotch Whisky Regulations 2009, which mandated that the only whisky that can be manufactured in Scotland is Scotch whisky, period. It either meets all the strict regulations, from raw ingredients to aging, or it doesn't exist. It is illegal to even age other whiskies within the Scottish borders. You can make cheap vinegar in Modena or cheddar in Roquefort, but there is no second-tier Scottish whisky below Scotch. The production of Scotch dates to the fifteenth century, and because only whisky meeting its high standards can be made in Scotland, it is perhaps the ultimate example of a Real Food, delivering what is promised. It is even illegal to use a brand that sounds like the name of a distillery but is not.

Nonetheless, to this day the Scotch Whisky Association fights constantly to protect its namesake product around the world, and there are numerous countries that have not afforded Scotch the legal protection it enjoys here in the States. Some play the same games we do with olive oil, using Scottish-style labels and names like "Royal Scot Blended Whisky" to create misleading implications of its origin. "Consumers and Governments around the world can be entirely confident that, when they buy Scotch Whisky, they are getting an unadulterated product," wrote lawyers for the Scotch Whisky Association, before stressing an important truth about Real Foods: "It is always important to remember that reputations can take years to build, but that they can be destroyed in a day."

There are three primary categories of Scotch whisky—single malt, single grain, and blended—but the name of the latter creates some misunderstanding. Single malts, made from only malted barley and water, are the product of one distillery, but not necessarily one production run or even one year. Typically, casks of various ages are vatted, or essentially "blended," but only with other malt whiskies made under the same roof. Single-grain Scotch is made the same way but can contain use unmalted barley or other approved cereal grains. Traditionally used solely for blending, single grains are becoming trendy and more widely available on their own. Blended Scotch combines single malts and single-grain whiskies from more than one distillery, often many, and a number of distilleries in Scotland do not produce their own bottles at all, but make whisky purely for selling to blenders. Blended Scotch is the best-selling style and includes well-known brands such as Chivas Regal, Johnnie Walker, Cutty Sark, and Dewar's, while single malts tend to be named for individual distilleries, such as Bowmore or Glenlivet. It is illegal to use a distillery name unless all the contents of the bottle were made there.

Niche categories include blended malt whisky, a mix of only single malts from multiple distilleries, the similar blended-grain whisky, and vintage single malts, made entirely from one year of production.

One interesting fact about Scotch whiskies lost on many consumers is that "age statements" are required to be based on the youngest whisky used, not an average, as is the case in some other wines and spirits. This is true whether it is a blend or single malt. When you buy a twelve-year-old Scotch, it is entirely composed of whisky at least twelve years old but often contains older spirits as well, one reason why it enjoys such consistently high quality.

Because of all this regulation, Scotch whisky is easy to shop for, at least in terms of avoiding fakes. Within Scotch there is a world of flavor differences, and some fans like only blends, some only single malts, some both. My favorite single malt is The Macallan, and for blends, I prefer Johnnie Walker, but as with Champagne, there is little, if any, bad Scotch, and finding what you like is a fun—and potentially lifelong—experiment.

## ✳ CONSUMER GUIDE TO CHAMPAGNE AND SCOTCH AND TERMS

### Champagne

*Nonvintage (or NV or simply without a year on label):* Most nonvintage champagnes are blends of wines from different years and must be aged at least fifteen months. About 95 percent of all Champagnes fall under this category.

*Vintage (with a year):* Champagne makers will declare exceptional harvests "vintage" years, something that is up to each producer and typically happens once every two or three seasons. By law, vintage Champagnes can only be made from the wines of that one exceptional year and must age at least three years. They are more expensive than NV.

*Prestige Cuvées:* Not a legal term, this refers to extra-high-quality flagship products of different producers, for example, Cristal from Louis Roederer, Sir Winston Churchill from Pol Roger, and

Dom Perignon from Moët & Chandon. Krug makes nothing else. Most are vintage, older, and more expensive than other vintage Champagnes.

*Rosé:* These are Champagnes made by allowing contact of wine with skins of black grapes or adding red wine. Many producers make a rosé version of all their Champagnes, and rosés are considered premium, with higher prices.

*Blanc de blanc and blanc de noir:* These Champagnes are made with only white or only black grapes, respectively, and are fairly rare.

*Dryness/Sweetness:* There are six levels of sugar content, always indicated on the label. From driest to sweetest they are extra brut, brut, extra dry, sec, demi-sec, and doux, but most are obscure specialties and the vast majority of Champagne is brut.

## Scotch Whisky

*Single Malt:* This Scotch can only contain malted barley and water, must be the product of one distillery and aged in wood for at least three years. However, single malts can contain a mix of different distillations, casks, and years. This allows brands like a twelve-year-old Glenlivet to maintain consistency and always taste the same, no matter when it's bottled.

*Single Grain:* Like single malt, this Scotch is a product of one distillery but can be made from other grains and/or unmalted barley. It is used mainly for blending and rarely sold on its own, though it is becoming more popular as whisky connoisseurship increases.

*Blended Malt:* This style, consisting of a mix of single malts from different distilleries, is not common.

*Blended Grain:* This style uses a mix of single grains from different distilleries and is also not common.

*Blended Scotch:* The most popular style in the world, including non-distillery names such as Johnnie Walker (red, black, and blue), Chivas Regal, Dewar's, Ballantine's, Cutty Sark, and so on. These are blends of single malts and grain whiskies from different distilleries, sometimes dozens.

*Vintage Year:* While there are really no "vintages" in the sense of better or worse harvests, as with wine, bottles with a year on the label can only contain whiskies made in that year. This will usually taste different from the same distillery's standard single malt—different but not necessarily better or as good.

# 8. Cheesy Cheeses

It's misleading to use these names for cheese made elsewhere, there's no question about it.

—LAURA WERLIN, James Beard Award–winning author
(personal communication, July 2014)

Gstaad is one of most storybook towns in Switzerland, authentically phony in a way Las Vegas or Disney World would envy. At first glance, it is just another classic Swiss alpine mountain town, straight out of *Heidi*, with nearly every building an almost identical rendition of the quintessential chalet: two or three stories high, wide and squat with a gently sloped, symmetrical peaked roof, a series of balconies on the front, and a white-walled ground level topped entirely with dark brown wood above this. Imagine a picturesque valley surrounded by snowcapped peaks in the Alps, with hundreds of giant cuckoo clocks strewn across the valley floor and lower slopes. Switzerland has lots of famous and beautiful ski towns like Zermatt, Interlaken, and St. Moritz, but Gstaad stands alone as perhaps the world's toniest, the Aspen of Switzerland so to speak, except with real estate prices even loftier than the mind-numbing ones in Aspen.

Switzerland has long been a safe haven for foreign funds, whether to avoid paying taxes or to simply keep assets safe, especially for those whose millions or billions were earned in a country where the current leadership might snatch the cash at any time.

For this reason, Gstaad has become a popular second home for Russian entrepreneurs and eastern European oligarchs, along with wealthy English bankers craving snow over rain and rich locals from Geneva and Zurich. Given the influx, Gstaad has become extremely protective about its character, with incredibly strict zoning laws. A fairly basic new chalet here runs twenty million dollars, and the more elaborate ones top a hundred million, while most fall somewhere in between, yet there is nothing flashy about Gstaad's architecture, because most of the glitz is kept behind locked doors (the cars, watches, and clothes are a different story). Main Street luxury boutiques are mingled with humble bakeries and butcher shops, and there are no trophy homes—unless the host invites you downstairs. That's because every new chalet must look just like the old ones, with construction capped at three stories. It is hard at first glance to tell the seven-figure "starter" homes from the nine-figure bad-guy-in-a-James Bond-movie lairs. Since you can't go up or sideways here, the answer is to go down, and some of these seemingly humble chalets have four, five, or six more floors belowground. Lower levels can contain full-sized pools, bowling alleys, full state-of-the-art gyms, movie theaters, even multilevel parking garages, all underground and out of sight. I saw the foundation being excavated for one such "chalet," and it looked like the worksite for building a new hospital. The old homes are old and the new homes look old, and all of them exist because the Swiss Alps are here. Recreation in Gstaad, summer and winter, revolves around the mountains. So does the rich cheese-making tradition, and while many of the chalets here are fake, the food is very real.

I often write about skiing and ski travel, and friends are always asking me whether they should try a European ski vacation over their standard trip to the American West or Canada. Every great ski destination has good months and bad months, good years and bad years. But, I always answer, if you go to North American ski resorts and Mother Nature is uncooperative, you are more often than not screwed—if you go to the Alps, at least you are still eating fondue.

There's a lot to be said for the cuisine of melted cheese, and when it comes to this specialty, Switzerland is the bomb. While fondue is the best-known variant, it is hardly the only one and, in my humble opinion, not even the best. There are so many decadent takes on the melted cheese main course that you can eat a different one daily, sort of like a carnivore plowing through the many unique cuts in Argentine steakhouses night after night without getting bored. And if, like me, you love these foods, you never have to look far—last year I went skiing in the Alps and was digging into my first plate (more like platter) of *tartiflette* before I even left the Geneva airport.

The restaurant I ate in, after customs but before exiting the main terminal, is exactly the kind of place that makes travel so worthwhile, and exactly the kind of place you would never find in a U.S. airport. It exemplifies why Switzerland is a food lover's heaven. Whereas domestic terminals typically offer chain pizza or burgers, this homey re-creation of an alpine shack served a full slate of authentic regional mountain dishes, with a focus on hearty sausages, stews, and cheese entrées. I had the *tartiflette*, an artery-clogging, soul-enriching casserole made by layering thick slices of cheese in an oval dish atop sliced potatoes and onions studded with lardons, substantial cubes of cooked bacon, baked until it is all melted together. It is delicious, rib-sticking alpine comfort food, and the concept would work with any number of cheeses, but here *tartiflette* always means reblochon.

Superb for melting, reblochon is a soft, washed-rind raw cow's milk cheese with a nutty aftertaste and AOC designation. It is delicious, but because the real thing is always made from raw milk, it has been banned in the States for more than a decade. If you see reblochon here, and you might, it is fake, and while there are near substitutes that produce a delicious melted mess, you have to cross the Atlantic to try a truly authentic *tartiflette*.

The most famous of these oozy cheese dishes is fondue, which has as many recipes as there are variants on how Italian *nonni* make their tomato sauce, and each household is just as passionate. The typical version combines Gruyère and Emmental, though no one agrees how much of each, usually melted in a bit of white wine. Beyond this base, some folks add cornstarch to help the consistency, kirsch, garlic, and/or cream, while people in the French parts of the Alps will often swap their beloved Comté for the Gruyère. Some use exclusively Comté or Gruyère, while some substitute vacherin or Appenzeller cheese for the Emmental in the blend. However you make it, the result is a pot of rich melted cheese dip, into which you immerse cubes of bread on a long fork until thoroughly coated and then eat them. The bread is a staple, but spreads are often augmented by other edibles that taste great dipped in melted cheese.

My personal favorite of all these alpine specialties is raclette, which is sort of reverse fondue—instead of dipping food in melted cheese, you spread melted cheese on top of food. Traditionally, a wheel of raclette cheese was sliced in half to expose a long band of the cheesy interior, which was placed adjacent to an open roaring fire until this edge melted. It was scraped off with a special wooden paddle resembling a painter's scraper or putty knife, the width of the cheese wheel. Diners would have their plates loaded with an array of bites from a buffet-style spread, including boiled potatoes, gherkins, pearl onions, mushrooms, and assorted cured meats, and take turns scraping the ever-melting exposed edge of the wheel. You end up with a paddle full of melted cheese, not as liquidy as fondue, and deposit this on top of your plate of food. You eat, then do it again. And again.

Today most restaurants have electric raclette machines, either individual or for the table, which take the place of the fire. These use a special bulb as the heat source, opposite an adjustable bracket that keeps the exposed edge of cheese the same distance from the heat as you eat it and the wedge gets smaller. You can back off the cheese from the heat when you need a break, then start again. It is a fun, communal, and delicious experience, and I think richer and more varied than fondue. Raclette cheese, made throughout both France and Switzerland, is a common style, like cheddar, rather than a strict AOC process, and it is widely available in the United States. That's key, because I have a raclette machine in my home.

There are three other major regional dishes in this family, all hard to find beyond the Alps. *Reblochonnade* is very similar to raclette, except using the same reblochon cheese as *tartiflette*, and its own special machine, in which pans of cheese are inserted under a broiler to melt, then scraped onto assorted tidbits. Berthoud pairs a ramekin of melted, seasoned Swiss Abondance cheese with a plate of various sausage, cured meats, and potato, sort of an individually portioned fondue/raclette stylistic cross. Crozet di Savoie is a tiny regional Swiss pasta, made from buckwheat, rolled into paper thin sheets and cut into squares about the size of those on a sheet of graph paper—really small. This is often cooked and then stirred with shredded grated local cheese such as tomme—it's a Swiss alpine take on mac and cheese. It is also used as a substitute for the potatoes in *tartiflette*, creating a pasta-based casserole variation called fittingly, *croziflette*. This is a hyperregional, old-school dish, and if you are lucky enough to see it on a menu, get it—you'll thank me.

While Gstaad is one of the wealthiest places you can set foot in, unlike many similarly upscale spots, farming is not only tolerated here but considered culturally indispensable and a most honorable profession. That's the reason for the zoning and why cows always have the right of way. The main street through the center of downtown is rightly known as the Promenade, and it is where many newly minted locals go show off their Ferraris and Bentleys and fur coats, while shopping for jewelry, watches, and more fur coats in the boutiques. Cheese making in the Alps is largely seasonal, and like many other mountain towns in Switzerland, the cows have to pass through town when they come down from the mountains in the fall and return in the spring.

Usually there is a designated day each season when the streets close to traffic for this migration, but not in Gstaad, where each farmer chooses when to move his herd, and in the fall, cows might block traffic on the Promenade for ten straight days. Each time they come through, the government sends a special cleaning crew to follow, because cheese making is that important here, not so much economically as culturally. That is why some fifty-two mountain peaks around Gstaad are privately owned, not by Russian billionaires, or ski resort operators, but rather by multigenerational farming families like the Bachs.

"Everything is done here to ensure that this is a farming region, that it looks like a farming region, and that it always will be a farming region," said Karin Bach, a former Swiss Air flight attendant who still carries herself with the grace of that profession, despite having been a farmer and cheese maker for far longer than she ever worked for the airline. She married into farming by way of a ski instructor with a "real" job in summer making the family cheese—Berner hobelkäse to be precise—which might just be the best cheese you've never heard of.

Switzerland is as serious about its cheese-making rules as are the French, with more than 450 distinct regional varieties, and hobelkäse is no exception. There are hard cheeses and then there are really hard cheeses, and this is the latter, an extra-firm spinoff of Berner alpkäse, a more common member of the Swiss alpine cheese family. The Berner hobelkäse is easily recognized when served in restaurants across Switzerland because its consistency requires the use of a special tool, a cheese planer, to serve. Many alpine cheeses are for melting, but not hobelkäse, which goes on charcuterie platters. Like a woodworking plane, the tool has a razorlike blade inset into a flat surface, and when a wedge of the cheese is pulled across it, the blade shaves off a paper-thin strip that naturally rolls into a cigar-shaped tube. These unique hollow, ethereal cheese tubes accompany platters of local sausage and air-dried beef.

Alpkäse and hobelkäse are both similar to Switzerland's more famous Gruyère, all in the general style of hard alpine cheeses, except with no holes, while real Gruyère sometimes has a few, though nothing like the faux Gruyère or "Swiss" cheese knockoffs sold elsewhere. By law, the Berner varieties can only be made with manual labor, even to the point where the milk must be heated only over a wood fire—no gas allowed. Tradition trumps volume in these mountains and valleys, and in the interest of consistent quality and flavor, the cheese is produced just in summer months when the cows can freely graze on high altitude grasses and flora that give the milk its flavor. In the winter, the herd moves indoors and the milk is sold off. These cheeses are higher in unsaturated fats than most others due to the cows' diet of alpine herbs, and they are never allowed to graze on land that has been fertilized.

The rules go on and on, and because the milk must be used so quickly after milking, most farmers have their dairies in buildings high in the mountains, where the cows and their milk are. After the milk is heated, cultured local bacteria and digestive natural rennet is added, curds form, and the cheese is put into round molds. It is aged twelve to eighteen months, when it is ready for human consumption. At this time it is still a bit soft, like Gruyère, so hobelkäse typically undergoes a secondary round of aging in a much drier setting, for at least another year but often more like three, until it reaches its signature texture and can be made into the delicate, melt in your mouth rolls on a charcuterie platter. Yet even the ultrastrict and traditional Swiss rules sometimes yield to technological advances, and as Bach recalled, "When my husband's father made the cheese, the molds were turned from wood. Now they are plastic. Everything else is the same."

The Bachs' peak is called Gummalp, and all summer long the couple, their herd of cows, and their Bernese mountain dog are up in what appears to be a backdrop from *Heidi*, milking, cutting firewood, and making cheese. "For three months we make cheese every day. People ask me what we do on weekends, but it's the same—the cows don't know it's the weekend. You can't ever skip a day." In similar fashion to the regulations for Parmigiano-Reggiano, no drugs, fertilizer, or anything unnatural is allowed, milk must be ultrafresh, and no ingredients except salt, bacteria, and rennet are added. "Today many visitors ask us if our cheese is organic, but here we never thought of it that way because everything has always been natural. It's the natural way, and not just the cheese, but everything we eat, the meat, the milk—it's all organic. But it is funny when people ask, as if it's special. I think it's the things that aren't organic that need special labels, because they are the exceptions."

Virtually no hobelkäse leaves Switzerland, and because it can only be made in summer, by hand, in a relatively small part of the Bernese Oberland region, there is not much to begin with, only about three hundred tons per year, of which the Bachs make ten, almost all of which is sold locally. Because it is not well known elsewhere, with little export demand, there has never been a reason to counterfeit it, with no profit in a fake version, and as far as I can tell, if you ever see hobelkäse in a store or on a menu it is real.

This cheese has been spared imitation by its lack of popularity. But when I ventured the hypothetical notion that someone in America might make and sell their own version of hobelkäse, Karin Bach simply could not wrap her mind around the notion.

"They couldn't . . . That's not possible . . . That's not right," were her responses no matter how I rephrased it. When I suggested that it would be legal in my country to make and sell hobelkäse, made from cow's, goat's, or even camel's milk, or from any animal fed any food, full of antibiotics, growth hormones, and steroids, without aging and loaded with artificial ingredients, and label it the same with pictures of the Swiss flag or Matterhorn, the idea seemed to come from another planet. So finally I asked, "Where do you think Gruyère cheese comes from?" She looked at me as if I had just said the stupidest thing she had ever heard, and answered "Gruyères, of course." Passionate, artisanal, and devoted to her ancient art, Karin Bach is also a very nice woman, and for her sake, I hope she never visits an American supermarket.

A few quick clicks on the keyboard take me to Amazon.com's online grocery store, where Swiss AOC Gruyère is selling for over twenty bucks per pound, while grand cru Gruyère is about four dollars less. Many geographically indicated products have gradations of quality, especially wine, where the labels "cru," "grand cru," and "premier cru" are frequently used to distinguish between better vineyards or different aging requirements. The same happens with cheese, where those aged longer often carry a special designation. In the case of Gruyère, Switzerland's rarest grade, Le Gruyère Premier Cru, is one of the most critically acclaimed cheeses on earth: it is the only one ever to win Best Cheese at the prestigious World Cheese Awards in London four different times. Its production is tiny and limited solely to Fribourg, one of five cantons (states) comprising the region that can legally make regular Gruyère, and it must be aged nearly three times the standard, a minimum of fourteen months versus the normal five. Reviews suggest it is a life-changing taste experience, but I haven't been able to try it myself because it is not imported into the United States and is hard to find even in Europe.

So unable to get my hands on the premier cru, I might be tempted to try the grand cru sold at Amazon, except for one minor hitch—there is no such thing as grand cru Gruyère. Real Gruyère comes in just three styles, mild (regular) at five months, reserve at ten months, and premier cru. Amazon's "grand cru" is "Produced in America with Pride" and "captures the distinct southern Wisconsin terroir." In the case of Gruyère, consumer confusion is even more pronounced than with the Parmigiano-Reggiano/Parmesan dichotomy because exactly the same Swiss name is used, rather than the translation, less is known about the cheese in general, and many of the knockoffs are not obvious low-end powdered imitations in cardboard tubes. The Wisconsin grand cru "Gruyère" sells for far more than lobster and most domestic "Gruyères" are pricy.

While Gruyère is widely used in fondue, its name is not directly associated with any actual dishes, and there is no such thing as a veal Gruyère hero or eggplant Gruyère. Only seven domestic producers even make an imitation of the venerable Swiss cheese, yet that was enough for the U.S. Patent and Trademark office to declare it "generic" and refuse Switzerland's request for trademark protection.

The entire category of "Swiss" cheeses, including the ubiquitous hole-ridden "Swiss" itself, accounts for less than 3 percent of domestic cheese production, of which faux Gruyère is only a slice. That seems like a pretty small industry to warrant such protection, especially given that real Gruyère was being made for more than six hundred years before the Declaration of Independence was signed, and for centuries before Columbus even set sail for the New World. Real Gruyère has been made the same way in the same place since 1115. Nonetheless, the U.S. Patent and Trademark Office refused the trademark application because "the existence of seven U.S. cheese manufacturers of gruyère cheese and the widespread generic internet and dictionary usage . . . clearly demonstrate that gruyère has lost its geographical significance and is now viewed as a genus of cheese."

America, not Switzerland or France or Italy, is the largest producer of cheese on the planet, as well as the largest exporter, responsible for about 30 percent of the world's supply. But compared to other top cheese-making countries, we don't really have any well-known signature cheese—the ironically best-known product, "American cheese" (which I admittedly use regularly because it is still the best choice for cheeseburgers), isn't even cheese at all. Bearing in mind that the United States has the most lax cheese-labeling laws of pretty much any developed nation, American "cheese," with its saturated fats, emulsifiers, and other additives, ventures so far from the basic definition that it can't legally be called cheese, and when I was younger, it used to be widely known as "American cheese food." Now it is more often called "processed cheese" or "cheese product." Kraft, the leading manufacturer, has gotten away from cheese altogether and simply calls its sliced version "American singles," and in smaller print "pasteurized prepared cheese product."

But when it comes to real cheese, America has plenty of great stuff, yet few are household names. Some of the most widely known are all original titles, such as Iowa's vaunted Maytag Blue, which has been giving Roquefort a run for its money for seventy years; California's Humboldt Fog; and Oregon's Rogue River Blue. I live in Vermont, which is the hotbed of the artisanal cheese industry, not just for the country but arguably the world. Virtually every type of cheese is produced here—hard, soft, from goat's milk, sheep's milk, and cow's milk—and many of them are among the best in class. Vermont is home to the nation's largest cheese-aging cave, and many of the products that come out of it, like Cabot's clothbound cheddar, easily rival anything made in Europe. Even as I write this, our country is enjoying a Golden Age of truly great cheeses, and with a few very notable exceptions such as Parmigiano-Reggiano and Spanish manchego, which have no near relatives here, you could eat gourmet cheese platter after platter without ever looking beyond our shores.

I personally buy more cheese from Vermont than from all of Europe combined, and I buy a lot of cheese. I was both excited and proud for my tiny hometown when I saw a very small production craft cheese made at a farm less than a three-minute walk from my driveway on sale in the fancy cheese shop at Seattle's vaunted Pike Place Market. American artisanal cheese has more than arrived; it dominates the dairy scene. There has been a huge surge in craft cheese making in the past two decades, and whether they are in the Pacific Northwest, California, New York, or Vermont, the folks involved have something important in common—very few of them steal Real Food names and produce Fake Foods.

Instead, the new model for high-quality American cheese makers has been to brand their entire dairy for excellence, rather than individual cheeses, the same approach taken by companies like Mercedes, whose name, rather than a particular model car, is synonymous with quality. Cypress Grove, the craft cheese maker behind Humboldt Fog, also makes the exquisite Midnight Moon, PsycheDillic, Sgt. Pepper, Bermuda Triangle, and Purple Haze, all whimsical names—and all individually trademarked. Vermont's Jasper Hill Cellars is one of the most acclaimed and awarded U.S. cheese makers, and it has a dozen different unbelievably good cheeses, none of which is called Parmesan or Gruyère or feta. Instead it has gone with choices like Constant Bliss, Moses Sleeper, and Bayley Hazen Blue.

Constant Bliss is one of my all-time favorite cheeses, and if you try it for the first time and like it, the name is far easier to remember than if you happen to try hobelkäse. The same is true for Midnight Moon or Bermuda Triangle. These dairies, and many others like them, have been very successful; their products are carried in cheese shops across the country, and they often sell so well they can be hard to keep in stock. Dairies like these prove that you can still do what every highly regarded brand name that connotes quality did at some point: build a reputation from scratch without the cop-out of stealing someone else's hard work and recognition. They did it by making high-quality products.

Even these visionaries, the best of the best American cheese makers, are hurt by the Fake Foods of their neighbors. Many of these award-winning cheeses are made in the style of European classics, sometimes improving on the original—after all, there are only so many kinds of cheeses and animals that give milk. In many cases, these producers could call their cheeses feta, Gorgonzola, Brie, and so on and be closer to the real thing than much of the industrial U.S. cheese, but they don't, and as a result, they suffer the same unfair competition that the original producers do.

As a consumer, you might say, "How can I buy PsycheDillic when I don't even know what kind of cheese it is?" That is a fair question, except if you look at it, it is pretty clearly a fresh round of soft goat cheese, and it says goat cheese on the label, so problem solved. On the other hand, when you buy domestic Parmesan, or Gruyère or manchego, or many other fake cheeses, you definitely don't know what kind of cheese you are getting, because these often have no relationship whatsoever to the real products whose names they have stolen.

"You cannot beat a true Spanish manchego if that's the style you want; there's nothing else like it," says cheese expert Laura Werlin, whom I first met at a cheese seminar she was conducting as part of the Cochon festival in Memphis, a celebration of all things swine. "The First Lady of Cheese," Werlin is a frequent presenter at top food festivals like Cochon, Pebble Beach, and Aspen's Food & Wine Classic. She knows a lot about all cheeses but is a big fan of and cheerleader for American cheese makers in particular. Two of her books, *The All American Cheese and Wine Book* and *New American Cheeses* deal exclusively with these and profile many of the country's best up-and-coming cheese makers. It's fair to say Werlin loves American cheeses, so when she objects to the copies made here, well, it just doesn't get any more credible than that.

Real manchego cheese only comes from Spain, where it is made from sheep's milk, and not just any sheep's milk, but only from the milk of the Manchega breed. According to its producers' group website, the cheese has been made for thousands of years, since the Bronze Age: "In Spain, archaeologists have found evidence of Manchego cheese production on the La Mancha plains well before the time of Christ." Its production is heavily regulated in terms of where the sheep live and what they eat; the aging process; and its purity, with only whole milk, salt and rennet allowed. "Real manchego has to be made a certain way," says Werlin. "But there are other cheeses called 'manchegos' made here in the U.S., and made differently, using cow's milk. Manchego is Spanish manchego and there's nothing like that." Of course, the average consumer likely has no idea what kind of milk manchego is made from, they just know it is famous cheese that is supposed to taste great, which is exactly what the fakers are taking advantage of.

While most of what I consider fake cheeses are pale imitations of real cheeses whose very names in turn are definitions of quality and purity, some is just totally phony, as with scam seafood and adulterated olive oil. Here we see yet again what happens anytime you cannot tell a more expensive ingredient from a cheaper one by looking at it—fraud—and few can tell what animal's milk a slice of cheese was made from with the naked eye. Yet cow's milk is cheaper than either goat milk or sheep milk, and that spells trouble.

Remember Dr. Mark Stoeckle, the DNA researcher at New York's Rockefeller University who first helped uncover the nation's widespread fake fish problems while helping his daughter test sushi samples for a high school science project? Well, his work aroused so much interest that his graduate students began conducting DNA tests for all sorts of other foods. "Cheese is another area I worry about," said Stoeckle. "We tested cheeses and found that some that said they were made from sheep's milk were cheaper cow's milk." This is an international problem, and cheese appears near the top of the list of most fraudulent foods (olive oil was number one) compiled by Dr. John Spink, director of the Michigan State University Food Fraud Initiative.

The cheese fraud problem has gotten bad enough that it has become a priority for one of the world's top research facilities dealing with such issues, the Institute for Global Food Safety at Queen's University in Belfast. Speaking at the Global Food Fraud and Safety Symposium, the institute's director, Professor Chris Elliott, outlined the growing breadth of criminal fraud, and described a cheese identification program similar to Stoeckle's species-based Barcode of Life for plants and animals. No one in the United States has done a comprehensive study of the various milks claimed in certain cheeses, but Elliot just finished such a review of the UK retail marketplace and the results were disturbing. Twelve percent of the goat cheeses tested contained milk other than goat's, in some cases almost no goat's milk at all. Elliott's researchers are busy assembling a database of identifiable characteristics for specific cheeses: "We are looking at developing molecular fingerprints for each cheese . . . so that whenever that cheese is sold anywhere in the world we can say, yes, this is genuine."

The institute is developing a handheld infrared scanner that you could point at cheese right in the store and literally get a red or green light as to its authenticity. Until then, in our country especially, it remains buyer beware, and all the more reason to seek out AOC or PDO cheeses whose production is at least regulated by some government. American consumers receive less protection against Fake Foods than do citizens of Colombia, El Salvador, Honduras, Nicaragua, Panama, and Costa Rica, all of which have entered into free-trade agreements barring the copycat use of protected names such as Parmesan and provolone. Canada, which has consistently been way ahead of the United States except when it comes to mock Prosciutto di Parma (see chapter 1)—signed a trade agreement with the European Union curtailing the nation's use of feta, Asiago, Muenster, fontina, and Gorgonzola, all protected geographically indicated products we never even would have heard of if some enterprising cheese maker in another country hadn't invented them. Under the agreement, products manufactured in Canada will be marketed as "feta-like" or "feta-style"), a simple solution requiring minimal rebranding or reeducation.

"I am a 12-year veteran of the American 'specialty' cheese industry," wrote American Liz Thorpe in the *Guardian*, "so Cheese-gate [the growing international debate over names] had me thinking: maybe those Euros are right. Yes, I thought: Parmigiano Reggiano, regulated down to its fat content and aroma and 'crust thickness,' really is a unique invention. Who are we to get all jingoistic in defending it as our own? Real feta, produced in Greece from sheep and goat milk, bears no relation whatsoever to the insipid salt crumbles most of us find in American supermarkets. You can't call Grade A beef 'prime,' right? And what's so bad about calling it 'Gorgonzola-style' anyway?"

Good question. The answer is that in nearly every case, those

opposed to respecting the protected names of foreign cheeses—
almost all of which predate the entire American cheese industry—
do so out of unvarnished self-interest, and the chief argument is
that the cost of rebranding, relabeling, and redefining themselves
to consumers would be onerous. This is an argument routinely employed by producers big and small, from Kraft to artisanal cheese
makers, and to all of them, I say, "Too bad." The only reason they
might face relabeling or rebranding costs in the first place is because they have already profited from riding the coattails of reputations established by others.

The "Muenster" cheese made at Wisconsin's Decatur Dairy
is a liquid brew made in huge batches in a thirty-five-thousand-
pound stainless-steel vat. Decatur owner Steve Stettler contends
that U.S. food makers have spent a lot of money building their
brands and asks, "How do we educate our consumers? People have
spent a great deal of money on labeling, building traditions, building a name on a product. And then not being able to use that
name would be kind of horrific." But what kind of name or history
has this imitation Muenster built? The "people" he refers to who
spent the money educating consumers and building the Muenster
brand and tradition were the French, not his company. France's
PDO Munster cheese (no "e"), which has been made in a specific
area under strict rules since the fourteenth century, is nothing
like most of the "Muenster" cheese made in this country. It is a
strong, soft-brined cheese with a creamy texture similar to Brie or
Camembert but with much more pronounced flavor. By law, it has
to be formed into flat discs about eight inches in diameter and
one to two inches thick, with a distinctively orange rind, which is
washed and brined regularly while aging.

U.S. senator Charles Schumer of New York, having realized
that artisanal cheese production is a growing industry across his
dairy-rich state, argued that small- and medium-sized family-owned

businesses could be "unfairly restricted" by protection of Real Food names and further states, "Muenster is muenster, no matter how you slice it." Except that it is clearly not, no matter how you slice it. In any case, Schumer was specifically talking about new companies, the ones that have the opportunity to begin with a clean slate and do not need to counterfeit Munster, saving them any costs of relabeling or rebranding. He also fails to notice that it is these very New York craft cheese makers he thinks he is protecting who are hurt by the use of fake cheese names. I seriously doubt he would take the same flippant attitude if a foreign government said, "An iPhone is an iPhone no matter who makes it." And given that Grimaldi's pizzeria, the famous Big Apple chain currently suing its illegitimate Chinese namesake, is one of Schumer's constituents, I wonder if he'll appease them with his same lame logic: "Grimaldi's pizza is Grimaldi's pizza, no matter who makes and slices it" (see chapter 2).

The other argument often employed is that of a slippery slope, as in, where does this end? Again, this is irrational, given that these products are real, existing, limited, and not theoretically infinite as opponents to geographically indicated protection would argue. Farr Hariri, president of California's Belfiore Cheese Company, which mostly makes original cheeses but does knock off Greece's feta too, said, "If all nations followed this mentality, where do you draw the line? Would all manufacturers—of spaghetti, lasagna, beef stroganoff, Hungarian goulash, hummus, salami, lavash—in this country someday fall victims to such irrational claims, which are purely motivated by greed and desire to artificially manipulate supply and demand?" Except there is no place called lasagna where the layered pasta was invented and is made under strict controls to this day. In fact, none of the products he mentions in his erroneous comparison are geographically protected, not even Hungarian goulash, the only example linked to a particular place.

This stew is a dish, not a product, akin to Chicago-style deep dish pizza or Texas barbecue, none of which have any standards for how they are made. This frequently used argument is simple fear mongering, and Hariri's conceit of using "greed" as a slur against the actual creators of the products being knocked off gives a pretty clear clue as to where the greed really lies.

The thing that seems to bother our senators, other politicians, and lobbyists is not the widespread ripping off of the American consumer but rather the roadblocks to Fake Food exports that the expanding global recognition of GIs is causing. Fake cheese pirates from the world's largest exporter are finding fewer safe harbors. Shawna Morris of the U.S. Dairy Export Council noted that since the European Union started putting restrictions on food names in the mid-1990s, they've spread to other countries, and as an example, one trade agreement "banned the sale of U.S. feta, asiago, gorgonzola and fontina to Korea." She added that Costa Rica recently barred American provolone and Parmesan, and other South and Central American countries have similar restrictions, which may signal a small shift in the right direction.

But at the same time, folks at the U.S. Dairy Council, who call the hijacked terms "common names," have been expanding exports to the world's largest market. "Recently concluded trade talks with China have resulted in stronger protections for common cheese names [common only to U.S. and China]. The U.S.-China Joint Commission on Commerce and Trade is expected to facilitate export of cheeses like feta and parmesan to China, with the agreement calling for strong market protections for product names and recognition of the importance of common name preservation to U.S. exports." Obviously these "stronger protections" for fakes hurt makers of the real thing who would presumably sell to Chinese consumers.

The lack of protection for cheese names allows domestic producers to steal sales from the real thing, and we are not talking about chump change. The U.S. market just for "hard cheeses named Parmesan using a misleading reference to an Italian origin" is a billion dollars or around 100,000 tons, according to the Consorzio Parmigiano-Reggiano. The group readily admits that not everyone who currently buys cheap, low-end products like grated "parmesan" in a tube would buy the real thing instead if fully informed, and "a prudent estimate of the loss of market share in the U.S. market would correspond to 150,000 wheels." So instead of a billion, the craft producers of Parma, mostly small family-owned dairies, are "only" losing about seventy-five million dollars a year to Fake Food.

But it remains the American consumer who loses the most, sometimes economically, sometimes in terms of health, almost always in taste, and often all three. In 2014, leading culinary website Serious Eats did a series of taste tests to find the best-tasting "Parmesan," ostensibly for when readers wanted to save money. The project had two surprising conclusions: first, there was no value proposition in the fakes, since many cost just as much—or more—and the most expensive cheese in the tasting was an inferior domestic imitation that sold for nearly 50 percent more than the real thing. But even more notable was the winner—none. Actually, the winner was real Parmigiano-Reggiano, but Serious Eats had to change the structure of the exercise to reflect the results. As reported by Daniel Gritzer:

> Maybe it seems wrong to have an imported Parmigiano-Reggiano win the domestic Parmesan taste test, but we simply can't, in good conscience, steer you to any of the domestic cheeses we tried when the real version is so much better. We rounded up as many domestic Parmesans as we could find in the New York City area . . . We bought any domestic cheese that was labeled as "Parmesan." I'll keep this short: The imported

Parmigiano-Reggiano whipped the pants off all the other cheeses. Furthermore, it was priced about the same as most of the other cheeses, which means that even from a quality/value standpoint, the imported one is the best option . . . Whenever a recipe calls for "Parmesan," there's only one thing I'll buy: real-deal imported Parmigiano-Reggiano. Sure, I see the domestic Parmesans in the supermarket cheese section. I just look straight past them. True D.O.P. Parmigiano-Reggiano is one of the greatest cheeses in the world, and I'm not generally interested in substituting it with an imitation.

Fortunately cheese is one of the easier foods to shop for as long as you know what to look for.

## ✽ FEW INGREDIENTS
By law, all cheeses sold in this country have to list their ingredients, and real cheeses tend to be made with just a very limited list, like milk, salt, and rennet, with the occasional additions of enzymes or spices like pepper. If there is a much longer list or laboratory-sounding names you are unfamiliar with, that's a sign it is an imitation.

## ✽ GEOGRAPHICALLY INDICATED CHEESES
There are more than 150 cheeses protected with GIs in the European, but the highest profile ones are Asiago, fontina, Gorgonzola, Grana Padano, Mozzarella di Bufala Campana, Parmigiano-Reggiano and Pecorino Romano (all from Italy); Comté, Roquefort, Munster, and Reblochon (France); feta (Greece); Gruyère (Switzerland); Stilton (United Kingdom); and manchego (Spain). Try to remember this short list and if you are buying any one of these cheeses, the real thing will only come from the respective nation. Feta, Muenster, and Gruyère are especially frequently copied elsewhere.

## ❈ DOMESTIC CRAFT CHEESES

Because of the substitution of cow's milk for more expensive claimed sheep's, goat's, or water buffalo's milk, I am wary of buying any unbranded cheeses, like those precut, wrapped, and tagged that read something basic like "Domestic Sheep's Milk Cheese." I'll only buy from actual manufacturers, and the best sell their cheeses already wrapped in proprietary labels—when you buy cheese from dairies like California's Cypress Grove, New York's Old Chatham Sheepherding or Vermont's Jasper Hill Cellars, they have their own distinctive packaging.

## RACLETTE FOR 4

🦡 The traditional preparation is scrape an oozy layer of melted cheese over plates already covered in foods like boiled pearl onions or chunks of sausage. Guest choose their meats and veggies and then top with melted cheese. If you have an electric raclette melter, by all means use it, but if you don't, there is a very simple alternative—the microwave. While these devices have a decidedly un-gourmet reputation, they work very well for melting cheese.

Any or all of the following:

Pearl onions, boiled
Baby potatoes or larger potatoes cut into bite-sized chunks,
    boiled
Gherkins
Assorted sausages/salamis, sliced into bite-sized chunks
Cured ham, such as Prosciutto di Parma or southern-style
    country ham, thinly sliced

1.5 pounds Swiss raclette cheese (at better cheese shops)

## DIRECTIONS

- Serve the onions, potatoes, gherkins, sausages and salamis, and prosciutto family-style as a buffet for guests to choose from and fill their plates.
- Slice the cheese into ½-inch-thick slabs, and one at a time, put a slice on a microwave-safe plate and microwave on medium-high for 30 to 45 seconds or until mostly melted and slightly bubbling.
- Immediately pass plate of hot cheese for guests to scrape on top of their vegetables and meats. Serve with glasses of white wine and repeat, often, until everyone is very happy.

# 9. Fine Wines and Not-So-Fine Wines

ME: I thought port could only be made in Portugal?
KEN PRAGER, PRAGER WINERY PORT WORKS: Well, the real stuff is. But I think we do a pretty good job.

Nineteen seventy-six was a good year for America—and for underdogs. Bicentennial celebrations lasted all year long, everything was awash in Stars and Stripes, and an unknown actor/screenwriter wrote and starred in what would become the Oscar-winning, highest-grossing movie of the year. Film's great underdog and everyman, Rocky Balboa, was an unranked heavyweight fighter given a shot at the title as part of America's patriotic birthday revelry. He lost the fight but won the girl, the moral victory, and the box office, with decades of sequels.

On the other side of the Atlantic, American winemakers were living out a *Rocky*-esque fantasy of their own (except for the losing part), winning both the red and white wine categories at the now-famous Judgment of Paris international competition. It was a sea change in the gourmet world, the very first time American wines were taken seriously outside this country, their quality loudly displayed on the global stage. Forty years later, every bottle labeled "Napa Valley" enjoys a price premium over most other wines, here and abroad, a success that stems directly from that fateful French spring.

Steven Spurrier, a British wine merchant (played by Alan Rickman in the movie about the competition, *Bottle Shock*) organized the high-profile tasting. Spurrier, who dealt exclusively in French wines, believed the Americans could not possibly win, and the invented contest was to some degree a publicity stunt. The overwhelmingly French judging panel (Spurrier was joined by one ex-pat American from a Parisian wine academy and nine very qualified French experts) tried the wines blind and ended up picking two California winners, a Chateau Montelena chardonnay and for the red, Stag's Leap Wine Cellars 1973 cabernet sauvignon. (Two years later, Spurrier reorganized the same blind tasting at the Vintners Club in San Francisco, with different judges, and underscoring the accuracy of the results, Stag's Leap won again.)

The red tasting in that first competition was higher profile and more important to the public, because it was billed as New World cabernet sauvignon versus Old World Bordeaux, the noblest and most lauded of the many noble and lauded French wines. Like Champagne or Burgundy, Bordeaux is both a region and a regulated wine style, but it is the most collected and coveted style. Strict quality rules rank just five Bordeaux vineyards out of hundreds as "first growth," or premiers cru, and all five have become household names among wine lovers, synonymous with luxury and quality: Château Lafite-Rothschild; Château Margaux; Château Latour; Château Haut-Brion; and Château Mouton Rothschild. These have long been considered among the greatest wines ever made, yet an unsung American (barbarians!) cabernet sauvignon using newly planted vines (unthinkable!) and only in its second vintage bested them all. It was a great day for American winemakers.

The only catch was that the 1973 Stag's Leap wasn't really a cabernet sauvignon. It was a blend of cabernet and merlot, a classic combination used regularly in—you guessed it—the great wines of Bordeaux. It was labeled cabernet sauvignon as both a convenience and a result of surprisingly vague U.S. laws on the contents of wines—plus, we didn't yet have a name for Bordeaux-style wines in this country. That would come twelve years later.

There are six varieties of grapes allowed by law in the making of red Bordeaux, but the traditional "Bordeaux blend" is a trio of mostly cabernet sauvignon, merlot, and cabernet franc though some are made with only two grapes, just as the Stag's Leap was. Similarly, there are nine permitted varieties for white Bordeaux, but many winemakers blend just two, a semillon and sauvignon blanc. Like a favorite recipe for chocolate chip cookies, these combinations of grape varieties are time tested and proven to work very well together, so winemakers worldwide have adopted similar blends, variously called Bordeaux-style, claret (a traditional British term for dark red Bordeaux wines), table wine, or vintner's blend.

The problem, especially in the United States, is that these terms don't have any discernible meaning, and they might refer to a traditional Bordeaux-style blend—or something else. Claret is the most distinctive, but few Americans know dated British slang. One who does is filmmaker turned winemaker Francis Ford Coppola, who is fond of using the old-school label, and in his case, he follows tradition, producing claret that is a "cabernet-based wine blended in the classic Bordeaux-style." Then again, Coppola is a Real Food guy who also grows his own olives, presses olive oil, and makes salami on one of his California estates, not for resale like the wines but rather for family meals. "If I have my name on something, it's a personal decision and one I don't take lightly. The public can trust that our wines will be of the best quality and authenticity," he told me. He recounted growing up with wine as an integral part of gatherings and big family meals in his Italian American household and explained that he wanted to make wine before he wanted to make films. As soon as he got his first big paycheck, from *The*

*Godfather* back in 1975, he sunk it into vineyards—and almost went broke in the process.

But forty years and a couple of sequels plus one *Apocalypse Now* later, he's more than landed on his feet as an extremely successful winery owner. In 1995, he purchased the famed Inglenook Vineyard and its Chateau, one of the nation's most historic winery properties, and in 2010 he opened the Francis Ford Coppola Winery in Sonoma's Alexander Valley, among the most impressive public wine facilities in the world, an oenophile fantasy land. The claret is part of his mainstay Diamond Collection series, an affordable lineup with diamond-shaped labels, which also includes a distinctively California-style Diamond Red Blend with zinfandel, syrah, and several other grapes. Both are blends, one a traditional Bordeaux-style, one a more fruit-forward New World wine, and both are good, but if you don't follow individual winemakers like Coppola, you would have no way of knowing which was which.

That's where meritage comes in.

Consumer confusion over wine in this country is exacerbated by the different approaches Americans and Europeans use in labeling. We tend to go with the names of grape varietals, such as merlot or zinfandel. European wines have long been known by their regional styles, so when you buy a red wine from Italy's Chianti region, as a consumer you are expected to know that is sangiovese and, likewise, that white wine from Burgundy's Chablis is entirely chardonnay.

The problem with Old World labeling (Burgundy, Côtes du Rhône, etc.) is that to understand it, you need to memorize every regional style of winemaking and the grapes they use. The problem with New World labeling by grape variety (chardonnay, merlot, etc.) is that not every chardonnay tastes like some general notion of chardonnay. In addition, most American consumers erroneously but understandably believe label terms to be absolute, with the same 100 percent meaning as something like orange juice or milk.

But U.S. law long required only that the majority—51 percent—be the varietal on the label, with the remaining ingredients unlisted. So while cabernet sauvignon is a premium grape commanding higher prices, a bottle of cabernet could be cut with almost half whatever grape was selling cheaply that season. On the flip side, the 51 percent rule allowed for a lot of creativity in blending, and U.S. winemakers like Stag's Leap could make "cabernet sauvignon" in the traditional Bordeaux style, perhaps a very typical mix like 70 percent cabernet, 15 percent merlot, and 15 percent cabernet franc.

In 1973, U.S. law raised the varietal minimum to 75 percent, where it remains today. Wines made from 100 percent of the varietal displayed on their label are still the exception in this country, and very few zinfandels are made of just zinfandel. So if you buy real Chablis (only from France), you get 100 percent chardonnay, always. If you buy chardonnay in the States (regardless where it is made) you get three-quarters chardonnay, one-quarter mystery. But if you buy fake domestic "Chablis," you might get some chardonnay—or none. It might not even be white. Go figure.

The Judgment of Paris dramatically raised interest in the new California reds being made with classic Bordeaux grape varietals. At the same time, the 1973 law change meant a blend with just 60 to 70 percent cabernet could no longer be sold as cabernet. "Suddenly these had to be called something else—like red table wines," said Mitch Cosentino, a highly respected longtime Napa winemaker who sold his eponymous Cosentino Winery in 1992 but continues to work as a winemaker and consultant. Today he is president of the Meritage Alliance and runs PureCru, a small-batch artisanal winery. I met with Cosentino and several of his winemaking peers at the Dry Creek winery in Napa, which among other niceties has a beautiful self-guided garden trail, sells an interesting assortment of locally made artisanal foodstuffs, and offers visitors the rare opportunity to make their own hands-on blends. It's a very friendly winery, but few who visit know Dry Creek's vital role in wine history—this is where the first ever meritage was produced.

The 1973 labeling change created the need for an alternative term for Bordeaux-style wines made outside of Bordeaux. Just as quality sparkling winemakers in this country won't erroneously use "Champagne," the best Napa and Sonoma vintners sought an original name. The Stag's Leap win propelled rapid growth in the highest-quality tier of the American wine industry, and many wineries launched individually named proprietary wines made with Bordeaux-style blends, the same marketing trend seen today in America's finest artisanal cheeses. These include such coveted labels as Opus One, Joseph Phelps's Insignia, Dominus, Dry Creek's Mariner, Franciscan's Magnificat, Justin's Isosceles, Beringer's Alluvium, Cosentino's The Poet, and Cain Five (so named because it contains all five contemporary Bordeaux grape varietals) and so-called cult wines Harlan and Colgin, which are very hard to find and easily fetch between five hundred and one thousand dollars a bottle.

The success of these top-shelf wines, all among America's best and many costing in excess of one hundred dollars, trickled down, and winemakers began rolling out much more affordable Bordeaux-style blends. The only problem was consumers, who had no idea what they were. It is one thing when two of the world's most famous wineries, Robert Mondavi and premiers cru Bordeaux maker Chateau Mouton Rothschild collaborate to jointly make Opus One, which had a big marketing budget, was reviewed in every wine publication, appeared on top restaurant lists, and sold for over two hundred dollars a bottle. A wine like this creates its own market, which cannot be said for the ten-dollar "red blend" in the supermarket. France has plenty of inexpensive red Bordeaux, but just the fact that it is Bordeaux tells the consumer a lot. America needed its own brand, and in 1988 a group of about a dozen progressive California winemakers got together to do just that. They held a contest to pick the new name. Several of them, including Mitch Cosentino and Dry Creek's president and second-generation owner Kim Stare Wallace, joined me around the winery's conference table fifteen years later to retell their story.

"We wanted a new classification for Bordeaux-style blends," said Wallace, one of the original members of the Meritage Alliance. "We were calling our blend Reserve Red—we hadn't come up with a proprietary name like Opus One. That's how the contest got started."

This was the pre-internet age, before things "went viral," yet much to their surprise, the contest really caught fire and got publicity all over the world. They ended up receiving an unimaginable six thousand entries. "We got it down to about ten names and I liked 'ameritus,'" recalls Cosentino. "Meritage was actually my second choice." Wallace also had another favorite: "One of the suggestions we considered was 'elevage.' We thought it sounded so elegant, but then we found out it had another not so elegant meaning having to do with something involving the multiplying of sheep. Meritage was made up from whole cloth and didn't have any baggage associated with it like some of the other names. The only problem is that consumers keep trying to say it with a French accent, but we don't really care as long as they keep buying it." Much to my chagrin, I discovered that I had been doing just that, and pronouncing the name wrong for, oh, about fifteen years. In the style of the wine, meritage was itself a blend, combining the words *merit* and *heritage*, with which it is meant to rhyme, not pronounced with a faux European accent.

"Our goal was to have the name recognized by the trade, in stores, and on wine lists so that these blends would not get dumped in with either cabernet sauvignon or the dreaded 'other red wines,'" said Wallace. They succeeded, and from such humble beginnings, with a dozen friendly rival vintners gathered around a table, meritage has taken off, and is now its own category in important wine competitions. There are more than 350 members of the Meritage Alliance, which has spread far beyond California: today, there are French wineries making meritage, because if they are not located in Bordeaux they face the same branding challenge. These wines are now also made in Canada, Argentina, Mexico, Israel, and Australia. The requirement to use the term is to blend at least two of the traditional Bordeaux grapes, with no one variety comprising more than 90 percent of the total.

Even big-box retailer Costco is an alliance member, retailing a private label meritage made for them. Grocer Trader Joe's does this as well, as do wine-store chains Total Wine and BevMo. The category has seen a recent boom in white meritage production, and today it is easier to find white meritage than white Bordeaux in many U.S. liquor stores. Even well-established proprietary brands like Mondavi's Opus One, which sat out the early days of meritage, have come onboard. Members include some of the most prominent names in California winemaking: Franciscan, St. Francis, St. Supéry, Sterling, Rosenblum, Rodney Strong, Kendall Jackson, Estancia, Flora Springs, B.R. Cohn, and many more.

I love the meritage success story because it shows that building a quality reputation from scratch, and quickly, is a viable alternative to stealing one, a common Fake Food strategy. Meritage is a controlled and transparent Real Food brand that has a defined meaning, which informs consumers, a rare success in the American wine world, where lower-quality pirated copies have long been the norm. "Burgundy, Chianti, Chablis, Champagne, and Rhône wines were never restricted legally here," said Cosentino. "And they were all widely used."

They still are. There is no better Fake Food wine example than the ubiquitous Gallo Hearty Burgundy, which bears little passing resemblance to any real Burgundy. Even the name is oddly disquieting, since real Burgundy is best known for its elegance, and "hearty" would be about the last adjective used in conjunction with the style. But more than just the name is flawed—almost everything about this wine is wrong.

"It was fifty years ago when the pioneering American winemakers Ernest and Julio Gallo first introduced a wine called Hearty Burgundy," reads a press release from the winery, celebrating the momentous—or from my perspective ignominious—half century of this wine's existence. "Hearty Burgundy was the favorite wine of the winery's founders Ernest and Julio Gallo. The brothers originally made it as an ode to the Italian wines they enjoyed when they gathered around the dinner table with family and friends sharing great food and conversation." I reread the press release several times trying to grasp the Gallo's fundamental misunderstanding of both wine and geography. I wonder if this "great conversation" ever involved a guest asking the brothers if they knew that Burgundy was in France, not Italy, and just what the hell were they thinking anyway? As long as they were stealing unrelated names, if they wanted an ode to Italian wines, why didn't they call it Chianti?

Of course, the Gallo brothers, born and bred in central California, grew up a long way from Europe, just as their parents had, and they may have been as ignorant about Italian wines as they seem to have been about French, wrongly thinking they had created some sort of Burgundy. The press release for the fiftieth-anniversary edition describes the "Varietal Origin," which would usually list grapes used, simply as "California," the only clue as to what the wine might be made from: some kind of grapes grown somewhere in California. Maybe red, maybe white, maybe some of each, or maybe whatever is selling most cheaply at the moment each

batch is made. You can't tell from the label, the press release—
or the taste. This is starkly in opposition to real red burgundy,
made with 100% pinot noir grown only in quality rated vineyards
in the Burgundy region (the one in France, not Italy). But then
again, real Burgundy doesn't sell in double-sized 1.5 liter bottles
for under ten bucks.

From another company press release, I was able to ascertain
that "although the exact varietal components have varied vintage
to vintage"—seemingly confirming my suspicion that the recipe
is based on fluctuating market prices—the wine always includes,
among many other possible grapes, both zinfandel and petite
sirah. The latter is popular in Mexican, Brazilian, and Israeli winemaking, not to be confused with the famous petite syrah used in
the Rhône region. It hardly matters, because any kind of petite
sirah or syrah, no matter how you spell it, along with all zinfandel,
is banned in the production of actual Burgundy.

The wine's label, which notes, "The Gallo Family is proud to
celebrate the 50th anniversary of Hearty Burgundy, America's first
iconic red blend," is full of contradictions. While celebrating its
blended nature and role in American wine history, it refused to
use an American name and instead chose one whose very definition means "never, ever a blend." This wine is low-hanging fruit,
so to speak, inviting mockery, but the problem with domestic fakes
runs much deeper. Like cheese, it involves the misleading use of
numerous geographically protected real wine names, each with
strict rules and definitions, allowing consumers to know with just
a glance exactly what they are buying. Specifically, the fourteen
wines routinely—and legally—faked in this country are Burgundy,
Chablis, Champagne, Chianti, Malaga, Marsala, Madeira, Moselle,
port, Rhine wine, sauternes, haut sauternes, sherry, and tokay.
All have been deemed semigeneric by the Alcohol and Tobacco
Tax and Trade Bureau (known as the TTB), the part of the U.S.

Treasury Department that regulates alcohol labeling and production. The TTB ostensibly does this under the guidelines of the Federal Alcohol Administration Act, which requires that "labeling and advertising of alcohol beverages provide adequate information to the consumer concerning the identity and quality of the product" and issues a mandate to "prevent misleading labeling or advertising that may result in potential consumer deception regarding the product."

No matter how many times I read those two statements that are supposed to govern the TTB, I cannot reconcile them with the ridiculous labeling they allow. Given that the TTB green-lights the sale of Korbel's "Champagne" and Gallo's "Burgundy," plus hundreds of similarly misleading products, it is pretty clear the bureau is flagrantly breaking both of the rules under which it is supposed to operate.

Few, if any, wines on the list has suffered as much as Chianti, the original "jug wine," which boomed in popularity after Americans returned home from Europe at the end of World War II with a newfound love of vino. This fueled a spike in demand that was met with a supply of exceptionally low-quality products, both from Italy and made domestically. In California, some wineries allowed customers to bring in bottles or containers and cheaply fill them from bulk tanks. In slang, this product became known as "Chianti," regardless of what kind of wine it was. In this case, the Italian wine industry's own lack of oversight and regulations helped open the door to low-quality fakes by allowing low-quality real and fake wines made in Italy. The country's wine business suffered from corruption, and when postwar demand grew, some producers simply "extended" their Chianti by adding cheaper southern Italian wines.

While the general structure for winemaking in Tuscany's Chianti region, in northern Italy, was laid out in 1716, it wasn't until

1996 that rules were sufficiently strengthened to provide consumer confidence. Among other upgrades, these legal changes introduced a new higher classification, Chianti Superiore. Today all Chianti is subject to Italian DOC and DOCG regulations, and even a very basic twelve-dollar bottle with a DOC sticker is a pretty reliable wine for the price, made from 100 percent sangiovese grapes grown in a top-rated vineyard region. The same cannot be said for the five-liter box of California-made Franzia "Chianti," the equivalent of nearly seven bottles selling for less than three dollars each.

Tuscany is not only one of the top wine regions on earth; it is also one of the greatest food regions. It is probably for this reason that Chianti has developed over the centuries to be one of the very best food wines, almost a no-brainer choice for pairing with heavier meals, Italian or otherwise. Chianti is the only choice to accompany the olive-oil-soaked, fire-kissed *bistecca alla fiorentina*, the signature steak dish of those parts. Tuscany is simply a spectacular tourism destination, and if I had to pick one last place to visit outside this country, one totally epic dream trip, I might well go back there, with the preserved medieval hill towns, fragrant olive trees, rich art and history, and wonderful climate. But the entire glorious region still has a dark shadow cast over it by America's bad "Chianti" era.

"Now, here's a hard wine to sell. Call it sangiovese and people don't know what you're talking about. Say it's a California version of Italy's famous Chianti, and people think you mean cheap, fruitless battery acid poured from straw-covered flasks into thimble-size glasses in pizza joints," wrote Fred Tasker for the *Chicago Tribune*. Fortunately, the oversized straw-covered bottles of low-quality domestic "Chianti" he was referring to, popular in the 1960s and '70s, have largely disappeared. But the damage has been done, and those infamous jug wines made a laughing stock out of real

Chianti, the reason some folks who lived through those days still won't drink the excellent real thing.

Chianti winemakers have undoubtedly been hurt by our domestic imitations for decades, and this continues today—few consumers who turn the spigot on a cheap box of imitation Chianti are likely to be so impressed that they run out and buy a pricier bottle of the real thing. Fortunately, consumers have become more educated and many copycats have gone by the wayside, while almost all quality domestic producers who have embraced the lovable characteristics of Chianti are labeling their bottles as the varietal, sangiovese. Like Champagne, the general rule of thumb is any domestic winery using the terms *Chianti, Burgundy, Chablis,* or others is probably of such low quality it should be skipped over.

Holdouts include producers such as California's Carlo Rossi, which bottles its "Chianti' in just three sizes: 1.5 liters, 3 liters, and a whopping 4 liters, hard to even pour because it is so heavy. Not surprisingly, Carlo Rossi is part of Ernest & Julio Gallo of Hearty Burgundy fame, and its jug lineup also includes several other geographically protected wines on the TTB's semigeneric hit list, including Burgundy, Rhône, and Chablis. According to the *San Francisco Chronicle,* Rossi's "Burgundy" is "a classic example of California jug wine, complete with a '100 percent grape wine' guarantee." I know I'll sleep better at night knowing that the wine is not made from soy beans.

My friend Dan Dunn is one of the leading experts on the American winemaking industry, especially at the big-picture level. A longtime wine and spirits journalist, author, and former host of the Sirius Satellite Radio show *The Imbiber,* Dunn has explored American winemaking from one end to the other, quite literally. For his most recent book, *American Wino,* Dunn took a several-month-long road trip around the country to see the different ways wine is made and perceived in every region, as well as to explore the cultural underpinnings of the domestic wine scene. Starting in Malibu, where he lives, Dan headed north through Pasa Robles and Santa Barbara, then Sonoma and Napa, up into the Pacific Northwest, across the plains and past Mount Rushmore, visiting winemakers in Wyoming and Nebraska and Michigan, on to New York's Finger Lakes region before arriving in northern New England and the wineries of Vermont, New Hampshire, and Maine, where wines are made with hardy grape varieties—as well as from blueberries.

It was at this point in his grand tour that Dan stopped and visited me, and we had lunch at Lou's, a classic diner-style eatery in the Ivy League college town of Hanover, New Hampshire. Along his journey, which had already spanned some sixty-five hundred miles of driving—and he was not yet halfway through—Dan had also decided to check out regional foods and specialties, so I steered him to a plate of buttermilk pancakes with Vermont maple syrup. Over this Real Food, Dan told me about his trip and his upcoming stops, and I asked him his thoughts on the use of protected foreign geographically indicated names in domestic winemaking. He had already visited almost every imaginable type of winery, big and small, corporate and family owned, even one in an Arkansas RV park, so Dan had a pretty clear picture of U.S. wine culture. "No one who cares about what they are making uses these terms; it's just industrial producers who have no other way to get you to buy their products." It is that simple, folks.

From New England, Dan was headed down the length of the East Coast and then back to California across the Deep South, Texas, and the Southwest. He would ultimately arrive home in time to present a seminar on American wine at the prestigious 2015 Pebble Beach Food & Wine festival. On his return leg, one of the stops he was most looking forward to was at Gruet, a revolutionary New Mexico winemaker that, along with California's

Schramsberg, first pioneered excellent domestic sparkling wine many years ago in the unlikeliest of settings, outside Albuquerque. "I just finished another article on domestic sparkling wine," said Dunn, who has written for everyone from *Playboy* to *Food & Wine.* "None of the good producers use the term *Champagne.* That only goes on the crap."

What about the proposition that many top wine names had become generic, the argument made by Congress, the TTB, and winemakers such as Korbel and Gallo? Dunn rolled his eyes and responded, "Ridiculous."

TO BE FAIR, many of these fakes are cheap low-end imitators, and few consumers who consider the price would set high expectations. But that is definitely not the case with the great fortified wines such as port, sherry, and Madeira, which as with real Parmesan cheese, often have fake domestic copies that sell for more than the real thing, and are packaged in more misleading ways.

"Port wine (also known as Vinho do Porto, . . . Porto, and usually simply port) is a Portuguese fortified wine produced exclusively in the Douro Valley in the northern provinces of Portugal," or so says *Wikipedia,* the twenty-first century's source of all factual knowledge. Many wine lovers would agree, except that the word "exclusively" in the definition overlooks all the "port" made in this country, one of the few pirate holdouts. Australia, long a major fake port and sherry producer on par with the United States, abandoned the practice in 2011 as part of its updated labeling requirements based on protecting GIs. "'Port' is a drink defined by its origin in the northern provinces of Portugal, near Porto," explained an Australian food trade publication of the changes. Canada stopped allowing domestic port and sherry at the end of 2013, as part of the Canada–EU Wine and Spirits Agreement. Contrary to what fear-mongering protectionists have claimed would occur from enacting such consumer protections in this country, neither the Australian nor Canadian economies, nor wine industries, have collapsed as a result.

Portugal, along with its neighbor Spain, is a fantastic food and wine destination, but beyond that, these two countries offer something really special to visitors. In Spain, they are called *paradores* and in Portugal *pousadas*, but the concept is essentially identical. Across the length and breadth of both countries, historically important buildings, including palaces, convents, monasteries, castles, mansions, and forts have been converted to small hotels or large inns, all owned by the government. The programs serve two important purposes, protecting and in many cases rescuing these centuries-old structures that otherwise could not afford maintenance and upkeep and offering tourists a distinctly immersive (and affordable) way to explore the countries.

In both cases, the historic hotels can be packaged into routes or circuits by theme or geography, so you can choose a ten-day driving package up the coast of Portugal, or loop through Andalusia in southern Spain, moving from one *pousada* or *parador* to the next. To explore a particular passion, you can opt for preplanned circuits revolving around golf, food, or religious pilgrimage. These hotels are all one of a kind, and there really is nothing like these programs anyplace else. One night my wife and I stayed in a former Portuguese convent, and the ceiling in our bedroom, towering above the four-poster canopy bed, was the highest I've ever seen, two to three stories, and all I could think about was how hard it would be to change the lightbulbs.

Every Portuguese *pousada* includes a restaurant emphasizing local regional dishes, a vital part of the group's cultural mission to showcase each destination's sense of place. We spent two weeks driving around the country, staying only in these historic properties, and at the famous *pousada* in Obidos, a crown jewel of the group, guests come from all over for the signature roast suckling pig with crispy, delicious skin. A UNESCO World Heritage site, this hotel is a sixteenth-century castle built right into the medieval city walls. After your pork, you can work off the meal with a stroll atop Obidos's high fortified exterior, literally a walk around town. It's a magnificent place. At another *pousada*, the regional specialty was translated as "chicken in red sauce." When my wife asked for more detail, the waitress beamed with enthusiasm and civic pride, and nearly shouted at us with glee that it was "chicken cooked in its own blood." To my wife's credit, she ordered it.

The *pousada* in Oporto, long the seat of the port wine trade, is in the waterfront Freixo Palace, a baroque civil monument built in 1742, complete with extensive formal gardens. As with the champagne houses of Reims and Épernay, aging is done in the city, but much of the actual production takes place in the countryside, in this case the Duoro River Valley. The barrels of port are then shipped by boat, in traditional craft that look like Viking ships specifically designed to hold casks, to the grand port houses in Oporto, where they are bottled and aged. One venerable port house after another is lined up along the waterfront of Oporto, with names like Graham's, Fonseca, and Dow's, and almost all welcome visitors. From the Pousada do Porto Freixo Palace Hotel, guests can simply walk down the street and visit port houses, enjoying a wide array of tours and tastings.

Port, sherry, and Madeira, all in the same general family of fortified wines, are unusually complex to produce, as different from other still wines as Champagne is. They are also inseparable from the local culture. While wine has been produced for as long or longer in other places, Portugal's Douro Valley was defined and protected as an appellation in 1756, making it the oldest official winemaking region in the world. Here, every step, from the varietals allowed to labeling rules, has been under the strict control of the Instituto dos Vinhos do Douro e Porto since its formation in 1932 and, before that, according to the 1756 regulations.

There are close to a hundred approved grape varieties in the region, but most are in tiny production, and red ports, by far the most popular style, generally feature five to eight grapes. Only one of these, tempranillo, is a recognizable wine varietal elsewhere, as the heart and soul of Spain's famous Rioja. Because the steep slopes above the river where grapes are grown are hot during the day and much cooler at night, over the centuries the farmers of the Douro Valley have developed a system of small terraced vineyard plots, which helps the soil retain heat at night, but also makes mechanization virtually impossible. As a result, pruning and picking are done by hand, and laboriously, with a lot of climbing up and down, just like in the eighteenth century. The terrain here is similar to that of the more visited Amalfi Coast in Italy, where gardens and vineyards are also terraced into the steep hillsides. While beautiful, my first thought upon visiting the Duoro Valley was, why here when there are so many much easier and more productive places to farm? The answer is simple: because this is where these native grapes grow best, which is why they are found here in the first place.

The port-making process starts by crafting traditional still wine from the indigenous grape varieties, but that's just the first step. Next, aguardente, a higher-alcohol spirit in the brandy family, made from the distillation of grapes, is added. This addition of higher-alcohol spirits is what makes port (and sherry and Madeira) "fortified wines," but it is not done simply to make them stronger. Rather, it stops the fermentation of the wine in its tracks, killing the yeast before it can consume all the sugar, leaving the wine sweeter and higher proof. Called mutage, this is the crucial step that makes them a distinctive category.

As a result, port, sherry, and Madeira look and taste different from other still wines, but they also last almost indefinitely. Because fermentation is stopped, the wine does not convert to vinegar over time, and it is possible to still open and enjoy bottles from the nineteenth century. Furthermore, most styles can be uncorked and then left open for long periods, a year or more. In this regard, fortified wines behave more like whiskey or brandy, where you can pour an after-dinner drink, put the cork back in, and have the next glass six months later. Don't try that with your zinfandel. I've got a bottle of Fonseca 2008 Late Bottle Vintage Port on my bar right now that I can't even remember when I opened, but it's still drinking just fine.

The process of making real port is laborious, but the results justify the effort. In its 2014 annual "best" issue, *Wine Spectator* magazine named the Dow 2011 Vintage Port the best Wine of the Year, with the highest score of any wine on the planet—99 on its 100-point scale. While quite an accomplishment, ports did not stop there: they took three of the top five spots, against every other style of wine made anywhere, with two other ports fetching 97 points. These three ports each outperformed every wine made in the United States or France at any price. As the magazine wrote, "The wine stands as a monument to quality and the modernization of the Douro over the past two decades, and a total of six Portuguese wines are ranked in the Top 100 of 2014, capping the nation's best performance to date. Like all ports, Dow's Vintage Port 2011 hails from the Douro River Valley in north central Portugal." But don't tell that to the port counterfeiters in New York and California, none of whom got anywhere near such accolades for their fakes.

There are several diverse styles of port, including the much less common white port, which usually has bit of a greenish tint and is traditionally an aperitif, served cold. Red ports are divided into ruby or tawny, the latter being allowed to oxidize into a brownish

color. Tawny ports are sold by age, like many whiskies, and can officially be labeled as ten-, twenty-, thirty-, or forty-year-old varieties,
but unlike Scotch, the age is an average of the components, not a
minimum. Rubies do not have specific ages, yet include the youngest and oldest ports and come in several tiers. Simple "ruby" is
the most like nonfortified red wines, fresher and fruitier, blended
from different vintages, and aged the least. "Late bottle vintage" is
a class of ruby port made from a single harvest and aged four to six
years, basically a less expensive way to get the rich, complex flavor
associated with "vintage" port. Vintage port is made only in exceptional harvest years, an average of three times each decade, and
solely from grapes picked that year. Because vintage ports can last
more than century, older bottles from years like 1966 make great
birthday gifts—as long as the person on your gift list happened to
be born in the same year as a stellar harvest in the Duoro.

Madeira is Portugal's other great fortified wine, made only in
the mid-Atlantic Madeira island archipelago (and knocked off in
Texas and California). It is similar to port, with one unusual and
important exception: it is heated during its initial production to
give it an even longer, sturdier shelf life. Back in the age of sail,
Madeira was the last European seaport for many long voyages,
the final chance to resupply, and the wine was created specifically
as a hardy stuff that could survive the extremes of tropical heat.
Island winemakers invented the heating process to make bottles
more stable.

Two hundred years before the Judgment of Paris jolted American winemaking, when the Founding Fathers toasted the signing
of the Declaration of Independence in 1776, they didn't pour
Champagne or Bordeaux or even rum, the most popular tipple
in colonial times, but rather Madeira. The drink has fallen out
of fashion here in the intervening centuries, even more so than
port or sherry, but I made a special trip to try some in Florida.

The legendary Bern's Steakhouse in Tampa, one of the nation's most iconic restaurants (its salad dressing is sold in supermarkets), has what is arguably the best wine program of any eatery in the country—if not the world—and certainly the best dessert wine list. It also has excellent dry-aged steaks, at prices significantly lower than peers' in New York, Chicago, or Vegas, making Bern's a top wine and steak lovers' road trip destination.

Bern's has a layout I have never seen in another restaurant: you eat dinner at a normal table downstairs, and when your main course is done, your entire party adjourns to an intimate booth upstairs for dessert and/or after-dinner drinks. A huge top floor is divided into these enclaves, laid out like library stacks, so many of them that it is easy to get lost if you visit the restroom. Because of the self-contained privacy of each room, there is a phone on the wall for calling in orders. The phone-book-sized wine lists—separate ones for dinner and dessert—include hundreds of after-dinner wines, with several dozen ports and an equal number of Madeiras. Many of these, even the much older ones, are available by the glass, a rare luxury, and after I gorged myself on Bern's luscious beef, I had a glass of Madeira from 1850, the oldest wine I have ever tasted—by more than a century (they serve even earlier offerings, but it was as far back in time as my budget could travel). They also package ports, sherries, and Madeira in a number of tasting flights, both by age and style, and if you ever want to sample an array of fortified wines, or any kinds of wines, Bern's is the place. But you still have to be careful—the huge list unfortunately also includes several fake "ports" from the United States. At least all the sherry is real.

Sherry is made in its namesake Andalusian town of Jerez (sherry is the municipality's anglicization), in hot southern Spain. Unlike port, sherry can only be made from three grape varietals, all little known and indigenous to the region. Like the specific mold found in the caves where Roquefort cheese is produced, one reason sherry has always been made here is because of a locally occurring wild natural yeast, flor, indispensable to the wine. All sherry is made from white grapes, and many styles are white, like manzanilla and fino, while others, namely oloroso and amontillado, are allowed to oxidize in wooden casks, giving them a tawny or golden color (the latter was key to the buried alive revenge plot in the famous Edgar Allen Poe horror story "The Cask of Amontillado").

The sherry process starts like port but gets even more complicated due to the *solera* aging system, which more closely resembles the production of fine balsamic vinegar in Italy's Modena than other wines. The *solera* system is a method of fractional aging in which liquids are moved from one barrel (the youngest) in an array of many to the next without emptying them, and so on. Each barrel has an increasingly older blend, and some fraction of the oldest wine always remains present in the final barrel. As a result, every bottle contains a trace of the original wine first put into the casks, and sherries do not have vintage years. There are still many sherries being produced in Jerez today, even as you read this, containing wines that predate American winemaking altogether.

The intricate process requires the climate of Andalusia, the local yeast, and the indigenous grape varietals found here—none of which are used in the production of the "sherry" from Brotherhood winery in New York State. The Korbel of the East Coast, Brotherhood has two important distinctions: first, it claims to be the oldest winery in the entire United States, since 1839. Second, it makes a staggering amount of different wines, both bizarre and copycat. The former category includes such offerings such as Ghengis Khan, a "blend of high-quality Korean ginseng with a sherry base." The name ignores the fact that Khan never set foot in Korea or Spain, the only place actual sherry is made. Other oddities include Sheba T'ej, from an old Ethiopian recipe made from honey; a take on mead simply called Mead; Señor Sangria; and Happy Bitch, a "perfectly balanced Rose." It's a bizarre catalog that also includes fake versions of "port," "sherry" and "champagne." The Brotherhood website boasted of once having 600,00 [*sic*] bottles of "Champagne" aging in its cellars, a figure that apparently is to real numbers what this wine is to real Champagne.

Back on the West Coast, the faux Champagne powerhouse Korbel also makes "sherry." To add insult to injury, the winery reserves about half of its annual production, blends this into the next year's batch, and then has the audacity to claim of this two-step process that "this 'solera' blending method is traditional for sherry, and is an important part of the style of sherry we produce," despite the fact that it bears almost no resemblance to the actual solera process. Korbel's "port" is made, like some of its "Champagne," mainly from zinfandel, a grape that cannot be used in the production of either real wine.

But while Korbel's ersatz Champagne sells for considerably less than the real thing, the "port" and "sherry" are comparable in price to the real wines of those names, and in wine and food, price often drives perceptions of quality and authenticity. In fact, Korbel's "port" fetches twice as much as bottles from respected authentic producers like Croft, Warre's, or Cockburn's—without any of the strict quality control and oversight of how it is made. There is almost no bad real port, so why would anyone pass up the genuine article whose quality is virtually guaranteed, for a far more expensive, younger imitation? Because they were duped. There really is no other explanation. But it gets worse.

As wine expert Dan Dunn pointed out, in the case of faux Champagne, Burgundy, Chablis, and Chianti, it is typically only the lowest-quality producers using these misleading terms. Not so for fortified wines. Otherwise respected winery Rodney Strong makes a vintage version called A True Gentleman's Port in a fancy bottle, which costs more than many real ports, and several other name wineries do the same. Prager Winery Port Works is located on the main tourist drag in Napa's St. Helena, the heart of American winemaking, alongside Duckhorn, Charles Krug, Raymond, Rutherford, and many other venerable wineries. Having visited the tasting room, it's clear to me that most of the customers, presented with a long list of "port" styles and ages in nice bottles at high prices, have no idea that these products would be impounded as counterfeits almost anywhere in the world.

Prager's cheapest bottle costs more than almost every twenty-year-old real port on the market—but is much younger. Prager's ten-year-old tawny costs two to three times what most acclaimed ten-year-old tawny ports cost. Prager's most expensive "port" is about the same price as the 99-point Dow 2011 Vintage Port rated the single best wine on Earth, while nothing Prager makes cracked the list. I tried some of these, and while they are distinctly portlike, there is no scenario for me under which a single bottle would be better than a substantially cheaper standout real port—let alone three times better. It's not like you can't easily buy the real thing, for less, so there is no void these copycats fill.

Ironically, even as Napa-based imitators like Prager and Korbel continue to knock off established foreign brands, their neighbors have joined in a heated fight to protect such names—including their own. Napa is the most respected and best-known appellation in the entire New World, and the advantage to Napa winemakers is dramatic—on average consumers will pay a hefty six dollars a bottle more for wines from Napa than other wines from California, which in turn command higher prices than wines made in the forty-nine other U.S. states. Considering that this Napa premium almost doubles the average price of a bottle of American wine, this is a huge advantage for the region. Because the Napa name carries such clout, it has been knocked off, both here and abroad.

Patterned loosely on France's AOC system, the American Viticultural Areas (AVAs) were established in 1978. The sole requirement for AVA labeling is that 85 percent of the grapes used be grown there. Likewise, vintage wines (those bearing a year of origin) in the United States must be made "mostly" with grapes from the listed vintage. Both rules sharply contrast the 100 percent requirement of just about every other top wine region in the world.

Yet despite the rules, several large and less expensive industrial producers like Napa Ridge and Napa Creek continued selling non-Napa wines under the name. Invoking the same protection used by folks like Korbel, they claimed that federal law effectively grandfathered them protection for their use of "Napa" as a semigeneric term because it was in use prior to changes in labeling laws. Bronco Wines owns both brands and lost a series of court cases, which ruled that California state law could preempt federal law and require the use of the 85 percent minimum even in grandfathered labels. After this, Napa Ridge began using Napa grown fruit. Bronco, which also makes the best-selling (more than three million bottles to date) Charles Shaw wines—aka "Two Buck Chuck"—exclusively for Trader Joe's stores, had previously pleaded no contest to charges of mislabeling grapes as a more expensive variety. Whether it's red grapes, red wine, or red snapper, it's a constant reminder what a confusing food world we live in.

While domestic imitators of the Napa name have largely been cleaned up, more important to Napa winemakers is defending their name globally. Napa wines were the first American product to receive official geographically indicated protection from the European Union. But outside the European Union, it is a different story, and thanks in large part to the U.S. government's unilateral refusal to respect most foreign brands, real Napa wines are only secure in about a dozen other countries. Napa Valley Vintners has been hard at work on this issue for decades but has had just piecemeal success and only received protection in China in 2012. Wine production in China has exploded in recent years, and it is already the fifth-leading producer, on pace to become the single largest winemaking nation in the world by 2018.

Napa most recently negotiated exclusivity for its own name, from of all places, Norway. It's not like Norway produces a lot of wine, but Norwegians do have among the highest per capita income and drink a fair amount. Until very recently they could import wines from elsewhere and relabel them "Napa," or simply import fake "Napa" wines from other unregulated countries—meaning most countries—which would almost always be less expensive than the real thing.

In 2005, representatives from major wine regions around the world gathered in the Napa Valley to sign the Joint Declaration to Protect Wine Place Names & Origin. Besides Napa, U.S. regions looking to protect their brands included Washington's Walla Walla Valley, Oregon's Willamette Valley, New York's Long Island, and California's Sonoma, Paso Robles, and Santa Barbara. Morgen McLaughlin, executive director of the Santa Barbara Vintners, explained that "winemakers worldwide know that when it comes to wine, location matters. The integrity of wine place names is a fundamental tool for consumers to identify the wines of great winegrowing regions." Foreign signatories included Porto, Jerez-Xérès-Sherry, Chianti, Rioja, Burgundy/Chablis, Bordeaux, and Champagne.

"Consumers worldwide need to know where their wine comes from," said Sam Heitner, director of the Office of Champagne, USA, who added, "Place names like Napa Valley and Champagne are integral to consumer understanding and to differentiating wines from different regions . . . we believe it is imperative that adequate safeguards be put in place to protect wine growing place names and stand with Napa Valley." This was a gracious gesture on behalf of real producers, given that as he said this he was standing just a few miles from some the largest producers of fake Champagne, port, and sherry in the world.

Centuries of refinement have gone into the production of real wines of high quality. There is no need to settle for imitations as long as you know what to look for.

## ✣ RENOWNED FOREIGN WINE REGIONS

There are a handful of places that have been associated with making excellent wine for so long that they have become household names. As a result, they are "semigeneric" in the United States, and neither their names nor American consumers are protected. This is not rocket science—you only need to know a few names, and chances are you already do. If you see any of these on the label, look closely for the country of origin, and if it is from the States put it back: Champagne, Chianti, Burgundy, Chablis, port, sherry, Madeira, sauternes. You do not have to worry about other top regions that came to prominence among American wine drinkers more recently, because these are protected here, including Spain's Rioja; Italy's Barbera d'Alba, Barolo, and Brunello di Montalcino; New Zealand's Marlborough; Australia's Barossa Valley; and France's Sancerre, Rhone, and Bordeaux.

## ✣ QUALITY DESIGNATIONS

Many European nations give seals of approval to wines made certain ways from the best vineyards. These are typically marks of reliable quality and authenticity: in France, AOC; in Italy, DOC and DOCG; and in Spain, DOC and VP (Vino de Page, or single vineyard/estate wines). Likewise, domestic wines from approved AVAs are allowed to carry an AVA designation or the words "Appellation of Wine Origin" for regions such as California's Pasa Robles. However, this just requires that 85 percent of the grapes come from the

AVA. It's better to look for "Estate Bottled" on domestic wine, as federal law states that 100 percent of the grapes must come from the AVA. If a particular vineyard, farm or ranch is named, 95 percent of the grapes must have been grown on that property. Napa Valley Vintners has also created its own higher standard, a seal proclaiming "100% Napa Valley Grown."

## ❋ MERITAGE

Owned and controlled by the Meritage Alliance, this term can only be used on blended wines made in the traditional Bordeaux-style. All meritage, red or white, must use only the designated Bordeaux grape varietals, and contain two or more, with no grape comprising more than 90 percent. Meritage wines are produced around the world, and the word is a good indicator of the grapes used and the style.

## JOINT DECLARATION TO PROTECT WINE PLACE AND ORIGIN

Whereas, it is generally acknowledged that there are a handful of truly extraordinary places on earth from which great wine is consistently produced.

Whereas, the names of these places are printed on labels side-by-side with the names of the producers to identify the origin of the wine.

Whereas, wine, more than any other beverage, is valued based on its association to its place of origin—and with good reason.

Whereas, even before modern technology allowed us to tie specific definitions to the soils, terrain, and climates of noted wine regions, winemakers were drawn to these special places.

Whereas, the names of these places are familiar, and synonymous with quality.

Whereas, we respectfully submit that the place where wine is grown plays a very important role in a consumer's selection process.

Whereas, we are furthermore united in our belief that the geographic place names of wine regions are the sole birthright of the grapes that are grown there, and when these names appear on wines that do not contain fruit from that region, they lose their integrity and their relevance, becoming merely words.

Therefore, be it resolved that we, as some of the world's leading wine regions, join together in supporting efforts to maintain and protect the integrity of these place names, which are fundamental tools for consumer identification of great winegrowing regions and the wines they produce.

# 10. The Other Red (and White) Meat?

Suddenly this hippie-food fad was mainstream . . . Moreover, marketers had a fresh dictionary of buzzwords, like "free-range," "hormone free," "organic" and "natural." As a journalist, I was fascinated with the new lingo. From a consumer vantage point it was often confusing, deceptive and ridiculous.

—KIMBERLY LORD STEWART, *Eating between the Lines*

I guarantee no other rancher you visit is going to open the gate and let you pet his bulls," said Leo Causland. The full-time architect and part-time cattle rancher, owner of High Country Highlands in Silverthorne, Colorado, was right. These two bulls, each tipping the scales at well over a thousand pounds, were the first I'd laid hands on, let alone gotten near. As Causland had promised, they truly were gentle giants, leaning in with their heads to be scratched like a dog and gently eating veggie pellets from the palm of my hand. They were decidedly petlike, despite the broad intimidating horns and thick, wild, hairy coats that made them look more like yaks than most cattle. But that was why I was able to stand there petting these behemoths and posing for pictures with them—because they weren't most cattle; they were Scottish Highland cattle.

Causland got married in Scotland in 2000 and, while on his honeymoon, first laid eyes on the odd looking beasts, a traditional fixture of the rugged Scottish countryside for hundreds years. Having only been exposed to American breeds, he was curious, as they are one of the few varieties where both males and females sport matching horns. An amiable, outgoing son of the Old West, he approached local farmers, made inquiries, and liked what he heard. "The Scots told me that they are really smart, friendly, and long lived, but also hardy and very low fat, 92 percent beef." Causland, who was already raising cattle as a sideline hobby/business with a partner, decided to give Highlands a try.

"We started with four animals, and all the attributes they told me were true. They are just perfectly suited to this environment. We are at about nine thousand feet here and get a lot of snow, and all the other people who raise cattle have to move them in winter, but not us. These guys stay here all year round." Because they have such thick, warm coats, they don't grow the protective outer band of insulating fat most cattle do, so while they are only eight percent fat, which is low, it is all found in the internal marbling. The result? "It's not dry like bison, and it's different from other beef, almost sweet. They are delicious."

Causland now raises the breed exclusively. He is president of the Mountain States Chapter of the American Highland Cattle Association and has sold breeding stock to farmers all over the country, but these friendly creatures remain very much a niche specialty, and he can't understand why.

I had been driving around Colorado for ten days writing an agri-tourism article for *USA Today* about artisanal cattle and buffalo ranches travelers could visit. When Causland found out that he was my last stop and that I was flying home that evening, he insisted I take a steak with me. We jumped into his pickup truck and drove to his house, a few miles from the ranch, where a fold of newborn calves and their moms were grazing in his yard—Highlands have their own group term, unlike the "herds" most cattle come in. Because of their size and horns, grown Highlands have nothing to fear from predators, but calves are susceptible to coyotes, so he keeps the babies close at hand. After petting some of the calves, with wary moms watching him closely, he ducked inside the house and returned with a strip steak from his personal freezer. It was such a gracious gesture and such an unusual piece of meat that I stopped at a supermarket to buy a disposable insulated cooler bag, which I stuffed with ice packs for the trip home. Despite my best efforts, it was half thawed by the time I got back to the East Coast, so I ate it that very night, recalling Causland's parting words: "You are going to be sending me an email telling me that it was best steak you ever tasted. You'll see."

Well, as much as I enjoyed his company and meeting the Highlands, which was a lot, I have to say it wasn't the best steak I've ever had, but it was a damn good steak, much better than most. If you told me that all the beef I could eat for the rest of my life would be Highland, I wouldn't fret. I wasn't especially surprised, because the Scots have been atop the beef world for just about forever, and being partially of Scottish descent—I've got the clan tartan head covers on my golf clubs to prove it—I'm proud to say that pretty much everything we think of as American beef comes to us by way of Scotland. I'm just not sure the Scots would be proud of what we've done to their gift.

In his aptly titled book *Steak: One Man's Search for the World's Tastiest Piece of Beef,* Canadian food writer Mark Schatzker explores everything related to the taste of steak, including the science of marbling, corn fed versus grass fed, and breeds. In search of the world's best beef—a quest spurred in part by the surprising taste-lessness of apparently well-marbled American industrial feedlot meat—he travels to Texas and Oklahoma, to the grassy pampas of Argentina, to France, Italy, and Japan, but—spoiler alert—his par-agon of steak, the closest to the ideal of red meat perception, is in

Scotland. Schatzker goes to try the country's much more famous Aberdeen Angus, but to his chagrin, falls for the furry Highland.

Having just tried the Highland, I set out to do this taste test in reverse and try the real Aberdeen Angus on my own recent visit to Scotland. I started my journalistic career largely writing about golf, a topic I'm still passionate about, so I have spent quite a bit of time in Scotland. Like our favorite beef cattle, Angus, America's love affair with golf is a bastardized version of the Scottish original. My previous trips were mainly thirty-six-hole per day marathons of every daylight hour, followed by pub meals of fish and chips or sausages washed down with pints and drams, and the odd distillery tour squeezed in.

This was a very short visit with just one free night in Edinburgh before touring Nike's new state-of-the-art golf club fitting and instruction center, so I made it my mission to spend that night in pursuit of the perfect piece of Aberdeen Angus. After all, I'd done Japan, gorged on the many varied cuts in Argentina, tried Charolais in Paris and the famed Chianina breed in Tuscany. I've had enough grass-fed Vermont beef to fill a freezer and enough corn-fed domestic beef to stop a heart. And thanks to Leo Causland, I'd recently had my first Highland steak. The major omission on my carnivore's résumé was true Aberdeen angus, and while angus is by far the most common source for steak in our country, this is a whole different animal, so to speak.

After consulting with the Scottish Tourist Board and running down various recommendations, I settled on a place in the shadow of Edinburgh Castle called Whiski Rooms, which, not surprisingly, given both its moniker and the fact that this is Scotland, where the brown spirit's very name was derived from ancient Gaelic for "water of life," specializes in whisky. But Whiski Rooms also has an impressive menu, with all meats sourced from award-winning Scottish butcher shop J. Gilmour, a multigenerational family operation that supplies many of Scotland's best eateries. J. Gilmour gets the Whiski Room's Aberdeen Angus from a nearby, grass-finished family farm. Since I had made my plans to eat this particular steak in this particular place many weeks in advance, it would be fair to say my expectations were high. It would also be fair to say they were not met. It was just fine, better than average but not better than average for a good steakhouse, and a far cry from its Highland cousin. I could make better at home.

I've spent a lot of time, probably too much time, pondering the nature of steak and the notion of the "best steak," which I've come to regard as an illusion, a quest akin to tilting at windmills. Yet I have not stopped thinking about beef, and especially about the differences among steak-loving cultures, which go far beyond breeds. Given that mixing meat with fire is the oldest and most universal form of human cookery, and not overly complicated, you'd think it would have become somewhat standardized. It has not. Cultural differences divide us sharply over what cuts to eat, cooking methods, temperature, the age at which cattle should be consumed, seasonings, and sides. The Italian notion of pouring olive oil over sliced T-bones is brilliant and delicious but shocking and outlandish in places that do not have this tradition, which means everywhere except Italy (and my house). Then again, the Italians would be just as shocked by the notion of smothering perfectly good beef in ketchup.

But the single biggest cultural beef divide between the United States and most of the rest of the world is not breeds, cuts, cooking styles, or how we eat steak, but rather it's how the steak eats. I now only buy truly natural, grass-fed beef, or to be more precise, naturally raised, grass-finished beef. In the simplest terms, I want cattle that has never been given unnecessary drugs and has eaten only grass—its whole life. But like so many other foodstuffs that involve labels, definitions, and especially profits, there is nothing simple about buying meat in America.

*Grass fed* was briefly defined, thanks to a USDA rule change in 2007, but this new, stricter label was rescinded in early 2016. Before the change, the term was often interpreted by meat producers as cattle that had eaten some grass during its lifetime, which is to say all cattle, since even the most industrial feedlots begin newborns with easily digestible grass before switching them to inedible force-fed diets. As demand for grass-fed beef rose, the label was increasingly slapped on all sorts of meat. The just-abolished rules dictated that 100 percent of the animal's diet be fresh or dried forage (hay), but now the term is once again part of a Wild West of undefined claims, though the USDA does still require labels making a "100% Grass Fed" claim to meet the higher all-grass standard. But what most consumers associate with the notion is what ranchers like Causland do, allowing cattle to roam free, eating actual vitamin- and nutrient-rich grass (this is called pasture-raised beef, though there is no regulatory definition of the term). Further, most ranchers who have adopted pasture-raised practices also opt out of drugs. But the USDA standard never required the animal to ever leave its stall or actually eat growing grass at all. A steer can be penned inside and fed exclusively hay its whole life, along with antibiotics, steroids, and hormones, a feedlot equivalent for "grass-fed" beef.

Conventional wisdom in the U.S. cattle industry has long been that an all-grass diet does not result in enough marbling, so true grass-fed beef does not taste as good. "Grass-fed beef is more natural but leaner and less intrinsically luscious. I like the flavor, but I don't think it's as complex," Steven Raichlen, the world's foremost authority on all things grilled and smoked, told me. A graduate of two of the most famous cooking schools on earth, Le Cordon

Bleu and La Varenne, Raichlen has literally traveled the earth, several times over, to see how cultures eat and cook steak, and is the author of nearly thirty books on cooking with fire. The host of three popular PBS television shows, *BBQ University, Primal Grill,* and *Project Smoke,* he has won five coveted James Beard Awards and a Julia Child Award and was named Cooking Teacher of the Year by *Bon Appétit* magazine.

"Grain-fed beef generally tastes better, with better marbling, richer mouthfeel and a more complex, well-rounded flavor. But grain, of course, is not a steer's natural diet, which leads the majority of growers to add antibiotics to the feed. What I do like about grass-fed is eating an animal raised on a healthier, more natural diet. It's a moral dilemma. Given the choice between factory feed-lot beef or tofu, I'd rather eat tofu," he said.

Raichlen proposed a middle ground that is now used by many so-called natural ranchers, which is to let the cattle eat grass their whole lives until shortly before slaughtering, then feed them grain the last few weeks to increase their marbling, which also raises their USDA grade and commercial value. "I see no harm in this as long as no antibiotics are involved."

This practice is called grass-fed, grain-finished beef, and many in the cattle business agree with Raichlen, including otherwise well-meaning family farmers. For more than a year, I bought "grass-fed" beef from a local ranch at my nearby farmers' market in Vermont. I would ride my bike past the pastures and see the cattle grazing freely. But one week I specifically asked the owners, who plainly stated that their farm follows the practice Raichlen described, finishing the mostly grass-reared cattle on grain to increase marbling and flavor. This happened to be a clear violation of USDA standards for what can be called grass-fed beef. It illustrates a rare case in which you are more likely to get sold Fake Food by local small producers than big corporate ones, because they fly under the radar of enforcement. Despite such farmers' market mislabeling, only producers who go through the USDA's optional process verification are now allowed to use one meaningful term, *100% grass fed.*

The problem with the grain-finished marbling theory is that it is off base in a few different ways. While the grain will drive up the USDA marbling scores, this ranking is not nearly as related to flavor as most people think but is based instead on appearance. Whereas the Japanese graders rate the quality of fat, we consider only quantity. The steak I got from Causland tasted far better than most USDA Prime beef I have eaten. So did most of the steak I had in Argentina, and much in Europe, all grass fed. I now buy my beef from a different Vermont farm that does only grass, and it tastes better than its predecessor. It's also healthier, and many believe that all the good done by the grass diet over a steer's lifetime is suddenly undone by the final few weeks of grain finishing.

When I sought out France's most famous native breed, the fine-dining restaurant I visited offered both standard French beef and an upgrade to the coveted Charolais, at a price premium, which I paid. The steak was not much to look at, gray and sinewy, not the single continuous slab of meat we usually get here, but rather a jigsaw puzzle of smaller pieces of meat divided by bands of connective tissue. It was also hard to cut, even with the sharp classic French Laguiole steak knife provided, and required a bit of sawing. Given this work and the fact that the French serve their steaks barely cooked, either *bleu* (literally so rare it's still bluish in the middle) or *saignant* (bloody), the meat itself, when I finally got it in my mouth, was shockingly tender, much more so than it looked, felt, or logically could be.

When it comes to steak attributes, tenderness is not one I normally prize, because it usually comes at the expense of flavor. But in some secret fashion, the Charolais managed to match its consistency with rich beefy flavor. I give it a big thumbs-up. The breed is raised here in the States in boutique fashion, but in France, Boeuf de Charolles has an AOC designation and all the regulations that come with that. This includes rules on what these cattle can eat, which is grass in summer and hay in winter, both only from the defined region. There are some mineral supplements allowed, but silage (a fermented liquid stew of grains like corn, which cattle do not eat in the natural world, supplemented with lots of antibiotics and hormones) is specifically excluded.

Charolais is not unusual in this respect, since pretty much all the beef in France is grass fed, also the norm in the rest of western Europe and the British Isles, as well as for beef-producing giants Argentina, Uruguay, Australia, and New Zealand. Even the "regular" steak for eight euros less was grass fed, and it may not be a coincidence that save only the tiny, remote island nation of Kiribati, France has the lowest rate of heart disease of any country on earth. It's certainly not a coincidence that the rate of coronary disease in the world's two largest beef consuming nations, Argentina and Uruguay, is appreciably lower than ours.

Despite a dramatic drop in meat eating in recent years that allowed Uruguay to sneak ahead and steal its longstanding per capita beef consumption title, Argentines, now in second place, still put away a handy 129 pounds per year per person (the historic high, a half century ago, was 222 pounds). In beef-famished comparison, the average American, with all his drive-thrus, Whoppers, and Big Macs, scarfs down just a paltry 57.5 pounds. The ability of the South American populace to consume such huge amounts of red meat without health repercussions might well be tied to both countries' devotion to grass-fed, drug-free, open-range cattle. All the countries that primarily eat grass-fed beef have much better numbers than ours, including Australia, Italy, France, Ireland, New Zealand, and even the United Kingdom, with its chip shops and love of all things sausage, fried, and wrapped in pastry. It's the place that invented the breaded, deep-fried Mars bar—yet more beef than fried candy bars are consumed there, and the United Kingdom sits next to Argentina at the low end of the world heart disease scale.

So why aren't we eating more grass-fed beef? The simple answer is money. It costs an estimated 17 percent extra to raise beef on grass than grain, according to USDA documents. Packing cows into indoor feedlots and forcing them to eat silage is cheaper.

Beef gets a bad health rap, despite the fact that humans are by nature designed to eat meat—and have been eating it for longer than most grains and other modern or cultivated foods. But the real problem may not be beef itself but rather our beef. The fat in industrial or feedlot beef—what the industry calls conventional beef, because this modern laboratory experiment has become the norm—is much less healthful than it should be. True grass-fed— and not grain-finished—beef is higher in vitamins A, E, and antioxidants, but most important, it's higher in "good" omega-3 fats and lower in "bad" omega-6 fats.

"When I was in Afghanistan with the [U.S. Army] Rangers, everything was about being the best we could be, moving faster and getting more done. I found that I could move faster by adopting the paleo diet, and I've been eating it ever since. But it has to be the right paleo diet, not just meat—it doesn't work with grain fed supermarket beef, because you are still eating grain," said Casey Cook, a former U.S. Army Special Forces soldier. So named because it mirrors the eating habits of our Stone Age Paleolithic ancestors, this now popular meat-centric diet is high in protein and very low in carbs.

But when Cook returned to Colorado after his service, he faced the same labeling issues and problems buying Real Food that the rest of us do. "None of it means anything, natural, organic, grass fed. It's all bullshit. *Grass fed* just means it ate grass at some point in its life, which every cow does. But then they can be finished on corn or grain, it's just feedlot beef, the nutritional value is terrible. When I left the military, I couldn't find any real grass-finished beef to eat, so I started raising my own. My cows have similar omega-3 to -6 ratios to wild sockeye salmon. You can actually eat the fat, while I wouldn't touch the fat in supermarket beef."

Cook now owns and operates Colorado Sustainable Farms near Boulder and offers tours to interested parties like me. Not far away, at the Sylvan Dale Guest Ranch, overnight guests can get a more complete dude ranch experience, including horseback riding, target shooting, roping, fly fishing, cowboy songs, bonfires, and much more. But what makes Sylvan Dale different from dozens of other similar working guest ranches across the American West is that they also serve lucky visitors real grass-fed beef from the farm as part of their stay. The ranch is owned by a brother and sister and their respective spouses, and the brother, David Jessup, gave me a tour. We had to drive quite a ways out to where the cattle were grazing on open ranchland, just like they would have all across the West a century ago.

Sylvan Dale was begun by Jessup's parents in 1946 and for more than fifty years just raised calves, which were shipped off to industrial cattle feedlots to fatten quickly through the miracles of alien diets and modern pharmaceuticals. But about ten years ago, the siblings noticed growing demand among local consumers— they are just outside of health-obsessed Boulder—for more natural drug-free beef. So they began keeping and raising some animals of their own to butcher and sell locally. Jessup, born and bred a real cowboy, right down to the boots, buckle, and hat, with a taut build and sun-weathered skin, quickly became an ardent student and late convert to grass-fed, truly natural farming. "At first, we used some grain to finish them because that was conventional wisdom, considered 'normal.' But then we really found out about the health benefits of purely grass-fed beef and how much better the kind of fats produced were, even compared to those fed just a small amount of grain. Now we raise all our cattle ourselves, from birth to slaughter, and they eat strictly grass." The problem for consumers is that unlike Cook and Jessup, many farmers still sell beef finished on grain as grass fed.

While the term *100% grass fed* can still be misleading, at least it is legally defined in a way that mostly makes sense, unlike *natural.* To me, there is nothing even remotely natural about beef raised on steady diet of nontherapeutic antibiotics, steroids, hormones, pig's blood, and chicken shit. Nonetheless, this is exactly how much beef cattle is raised, and it all qualifies for the natural label.

More than 80 percent of the antibiotics manufactured in this country—and 95 percent of the class considered "medically important" for treating humans—are not used to treat us, our pets, or to treat anything at all. They are food, fed directly to cattle, pigs, and poultry. In most cases, they are used for two reasons: as a preventive measure so that animals can be kept in conditions and fed things that would otherwise make them sick and as a way to cheaply help them gain weight. It was discovered that when used as a supplement, antibiotics encouraged faster growth—as do growth hormones and steroids, both also widely used in cattle. Hormones and steroids are banned in pig and poultry production.

There is no doubt that the widespread consumption of antibiotic-laden meat is bad for us. Ample evidence fingers this massive drug use in our meat industries as a key contributor to one of the biggest health concerns of the modern era, the rise of drug-resistant bacteria, aka superbugs.

This is not some future science fiction. It is killing people right now—lots of people. The CDC called antibiotic resistance one of the five greatest health threats facing the nation, and new drug-resistant strains are spreading worldwide. According to the CDC, in 2013 antibiotic resistance caused more than two million illnesses, an estimated twenty-three thousand deaths and over $20 million in health care costs in this country. And it's getting worse—quickly. In early 2015, President Obama issued a $1.2 billion National Action Plan for Combating Antibiotic-Resistant Bacteria.

"Most people who say they have not had an antibiotic in years are mistaken. Millions of us are exposed every day," wrote Dr. Martin Blaser, author of *Missing Microbes.* "The antibiotics themselves arrive in our food, particularly in meats, milk, cheeses, and eggs." According to Blaser, FDA rules intended to keep antibiotics out of eggs and other products often do not work, and studies throughout the past two decades have consistently shown that legal antibiotic limits are exceeded about 10 percent of the time, in both meat and related animal products.

Tom Colicchio is one of the most famous award-winning celebrity chefs, and since opening New York's Gramercy Tavern, one of America's best restaurants, more than twenty years ago, he has been on the culinary fast track. He owns or operates two dozen restaurants and a hotel, produces documentaries, writes critically acclaimed cookbooks, serves as head judge on television's *Top Chef,* and is heavily involved with charity efforts. Colicchio is also adamantly against the use of antibiotics in our food supply, and I interviewed him to find out why.

"Nearly three years ago I had neck surgery, and I got an infection while in the hospital. So I did all this research and found that overuse of antibiotics in this country is creating these superbugs immune to drugs, and something as simple a scraped knee can kill people. When you feed antibiotics to animals, the bacteria in their stomach becomes immune, and you can end up creating *E. coli* that if it gets into people causes bacterial infections, it can no longer be treated. We have got to get away from that." As a result, he switched to exclusively antibiotic-free chicken, pork, and beef in his restaurants. He remains a rare exception, though in one refreshing piece of news, fast-food giant McDonald's, the world's largest restaurant chain, announced that by 2017 it will serve only chicken raised without classes of antibiotics used in human medicine.

In addition to drugs, another alarming part of the diet of most of our meat cattle is meat, especially odd since they are herbivores and never, ever eat meat unless it is force-fed to them, which it is. This practice was routine until the FDA discovered that feeding animals to animals was causing outbreaks of BSE—mad cow disease—at which point they banned it. But like so many words related to our food supply that don't mean what they should, the "ban" has many exceptions. It is not only legal to feed our beef the blood, fat, and feces of other animals, it's standard practice.

While the word *natural* can still be slapped on the label of drug-laden, cannibalistic beef, there are some increased protections consumers can look for. In 2009, the USDA defined *naturally raised*, adopting the standards often called never ever three, or NE3. These are what most third parties and other countries trying to define *natural* have agreed on as a basic minimum, and they mean that at no point in its life did the animal consume any antibiotics, any growth promotants, or any animal by-products.

*Natural* used by itself refers to the processing rather than the raising of meat. It legally requires that the labeled product be "minimally processed," a subjective caveat, and contain no artificial ingredients or added colors. In a rather large loophole, this does not include hormones, steroids, or antibiotics, all clearly artificial ingredients not supposed to be found in steak. Here is the main way the USDA defines natural for meat: "All raw single ingredient meat and poultry qualify as natural." In one of the few cases where rules mean what they say, this defines every piece of every animal as natural. Additionally, "certain products labeled as natural may also contain a flavoring solution . . . The amount of solution added to products bearing natural claims is not limited."

So while the current USDA standard for *100% grass fed* does not prohibit drugs or animal by-products, and the naturally raised definition does not prohibit an unnatural diet of grain and silage, labels bearing both claims are pretty close to what consumers such as Tom Colicchio, Casey Cook, and I want to eat. There are also a few viable alternatives. The American Grassfed Association seal is issued by an industry group that requires its like-minded members to feed only grass and never confine cattle or use antibiotics or hormones.

If the drugs and by-products bother you, but like Steven Raichlen and many others, you don't mind grain-fed or grain-finished cattle, you can also look for the labels "USDA Organic," "Niman Ranch," and "Certified Angus Beef Natural" (as opposed to the more common regular Certified Angus Beef), all nationally available. The latter two are brands that require supplier cattle farmers to practice NE3 and feed grass for most of the animal's life. Niman Ranch products are a favorite of chefs and often show up on restaurant menus.

Additionally, the USDA has approved the use of label terms "no hormones administered" for beef and "no antibiotics added" for beef, pork, and chicken. In both cases, sufficient documentation is required of the producer to show that no hormones or antibiotics were ever used in raising the animals. (However, when Tyson, the nation's leading industrial chicken producer, slapped it on birds that had been given antibiotics, the USDA revoked its label approval but allowed them to keep selling the falsely labeled chicken until new labels became available.) On the other hand, terms such as *pasture raised, pasture finished, no additives, no animal by-products, free range, free roaming, green fed, humane,* and *pesticide free* are all allowable—and all totally meaningless.

Hormones and steroids are completely banned in domestic pork and poultry production, but some producers slap a "no hormones added" label on pork and chicken because it has been proven to trick consumers into paying more—and it is technically true. The use of antibiotics is standard in poultry and even more widespread in pigs than cattle. Pigs don't eat grass and are omnivorous foragers, so there is no equivalent of grass-fed pork. The most reliable pork and chicken label is "USDA Organic" (used mainly for meat and much different from the FDA's version of organic), which requires a 100 percent organic diet, no antibiotics (ever), and bans feed made with synthetic pesticides. For poultry shoppers, Smart Chicken is a national brand owned by Tecumseh Poultry, founded in 1998 to fill the void in the quality chicken market. It comes in organic and regular versions, both of which are completely antibiotic and animal by-product free, using a 100 percent vegetarian or 100 percent organic vegetarian diet. I buy Smart Chicken regularly. For pork, the Niman Ranch brand is antibiotic free with a 100 percent vegetarian diet. As for heirloom and heritage breed pigs, they do usually taste better, if they are indeed heirloom and heritage breeds, but these increasingly widely used terms are unregulated.

If memorizing label terms becomes a mind-numbing experience, the quickest and easiest shortcut to idiot-proof shopping for healthful red meat is to buy buffalo. At least until it gets popular enough to be exploited, pretty much all commercial bison operations in the country are free ranging, with no fences, eating an entirely natural diet of grass and forage without drugs. It is arguably better for you than beef anyway, tastes good, and there is no such thing as a bison feedlot (technically for scientists, buffalo means African or water, and ours are all bison, but we've been informally using buffalo as a synonym since the Old West).

Media mogul Ted Turner is one of the nation's largest private landowners and its largest bison rancher, supplying his very good chain of buffalo-centric Ted's Montana Grill restaurants. The next largest single herd can be found at Colorado's Zapata Ranch, owned by the Nature Conservancy. Half the vast property is used for grass-fed cattle and half for bison, and when I visited it was easy to see the difference. The bison, about two thousand head strong, simply do what they want, where they want to, within a single fifty-thousand-acre enclosure until it's time for them to become steaks. Buffalo meat is increasingly available in supermarkets, and I buy it at warehouse store BJ's. It is an especially good choice for ground meat because it doesn't have all the nasty additives and heavily processed filler allowed in many beef-based burger products. A Real Food, bison offers the advantages of the purest grass-fed beef without the concerns over getting swindled.

New Zealand lamb is another easy meat shopping choice, as it is all grass finished, widely available in this country, and country of origin claims for single-ingredient products like lamb tend to be better enforced than other label terms. Domestic lamb production, on the other hand, is very similar to beef, in that there is a niche market in pasture-raised product and a much bigger "conventional" market built on antibiotics, growth promotants, and nonnatural diets.

THE REASON I made such an effort to try a steak in Scotland is because in our country, "Angus" beef may or may not come from Angus cattle. Aberdeen Angus is a very particular breed, and in many ways, a victim of its own success. Nicknamed the "Butcher's Breed," it has become the standard for the beef industry worldwide. But while originally suited to a particular Scottish terrain and colder climate, many prime cattle raising areas are warmer, and after centuries of the cattle being widely exported, then crossbred with local stock, today traces of Angus are found in all sorts of different creatures. This has reached the point where few agree on what is and isn't Angus anymore. But what everyone does agree on is that the word *Angus* on a meat label or menu increases the consumer's perceived value and thus the price.

Otherwise, *Angus* has little meaning. Because most actual Aberdeen Angus cattle—and most beef cattle period—are predominantly black, though there are red Angus, the USDA defines the term by color, not breed. To be labeled "Angus," meat must come from a steer that was at least 51 percent black. Menus often describe steak or burgers redundantly as "black Angus" to impress buyers, whatever kind of cattle it came from.

"Real Aberdeen Angus is among the very best meat breeds on earth," says Thomas Schneller, the head chef instructor in the meat department for the main campus of the Culinary Institute of America in Hyde Park, New York. Schneller also wrote the CIA's textbook on the subject, titled simply *Meat*. He often buys beef from Amy Goldstein, a local farmer in upstate New York, one of the few raising actual purebred Aberdeen Angus. I visited the campus's meat department as Schneller, in his white lab coat and wielding a meat hook and huge knives, was teaching a class of students how to break down a side of beef into the different cuts. Unlike most college professors, he finished class slightly blood spattered. Afterward, he took me through his meat filled walk-in freezers, showing me different cuts from different cattle, several labeled "Angus." "Some are Angus based on color, some on genetics, some on marbling, and some are just jokes." While far from a guarantee of quality, or of anything, *Angus* is one of the more harmless Fake Food terms thrown around the meat industry.

By looking for "naturally raised" in conjunction with "USDA Organic," or similar alternative labels, you can buy meat that is Real Food, the way nature intended it. But there is one last thing to think about when shopping. If the meat you are eyeing is already packaged, as most supermarket steaks are, sandwiched between a foam tray and clear plastic wrap, don't rely on its vibrant appearance to make your decision. Meat marketers use what is known as modified atmospheric packaging, or MAP, to make products look artificially fresh. Basically, they fill the package with small amounts of carbon monoxide, the same stuff unhappy folks use to kill themselves in garages. This doesn't actually preserve meat, but it does keep it bright red—even if it has already spoiled (seafood lovers, as if you didn't already have enough problems, they do the same thing with tuna—real and fake).

The beef industry argues that the sell-by date protects consumers in regard to freshness, and it certainly can, but obviously there's a risk in making food that is spoiled and should look spoiled appear unspoiled. Consumers Union tested supermarket packages of ground beef using MAP and found that 20 percent (one in five) were spoiled, still on shelves, and looked yummy. While the USDA regulates the meat in the package, the carbon monoxide is considered a food additive, so it comes under the purview of the FDA, which in turn does not require it to be listed on the label. The FDA received a citizens' petition to ban the practice for reasons of both "consumer deception" and "food safety risks." Under its own rules for the petition process, the FDA was required to respond on the MAP issue within 180 days. The agency has not done so yet, but don't hold your breath—the complaint was filed more than ten years ago.

## Steven Raichlen's Best-Ever Spanish Steak Recipe

This simple but delicious two-ingredient recipe was adapted by culinary author Steven Raichlen from Casa Julian, a famous steakhouse in Spain's Basque region outside San Sebastian. He taught me the salt cooking technique and I've made it ever since because it is a simple but excellent way to cook steak.

Spain is a steak-mad nation, and the country's signature cut is chuleton de buey, a very thick bone-in rib steak, often served for two. At Casa Julian the steak is two and half inches thick and it is the only entrée on the menu—you go there to eat this one dish and it is awesome. As in Argentina, it is cooked over a wood fire, but I've made this recipe on the gas grill and it works fine. A boneless rib eye may be substituted with equally good results. Serves 2.

2 bone-in grass-fed, naturally raised rib steaks,
   cut at least 1½ inches thick
1 cup rock salt or coarse sea salt

DIRECTIONS

– Oil the grill grates. Preheat a gas or coal grill medium-high.
– Place the steaks on the grill and cover their entire top surface with a ¼-inch-thick layer of coarse salt. Cook undisturbed for about 5 minutes or until drops of juice begin to appear through the salt layer.
– Flip and don't worry about the salt falling off. Repeat the salt application. Cook for 4 to 5 minutes for medium-rare, slightly longer if you have thicker steaks or want them more well done.
– With tongs, knock the sides of the steaks against the grill or hold the steaks and hit them with a knife to remove excess salt. Rest the steaks for 2 minutes, then serve.

# 11. Fakes, Fakes, and More Fakes: What Else Is There?

> One of the greatest problems facing this branch of criminal investigation—food forensics—is that consumers can't always tell when they're being defrauded . . . estimates the cost to the global food industry at $49 billion.
>
> —ROYAL SOCIETY OF CHEMISTRY

My next-door neighbor used to keep bees, and I have to admit, when I first moved from New York City to rural Vermont almost twenty-five years ago, as a city fish out of water, the hives sort of freaked me out, with a mess of bees buzzing freely around the backyard—it just seemed counterintuitive. But I got used to the bees pretty quickly: they became part of the scenery and never bothered anyone. Even my dog was uninterested in the busy, buzzy hives, and I occasionally scored some free homegrown honey out of the deal. I have always traveled a great deal for work, here and abroad, and when my wife traveled with me, my neighbor and her kids often took care of our golden retriever. Because she was a very avid hobbyist beekeeper, and really into honey, I got into the habit of bringing her home a souvenir jar from wherever my travels took me, usually sourced at a local market, and she was always interested in the regional differences. She got honey from places like Durango, Colorado, Peru, Tanzania, and even mainland China—that was the only time she told me it was bad, with a "chemical taste." Her family eventually sold their house and moved, and I've heard she is still making honey at her new place.

That was all years ago, long before I started writing about Fake Food, but the memory lingers because foods that can't be differentiated by sight will often be faked, and honey fills the bill. But honey has other problems as well, with the pirates on one side and regulators on the other. For starters, while we know for sure there is plenty of obviously fake honey, no one agrees on what the real thing is.

The American Beekeeping Federation is the industry group representing U.S. producers of non-ultrafiltered honey. They petitioned the FDA to create a "standard of identity" for honey, basically a detailed definition that sets legal standards. As with similar appeals for an olive oil standard, the FDA summarily denied this request. While it told the federation that it shared their "concerns about adulterated and misbranded honey," regulators chose to defer to *Webster's*, literally, citing the dictionary's definition as adequate: "a thick, sweet, syrupy substance that bees make as food from the nectar of flowers and store in honeycombs."

That sounds like honey to me, which is part of the problem—like most consumers, I don't know a whole lot about the intricacies of honey. The position of the American Beekeeping Federation is that real honey must have pollen, but lots of other domestic honey producers disagree and ultrafilter theirs to remove the pollen, which helps keeps the product from crystallizing. In Europe, most consumers are used to honey in this original state, but Americans vote with their dollars for the more liquid filtered version, sans pollen but with nothing necessarily added. I say "necessarily" because pollen is a fingerprint for honey that can be tested to show where the plants the bees visited lived and prove country of origin.

One legitimate fear is that countries like China use the

ultrafiltration or ultrapurification processes to mask the origin of the honey, which is then transshipped and sometimes mixed with a small amount of pollinated honey, from say India, to throw off testers. Sometimes Chinese honey is cut with much cheaper corn syrup or fructose syrup to enhance profit margins, and sometimes Chinese producers even feed corn syrup to the bees to get it into the honey more "naturally." The importation of Chinese honey is specifically banned by the USDA because it is so often adulterated.

Unlike the FDA, the USDA has chosen to get more precise about what honey is—sort of. They created a voluntary grading system that lets producers slap Grade A, Grade B, or Grade C on their labels, with zero enforcement. Sound familiar? The USDA did the same thing with olive oil grades, leading pretty much every producer to choose the highest extra-virgin grade designation, regardless of what was in the bottle. In this case, the USDA created very detailed honey grading rules—and lets them all be ignored. The formula scores five specific elements like moisture content and "absence of defects," but the grading rules skip vitally important factors, such as whether nonhoney ingredients (such as corn syrup) can be added. Additionally, honey and maple syrup are in a special category, and unlike almost every other product it regulates, the USDA allows use of its grading marks without any inspections, ever (oil is theoretically subject to inspection, though it almost never is). As the *Federal Register* reads, "Honey does not require official inspection in order to carry official USDA grade marks and . . . there are no existing programs that require the official inspection and certification of honey." Enforcement is based solely on responding to complaints.

Honey-obsessed website Honey Traveler concluded, "Two honeys could be legally graded as Grade A honey and be identically labeled as, '100% Organic Clover Honey from Arizona—USDA Grade A' yet be entirely different honeys. They could be a blend of honeys from all over the world, some heated to 180 degrees to make it easy to filter, contain antibiotics, chemicals and corn syrup, not made from Clover at all nor actually be from plants in Arizona!" While this is often the case, the site's claim is not entirely accurate, because there is a legal standard for the term *organic* in agricultural products, including honey. However, actual organic production of honey is almost impossible for producers to control, because bees roam freely and choose plants that may or may not have been organically farmed. Also, "100%" is a widely misused food label term that often means a particular ingredient, not the entire product, is 100 percent something.

But the bottom line is that legal or not, "you may be paying more for honey labeled 'certified organic' or feel reassured by the 'USDA Grade A' seal, but the truth is, there are few federal standards for honey, no government certification and no consequences for making false claims. For American-made honey, the 'organic' boast, experts say, is highly suspect," noted the *Seattle Post-Intelligencer*. "Major supermarkets offer dozens of different brands, sizes, types and flavors of honey for sale. Consumers might walk away with the finest-tasting, highest-quality honey there is. Or they could end up with an unlabeled blend, adulterated with impossible-to-detect cheap sweeteners or illegal antibiotics." Suddenly that innocent plastic bear on your table sounds like lots of other Fake Foods.

There are debates over whether or not pollen makes the honey healthier and/or tastier, so your definition of real honey depends which side of this divide you are on. But in either case, most consumers expect real honey to contain just honey, whether filtered or not. But when the FDA opened a comment phase in 2014 on proposed draft guidelines that may someday exist, one question was whether to bar honey cut with other sweeteners from calling itself honey. If such regulation passed, it still might not stem the tide, since honey is an easily faked and expensive product that's mostly sugar. Reports of widespread counterfeit honey, made with glucose and just enough actual honey to give it flavor, plus the occasional body parts of bees to make it look authentic, date to at least 1881.

The rare and prized manuka honey, about the priciest kind, comes from bees visiting the manuka bush, found only in New Zealand and a small part of Australia, an excellent example of *terroir*. Fans believe it is both healthier and better tasting than all other honeys. It certainly costs a lot more. A 2014 investigation in the United Kingdom, where manuka honey is especially popular, found that just one of seven brands in supermarkets labeled as such was the real thing. According to a comprehensive overview of Fake Foods published in the *Journal of Food Science* and coauthored by Dr. John Spink, director of the Michigan State University Food Fraud Initiative, honey is the third most faked food in the world. And Americans buy and eat more honey than anyone, nearly four hundred million pounds every year. Much of the fake stuff ends up in processed "honey"-flavored foods.

The FDA's honey guy, Martin Stutsman, who also "monitors" olive oil, told *USA Today* that cane sugar or high-fructose corn syrup used to be most commonly used to thin honey. But an isotope test easily spotted this adulteration, so savvy counterfeiters switched to beet sugar, with a chemical profile much more similar to honey. The FDA, in turn, switched to a much more complicated, multistep test. "But once we started catching people, they create a moving target. They'll switch to something more difficult (to detect)," said Stutsman.

At least honeys cut with sugar substitutes like corn syrup and beet sugar aren't poisonous. That's not the case with chloramphenicol, a powerful antibiotic that can lead to a potentially fatal bone marrow disorder, the reason the drug is not is not approved for food use in the United States. But it is a common contaminant in adulterated Chinese honey. While the import of Chinese honey is banned, its price difference is big enough to make it worthwhile for smugglers to relabel and transship.

This can be big business for organized criminals, not just a few jars in the lining of a suitcase. One German honey distributor did this kind of illegal transshipment for seven years, obscuring and importing some eighty million dollars worth of banned and sometimes adulterated Chinese honey into the United States before getting caught. "Chinese honey was often harvested early and dried by machine rather than bees," reported *Businessweek*. "This allowed the bees to produce more honey, but the honey often had an odor and taste similar to sauerkraut. Fan [a worker] was told to mix sugar and syrup into the honey in Taiwan to dull the pungent flavor." Just as with the transshipped banned Chinese shrimp that went via Indonesia—also contaminated with dangerous and forbidden drugs—investigators noticed a sudden spike in honey imports from Indonesia, Malaysia, and India after banning Chinese honey. The scam was so large that honey exports suddenly totaled more than those three countries produce annually, combined. According to *Businessweek*, this operation was the single largest incident of food fraud in our country's history. More accurately, it is the largest case where someone actually got caught.

What's especially sad is that it is easy to buy real honey, made by small producers all around the country, and widely available at farmers' markets and gourmet stores. By simply avoiding big supermarket brands and buying it from someone who makes it locally, you should be safe. But what other Fake Foods do you need to know about?

COFFEE IS THE world's fifth most faked item on Dr. John Spink's Michigan State University Food Fraud Initiative list—yet tea drinkers might fret as well. Much of the fraud with both products has to do with labeling and origin, simple substitution of cheaper products for more expensive ones. Tea lends itself more to outright adulteration than coffee, which in its whole-bean form is harder to fake. Ground coffee, on the other hand, is more widely purchased by consumers than beans, and cutting it with cheaper substances has been common practice for over two hundred years. In the old days, virtually any dried powder would do, from ground acorns and parsnips to sawdust, mixed with some burnt sugar for color. Contemporary researchers have found twigs, roasted corn, ground roasted barley, and even roasted ground parchment. Adulteration is more extreme in powdered instant coffee, where substances found have included chicory, cereals, caramel, parchment, starch, malt, and figs.

Coffee is the world's number-one dollar volume foodstuff and second-most-valuable commodity of any kind, ahead of sugar, corn, and beef as well as coal, gold, and diamonds, behind only oil. We consume some twelve billion pounds of it annually from twenty-five million different farmers in more than fifty countries, many of them less developed. Not surprisingly, like seafood, it is hard to keep track of a supply chain with so many middlemen, distributors, processors, and other moving parts. According to *Chemistry World*, "There are currently very few ways to tell if the coffee we buy and drink contains things it shouldn't . . . There is a huge global demand for coffee, and when supplies are low the price rises, which encourages fraud. Increasingly, ground coffee is being mixed with cheaper ingredients such as maize, soybeans, sugar and acai seeds."

The simplest solution for coffee drinkers is to buy whole beans, which is what I do. But while this eliminates the addition of unsavory ground additives, it still isn't enough. First, the world's commercial coffee industry consists almost entirely of two varieties of beans, the far cheaper robusta and the more desirable arabica, which sells for two to three times as much. Of course, they look the same. This makes it tempting and profitable for producers or suppliers to cut real coffee beans with other real coffee beans. Also, aficionados pay a large premium for coffee from higher-quality production countries and regions, but it is impossible for consumers to tell if the beans actually came from there.

In 1996, the owner of a California coffee distributor, Kona Kai Farms, was indicted on federal wire fraud and money laundering charges after he was caught repackaging cheaper coffee from several Central American countries into bags labeled Hawaiian Kona coffee. Frequently cited as a standout example of an American appellation, and one of our few legally protected geographically indicated products, Kona is one of the most famous gourmet coffees in the world. As such it typically commands among the highest prices and all of it is grown only on about two thousand acres on Hawaii's Big Island. Like the German-Chinese honey fraud, this labeling scam went on for years, and one industry site reported that the company had successfully swapped several million pounds of beans, while the total production of real Kona coffee is less than two million pounds annually.

Even without this criminal fraud, Kona fans often wind up on the short end of the Real Food stick, thanks to Hawaii's own state coffee labeling law. It can come in many wildly different forms, from pure Kona coffee to Kona blends allowed to use the geographic designation on their labels while containing just 10 percent real Kona beans. If the product says "100% Kona coffee," it is supposed to be just that, but if it reads "Kona blend," "Kona roast," or "Kona style," it is more likely 10 percent premium beans and 90 percent whatever is cheapest. Under state law, the origin of this 90 percent anything else does not have to be indicated. As with olive oil and its faux Italian roots and Tuscan farmhouse images, this allows for enormously inflated profit margins by selling barely Kona blends with labels exploiting Hawaiian place names and images.

While it's widely believed that the use of sawdust to cut coffee is past history, that's not the case for tea, according to the Congressional Research Service. In its broad report to Congress on food fraud in 2014, it found that sawdust, along with coloring agents and leaves from other plants, were used to extend tea. In 2008, two sophisticated large scale tea adulteration factories using poisonous chemicals were uncovered in India, a huge tea supplier to the world. One of the companies was an ISO 9001–certified facility that exported large quantities of tea to many countries around the world, and Indian officials ended up destroying more than twenty-eight tons of tainted tea. In bag form, it is even harder for consumers to look critically at the ingredients, and this is especially true of herb teas, which can look like almost anything.

After tackling fake seafood and cheese with his DNA testing, Rockefeller University's Dr. Mark Stoeckle and his students turned to other foods, including herb teas, and again found adulteration pervasive. "There is a lot of substitution going on in food," he said. "We tested herbal teas and a third of them had things not listed on the label, like 'weeds.' It didn't matter whether they were low end or high end, we bought them from all different stores, from Starbucks, it didn't matter. As a consumer, there is no easy way to look at a bunch of dried twigs and tell what they are."

Darjeeling, a geographically indicated brand name of immense value in the tea world, is owned by the Indian Tea Board, which actively defends the brand's reputation and purity worldwide. The board is lucky enough to have done what Champagne and Parmesan could not and obtained a protective trademark for its name in the United States; it also has EU protection. Nonetheless, it is estimated that consumers worldwide drink more than four times as much "Darjeeling tea" as is actually grown each year. Real Darjeeling tea, grown only in India's Darjeeling region and widely considered a premium product, carries a green logo of a woman holding a tea leaf along with the word *Darjeeling*. Like European AOC or PDO seals, and unlike Hawaii's Kona coffee, the Indian Tea Board only allows this logo to be used on 100 percent pure Darjeeling tea products.

Another popular Indian premium food frequently duping consumers, especially in the United States, is basmati rice. Basmati is a texturally light variety of long-grain rice, prized for both its delicate consistency and fragrant flavor. It works exceptionally well as a base for stews, curries, and sauces, where because of its fine texture it does not overpower or weigh down the main course. The real thing is grown only in specific regions of northern India and across the border in Pakistan, but like so many widely accepted geographically indicated foods recognized by the rest of the world it remains unprotected in the United States, so any kind of rice can, and often is, sold as basmati rice here. This is just another in a long line of economic and quality cheats facing American consumers. In some ways basmati mirrors the wagyu beef situation, with various rices similar to or actually derived from basmati strains cultivated and sold domestically that closely mirror the basmati-style, while other "basmati" does not even remotely resemble the real thing.

Spices, especially when sold dry—as most are—have lots of similarities to tea, so there is plenty of fraud. When New York's CBS station, Channel 2, investigated "spiked" spices in early 2016, half the spices they bought at several stores were adulterated. Samples were shipped off to IEH Laboratories in Washington State, and testing revealed problems, especially with oregano, turmeric, and nutmeg. "As you know, turmeric is yellow powder, and we found a good amount of corn in it," said IEH's Mansour Samadpour in the segment. Nutmeg was cut with pepper and "pepper is cheaper than nutmeg any day." He's seen spices diluted with wheat flour and peanut flour, which poses special health risks. "It's economic adulteration and if you're allergic, it can really be a bad situation." Oregano "contained other unknown plants, possibly weeds," and this corresponds to a similar study that found a quarter of all dried oregano sold in the UK was cut with "other plant matter."

Fruit juices show up on just about every list of commonly faked items, and the top ten from the Food Fraud Initiative includes both apple juice and orange juice. Fake juice takes many forms, legal and illegal. Not so long ago I went grocery shopping, and my wife asked me to pick her up some cran-blueberry juice. Despite the fact that I should know better, I fell for a classic trick, buying into a premium-looking, feel-good, natural-looking package. I bought a bottle of R.W. Knudsen's organic cranberry blueberry juice that was prominently labeled "100% juice." The label was entirely illustrated with pictures of blueberries and cranberries, fifty-fifty, side by side. It came in a glass bottle, was in the section with the other fancy "natural" products, and cost about twice as much as the store brand. So I foolishly assumed it was actually made from blueberries and cranberries. It did not occur to me that the main label "Cranberry Blueberry" and the "100% juice" were two different and unrelated claims—it did not actually say "Cranberry Blueberry Juice."

It wasn't until I got home that I looked at the ingredients, listed in order of volume, and found that the number one was neither of the berry juices but rather apple juice concentrate. This is deceptive for several reasons, not the least of which being that apples are neither blueberries nor cranberries, the only two fruits listed on the front of the bottle. Nor are there any pictures of apples on the label with the berries shown, despite the fact that it has more apple juice than either. Then there is the sticky matter that most of the apple juice concentrate used in this country comes from China and has a bad reputation—deservedly, as it has frequently proven tainted.

I didn't want apple juice, which my wife and I also feel is nutritionally less desirable than either blueberry or cranberry juice. In short, I got ripped off, in completely legal fashion, because I failed to follow my own advice and didn't read the ingredient label, which by the way also lists lemon juice, and of course, there is no mention or pictures of lemons on the front. It is no coincidence that both blueberry and cranberry juice are more expensive than apple and lemon juice, so accurately depicting what's in the product might make consumers realize it is not worth as much as they paid. I took a look at Knudsen's website, which described the clearly labeled "100% juice" product as a "flavored juice blend of four juice concentrates with other natural ingredients."

"Other natural ingredients" seems impossible to reconcile with "100% juice," especially using the mathematical definition of *100 percent*, which means "all." How can something be entirely juice while also containing nonjuice ingredients? Only by using the same "logic" as in the case of 100 percent beef hot dogs, where it doesn't mean that the hot dog is all beef, just that the beef in it is beef. Apparently the same holds true for juice, which contains some juice made of juice. Apple juice is also the number-one ingredient in Knudsen's açaí berry juice blend, also labeled "100% juice." On the label, "juice blend" appears in smaller letters and a different color that "blends" in with the background and makes these words less readable, on a label covered only with pictures of açaí berries (it actually contains the juices, purees, or concentrates of five different fruits). According to Michael Roberts, a professor of food law and policy at UCLA and director of the Center for Food Law and Policy, most juice in pretty much any kind of juice (except orange) you buy is apple, even if it's labeled blueberry or cranberry: "Apple juice is the cheapest, and manufacturers aren't required to list percentages on the label."

Interestingly, while the FDA requires items on the ingredients list to be in order of the amounts used, they specifically have a different policy for the front label and names of products that contain multiple ingredients. If FDA rules were consistent across the entire label—we are talking about a few square inches of consumer protection—then the juice I bought would have to be called apple-cranberry-blueberry-lemon. But they are not. That's why Coca-Cola, following the letter of the law, labeled its juice "Pomegranate-Blueberry," despite containing almost no pomegranate juice at all—0.3 percent to be precise. POM, a leading maker of actual pomegranate juice, sued, and the case went all the way to the U.S. Supreme Court. The company argued that FDA rules allowed it to name food products based on minority ingredients, but that did not sway Justice Anthony Kennedy, whose written opinion called these sorts of labels "practices that allegedly mislead and trick consumers, all to the injury of competitors." In a rare 2014 victory for consumers, the Supreme Court ruled— unanimously—that the lawsuit could move forward. That was just the beginning, and Coke vowed to fight on.

But juice can be more than just misleading. The 2014 Congressional Research Service report called fruit juice one of the leading food categories with reported cases of food fraud noting, "Juices might be watered down, or a more expensive juice (such as from pomegranates or other 'super' fruit) might be cut with a cheaper juice (such as apple or grape juice). Some juice may be only water, dye, and sugary flavorings, although fruit is the listed ingredient on the label. Orange juice has been shown to sometimes contain added unlisted lemon juice, mandarin juice, grapefruit juice, high-fructose corn syrup, paprika extract, and beet sugar. Apple juice has been shown to have added unlisted grape juice, high-fructose corn syrup, pear juice, pineapple juice, raisin sweetener, fig juice, fructose, and malic acid." The report also said that some fruit juices may be made from or diluted with juice from rotten fruit and may contain toxic mold—including of course, those from China. Even if the apple juice you buy happens to be real apple juice, you still may not want to drink it. The vast majority of apple juice sold in the United States is from Chinese-made concentrate, which as I have mentioned has repeatedly been found to contain banned pesticides and other chemicals.

In her book *Swindled*, on the history of food adulteration, Bee Wilson described a common practice of cutting fruit juice with water, sugar, and pulp wash, "a liquid extracted by repeatedly washing the exhausted pulp left over from making Proper Juice." She further reported that in the 1990s an estimated 10 percent of all fruit juices in the United States were fraudulent, and at the same time, a UK study found that sixteen out of twenty-one leading brands of supermarket orange juice contained adulterants such as beet sugar.

Krueger Food laboratories is an independent testing facility in Massachusetts that among other things specializes in fruit juices. In a presentation on food adulteration for the University of California, Davis, Dana Krueger noted that fruit juice could be "extended" with sugar or high-fructose corn syrup costing a fifth as much as the actual juice, as well as cheap specialty sweeteners such as insulin syrup and rice syrup, while juices could also be "enhanced" with improper additives like colors and acids. More expensive juices were cut with cheaper apple, white grape, and pear juices as well as by-products like fruit pomace extract and peel juices, while in the case of the most expensive berry and pomegranate juices, "almost anything" made economic sense as an adulterant. She detailed a long and continuing history of major fruit juice scandals in this country: apples in the 1970s and again in the

1990s; oranges in the 1980s; cranberries in the 1990s; and problems today with both lemon and pomegranate juices, as well as the suddenly hot category of coconut water.

In the spring of 2014, the FDA issued an "Import Alert" after ascertaining that pomegranate juices or concentrate, lemon juices or concentrate, and the vaguer "other fruit and vegetable juice or concentrate" labeled "100% juice" in fact contained undeclared ingredients. This alert noted that "the products were not as they were represented to be on the labels and were therefore adulterated and misbranded." It covered almost every kind of juice you could buy ranging from Canada, Italy, Iran, Peru, and Turkey, spanning three continents. These types of alerts are temporary in nature, issued on a case-by-case basis, aimed at retailers so they can pull tainted products from shelves. The alert was updated in June 2015 to allow "detention without physical inspection" (confiscation) of juices from certain producers in Iran and Turkey after FDA tests found undeclared ingredients and a determination of "substitution, misbranding and adulteration."

It's a tenet of the real-food world that whole foods are generally better—it is safer to buy a blueberry or cranberry than blueberry cranberry juice. It is hard to fake a tomato or banana when you buy it whole—but not impossible. In recent years many food lovers have complained about the bland tastelessness of supermarket tomatoes, and the consensus seems to be that the flavor, texture, and succulence has been bred out of them. That is partially true, and like almost all fruits and vegetables, there is a directly inverse relationship between quality and durability. Tomatoes have been bred to specifically enhance their qualities for shipping and storage at the expense of flavor. But that is not enough for profit margins.

Science has found a way to make tomatoes even more cost efficient to produce, ship, and store, which is to pick and sell them before they ripen. Every day less any produce spends on the plant equals less risk for the farmer, less chance it will get eaten by an animal, attacked by a bug, or contract a disease. Rock hard green tomatoes are also less likely to be damaged in transit and they store better. The only problem with this plan—besides the fact that they taste crappy—is that consumers are too smart to buy green, unripe tomatoes. So if you can't sell someone a green tomato because that is too obvious, what's the next best solution? Painting them red won't work because that's ridiculous, and unlike farmed salmon, no one has figured out a way to make the tomato eat dye so it looks like the real thing.

But where there is a will there is a way, and science has come to the rescue of the bland tomato industry, which gases the green tomatoes with ethylene, triggering a ripening response—or more accurately a reddening response—in already-picked tomatoes. "You can take green tomatoes, gas them, and they turn red within twenty-four hours, but while they may look red, they are still green, as in not ripe, and they taste terrible. Maybe 95 percent of the field grown tomatoes in the U.S. are gassed and not truly ripe," said Dr. Howard Resh, one of the world's leading authorities on hothouse gardening and hydroponics. Resh oversees the vast kitchen garden program at the Cuisinart luxury resort on Anguilla, the largest hothouse program of any resort in the world, and he gave me a tour. The facility supplies much of the produce to the resort's restaurants, and the program is so successful that Cuisinart has repeat guests who return just because the salads here taste so good. Hothouse tours are regularly offered to guests.

Resh explained that while ethylene works magic on tomatoes, it does nothing for bell peppers. (His hothouses contained such gorgeous examples that I wanted to pick one and eat it like an apple.) Peppers naturally go from green to red, yellow, or orange as they ripen on the vine, the same pepper, different stages.

Contrary to what many people think, the green bell peppers in the supermarket and the red ones next to them are the same vegetable, maybe from the same plant, just at varying stages of ripeness. Because green peppers are sturdier and picked earlier with less risk, they are cheaper but less ripe. According to Dr. Resh, you should "always buy colored peppers. It's worth the extra money, better tasting, better for your health, more nutritional value." I've followed his advice ever since, and the orange and yellow peppers do clearly taste better. But even the greenest pepper tastes a lot better than a green tomato.

Have you ever heard the old tip about putting an apple in a paper bag with other fruit you wanted to ripen in the kitchen? It works, according to Christopher Watkins, because apples are a natural source of ethylene. Watkins, a horticulture professor at the Cornell University College of Agriculture and Life Sciences, walked me through the process. "In California and Florida, two major production areas, it is quite common to pick tomatoes while green and apply ethylene afterward to stimulate postharvest color development. It does also ripen them to a degree, but we sacrifice quality. There is no doubt that a fruit that's harvested on the vine when really ripe is of superior taste and quality."

Ethylene ripening cannot be used on tomatoes labeled organic, and in recent years you may have noticed in supermarkets a lot more tomatoes, often in plastic clamshell boxes, labeled "hothouse grown." "Field grown" seems a virtuous adjective when it comes to fruits and vegetables, and given that it is more natural to think of a field of tomatoes under the sun than in the artificial confines of a hothouse, I always viewed the latter as a winter substitute or otherwise second rate. I was wrong. Next time you go to the supermarket, take a look, and you will see that hothouse tomatoes almost always sell for a higher price, often much higher, than the more romantic sounding field-grown tomatoes. But the hothouse fruits actually ripen on the vine, the way real tomatoes are supposed to, and they taste better as result.

Watkins is quick to defend his region and point out that in parts of the United States, especially the Northeast, field-grown tomatoes do ripen on the vine but typically only in summer. Hothouse tomatoes are available year-round. I learned from Resh that the big-box warehouse stores, like BJ's and Costco, tend to contract directly with large hothouse operations and buy their entire supply, and these stores are often an excellent place to get reliable ripe tomatoes and colored peppers, which he described as "higher quality than most supermarkets."

As the apple-in-the-bag trick suggests, ethylene does work on a few other fruits, most notably bananas. I eat a banana almost every day and was shocked when Watkins told me these too are routinely picked about two-thirds ripe, then later treated with ethylene. Both apples and bananas are shipped green or greenish, stored in distribution warehouses around the country, and gassed as needed to change their color just before putting them into stores. That's why green-tinged supermarket bananas ripen in just a day or two at home, even though they have been sitting in a warehouse green for weeks before gas. The "USDA organic" label bars the gas, but in this case green-picked bananas are just moved through the supply chain faster, and still "ripen" after picking.

What would an actual tree-ripened banana taste like, I wondered, having seen the huge difference in fresh tomato quality from my own garden? Watkins told me that as a typical American consumer I'd probably never tried one, and it is something I will make a point to seek out next time I go someplace where bananas are grown. Had he ever had one? "I had a fully ripened greenhouse banana once. It was amazing. We are so used to the supermarket version here that the ripe one might have too much flavor for some people."

Here in Vermont, our most famous agricultural product is maple syrup. Like honey, it is specifically exempted from USDA inspection, and thanks to lax labeling laws, there are many part-maple or pseudo-maple "100% natural" syrups pretending to be the real thing. But a more pervasive problem is the number of maple-flavored products that contain no maple at all. Each year the Vermont Maple Sugar Makers Association puts on a statewide series of open houses at "sugar shacks," which is what the outbuildings where sap is boiled down into syrup are called. Since most maple producers are mom-and-pop operations, most sugar shacks are small cabins on residential property, and during sugaring season, usually in April, all over Vermont you can smell the sweet scent of boiling maple sap.

I chose to visit Echo Hill, a fifth-generation maple farm in northern Vermont. Husband and wife owners Randi and Louise Calderwood, the fourth generation, are keeping up a ninety-three-year-old family tradition, along with their kids and Randi's elderly mother, who still sells syrup twice a week at farmers' markets in the summer. When he is not tapping trees or boiling sap, Randi is the assistant chief of the volunteer fire department in nearby Craftsbury. I asked him if he ever thought about expanding his orchard, and he laughed, explaining that it takes about forty years for a maple tree to mature from sapling into a syrup producer. No one gets into the real maple business overnight.

Randi, Louise, and I chatted with Matthew Gordon, executive director of the Vermont Maple Sugar Makers Association, about the Fake Food challenges to the industry. "This is the image of the maple syrup industry," said Gordon, gesturing around at fire chief Randi in his flannel shirt and work pants, boiling sap in this farm outbuilding set among snow-covered forest off a dirt road, a back road so far back I got repeatedly lost trying to find it, a long way from any cell service or Google Maps. It was a down-home scene, a Norman Rockwell painting brought to life. "But it is an accurate image, and clearly one that these bigger companies are trying to trade on."

Gordon produced two plastic shopping bags. On the way from his office in the state capital of Montpelier, he had stopped at a supermarket and went down the cereal and snack aisles, buying every allegedly maple product he could find. He had several boxes of maple and brown sugar granola bars, and oatmeal, from a wide range of both huge national manufacturers and more specialty "natural" producers. One thing they almost all had in common—besides the word *maple*—was the distinctive image of a maple syrup jug on the package. They almost all had something else in common too—only one contained any actual maple syrup. "It really burns me," said Gordon. "You look at the box, the name, the picture of the maple syrup and clearly you would be confused because there is no maple syrup in it. The FDA says for it to be deceptive the average person would have to be confused, and that is clearly the case, most people would think these have maple syrup in them. How can Quaker Oats make maple oatmeal with a picture of maple syrup but no maple in it?"

It's a very good question and the technical answer is usually a combination of high-fructose corn syrup and/or maltodextrin combined with fenugreek seed or anise. In particular, a lot of "maple" flavor comes from fenugreek oleoresin, a "natural" plant product obtained by extracting it with alcohol or acetone. Of course, while you know the flavor doesn't come from real syrup, you will likely never know exactly where the maple flavor comes from because it's listed vaguely as "artificial and natural flavorings." I was skeptical of Gordon's claim, but I looked at each box, and as promised, Quaker Oats maple and brown sugar instant oatmeal has nary a drop of maple syrup in it, though it has both kinds of flavors, natural and artificial, and does as advertised, contain sugar, though there is no evidence it is brown, which may just be the added caramel color. Chex oatmeal with maple and brown sugar is actually pretty wholesome, the ingredient list comprising just whole grain oats, sugar, salt, and natural flavors—but still no maple syrup. Kellogg's maple and brown sugar–frosted Mini-Wheats? Nope.

My wife eats Nature Valley Granola Bars, so I was especially interested in those, and to my relief, while Nature Valley's bars also have a picture of a glass jug of syrup and claim in the online description, "Maple Brown Sugar Granola Bars combine whole grain rolled oats, crisp rice, maple syrup and brown sugar to produce a sweet and wholesome snack," they actually do contain maple syrup. Of course, there's less real maple syrup than high-fructose corn syrup, but there is some, apparently enough to live up to the company's "straight from nature" slogan. I close my eyes and conjure up images of farmers picking high-fructose corn syrup in sun-kissed fields.

I asked Steven Kronenberg, the attorney specializing in food fraud, how companies like Quaker Oats get away with it and he explained, "If something says it is maple flavored, there are certain requirements about whether it has to be identified as artificially or naturally flavored. It doesn't need to actually contain maple syrup per se, unless it says 'with maple syrup.'" As for the deceptive images? "It's a fine line when it comes to what is 'misleading.' It's tough to say what would confuse the average consumer. Just showing a picture of a jug that appears to be maple syrup and that you and I would commonly associate with maple syrup may not be enough to get you through the courthouse doors."

Read the list of ingredients—it might not be accurate or honest, but it is your first line of defense.

## Maple Syrup & Brown Sugar Oatmeal

⁂ Real oatmeal is an extremely healthful food, full of whole grain goodness and heart-healthful artery-cleansing properties. It is so easy to make the real thing there is just no reason to buy that artificially flavored instant processed crap. Pure oatmeal is widely available. Two brands I like are McCann's (look for the steel-cut Irish oatmeal in a distinctive white can) and Bob's Red Mill (a Scottish-style oatmeal from a natural and unprocessed specialty grain company out of California). You can increasingly find Bob's Red Mill products in gourmet stores, better supermarkets nationwide, and of course, on Amazon.com. Just about everything from this company's oatmeal to pancake and waffle mixes to flour is first rate.

100% pure steel-cut oatmeal or rolled oats
Pure maple syrup (ideally from Vermont!)
Brown sugar

DIRECTIONS

– Make the oatmeal according to the directions on the box. Add maple syrup and brown sugar to taste. Enjoy!

# 12. In Conclusion

> How did we ever get to a point where we need investigative journalists to tell us where our food comes from?
>
> —MICHAEL POLLAN, *The Omnivore's Dilemma*

Lions are what are known as opportunistic hunters, meaning they will eat almost anything that's easy for them to catch, even when they are not particularly hungry. Antelope, wildebeest, warthogs, and birds are on the menu if they make the mistake of becoming convenient prey. The lion never knows when or where its next meal is coming from—it takes what it can get.

Humans are much better off. The good majority of us eat for pleasure as well as sustenance, and compared with any creature on earth, we have an unparalleled wealth of food choices. It is how we make those choices that matter.

Like a stone tossed in a pond, deciding what to eat has a ripple effect that goes far beyond the calories needed to carry us from breakfast to lunch or lunch to dinner. When you choose to eat Real Food, your immediate benefit is that it tastes good. Your long-term benefit is that it is almost always healthier. In many cases it is also more sustainable, healthier for the environment, and supports people whose work, methods, and entire communities make the world a better place.

Conversely, when you choose—or are duped into eating—Fake Foods, you usually get things that taste worse, are less healthful, and sometimes truly dangerous. Eating them supports production methods that are often unsustainable and sometimes illegal. Slavery is the extreme end of the Fake Food immorality spectrum, but destruction of the oceans, tens of thousands of deaths annually from antibiotic-resistant superbugs, increases in coronary disease, massive exposure to known carcinogens, and widespread consumption of banned dangerous chemicals are commonplace in the Fake Food world. For me, though, the economic fraud, being ripped off by pirates and counterfeiters at the expense of hardworking artisans, is reason enough to change.

Change comes at a cost, and some of the foods described in the previous pages, like Kobe beef and Champagne, cost a lot. But eating Real Foods is not reserved for the rich. I'm far from wealthy and aspire to someday being described as upper middle class. It pains me when I go to buy my real beef, truly natural, grass finished, and chemical free, and it costs dearly, while right next to it is an industrial version for a third of the price. That's a big difference, and not everyone can afford good steak. My solution? I eat less beef than I used to, but when I indulge, I make it count.

Fortunately, not all quality food is prohibitive. Truly natural chicken costs more than industrial poultry, but not that much more, and it is far more affordable then beef, so I eat more chicken now, but I only eat real chicken.

Consider one of the most affordable and satisfying foodstuffs on earth, pasta. The pasta I buy is made in Italy, and is certified both USDA Organic and Bio, the latter being Italy's (stricter) version of organic. It is 100 percent whole wheat, which I think is healthier than white pasta. But otherwise, it is regular dried pasta that can last two years on my shelf. It tastes great and is a cinch to cook. As food labels go, it is also very easy to shop for, since it has only one ingredient: organic whole durum wheat flour. So why does the nation's leading brand of supermarket pasta require a whopping seven ingredients? Of these, only three are readily identifiable by name, two kinds of flour and iron. Four—the majority of ingredients—have been coded ASP by the FDA, which means that for some reason they were deemed suspect and "full up to date toxicology information has been sought." This may have been years ago, maybe decades, as the FDA moves imperceptibly slowly. While we await those results, I'll stick with my pasta, which is more nutritious, has no potentially dangerous additives, and as an added bonus, yields significantly fewer calories than the more processed version. But it costs almost twice as much. That sounds like a lot until you consider that the actual difference is less than a dollar, for a bag that serves a family of four. Yes, a twenty-five-dollar steak is a luxury, but most of us can afford a splurge of twenty cents per person on our diet. And there are many cases, as we saw with my beloved Parmigiano-Reggiano, in which the real version is cheaper than the fake.

I KNOW PEOPLE, especially here in historically counterculture Vermont, who are convinced of some grand conspiracy theory and think the food industry and our government are conspiring to make us sick. That's not true—they are making us sick because for decades the sole focus has been on making food cheaper and because lobbyist dollars carry more clout than consumer outrage does. A lot of the blame for our Fake Food mess falls on regulators.

It is important to understand that the USDA and FDA are different entities with different missions. The USDA was not created to protect the American public; the FDA was. The USDA was originally not a cabinet-level department. It became so only as a result of the lobbying of the food industry. Since its inception, part of its duty has been to foster industrial agricultural production, and it has done this very well. To say the USDA is in bed with big industrial producers sounds like an accusation, but it is essentially its job to be in bed with them. The first six words of its official vision statement are "to expand economic opportunity through innovation," not to make sure the public eats healthful meat.

Nonetheless, to the USDA's credit, it has finally put much of the framework in place that we need to do just that. The last decade or two has seen a world of changes in both meat and the larger organic food labeling. While I have serious complaints about its lack of will on the "natural" issue, and the sickeningly widespread use of drugs, at least the USDA has given the American consumer better shopping tools. By demanding clarification of *natural*, as consumers did for *organic*, and by participating in the many public comment opportunities the department offers, you and I have an ongoing opportunity to help effect even more change for the better. The USDA has also done a fantastic job of assuring that outbreaks of diseases like *E. coli* can quickly be contained and traced back to a specific source.

The FDA is another story altogether. The mission statement of this agency is "protecting and promoting your health." It has a funny way of showing it.

When it comes to food labeling, the FDA is concerned almost entirely about nutrition information and what it randomly defines as health claims. Put a "Heart Healthy" label on the box and you better have clinical studies to back it up, just like a drug. But from its perspective, "all natural" is not a health claim, so put that on the box and the agency doesn't care. In fact, the FDA has repeatedly, intentionally, and actively chosen not to care. Ironically, in late 2015, it once again solicited public comments on the meaning of the word *natural* "in the labeling of human food products"—something it did a quarter century earlier, then ignored the comments.

In 1993, two years after the comment period, the FDA concluded, "We noted that we had received many comments on the subject, but that [n]one of the comments provided FDA with a specific direction to follow for developing a definition regarding the use of the term 'natural.' We stated that at that time we would not be engaging in rulemaking to define 'natural.'" As of 2015, fully one in four new food products introduced in our country—across all categories—included the word *natural* on packaging.

It is the same for lots of other words that carry obvious and important health implications. Why does *low fat* have a detailed definition while *pure* has absolutely none? There is no good answer, but the bad one is that the FDA has also long and adamantly refused to give various foodstuffs definitions, which are legally necessary for it to provide oversight.

The FDA is schizophrenic on health concerns in food labeling, caring that consumers looking for whole grains are able to get the exact amount a product contains, while allowing the same package to contain hidden substances known to be toxic or carcinogenic. At the same time it was extensively redesigning the nutritional information panel to be clearer and more precise, the FDA allowed the list of ingredients that don't have to be shown on the label at all to expand dramatically—including many proven dangerous. The FDA lets manufacturers hide everything from lice killer to antifreeze in many of our most beloved foods and gives the same companies that invent new food additives the power to decide whether they are "safe."

These companies are not even required to inform the FDA when new inventions are created and added to products. Really. As a result, no one, not the USDA, not the FDA, not even the CIA, knows how many of these invented "approved" food substances there are, what they are, where they are manufactured and imported from, or how they are used in our foods.

Most recently, in late 2015, the FDA moved to allow the sale of genetically modified salmon—dubbed Frankenfish by its critics—without any additional labeling. It is the first such modified animal of any kind approved for sale in this country and is made in a way that eerily mirrors the fictional dinosaurs of *Jurassic Park* fame, by splicing in genes from fish other than salmon. While the genetically modified organism (GMO) issue is complex, and there is an argument to be made that such modified foods are truly safe, research has shown that the majority of Americans (58 percent) want to avoid buying these foods. Nonetheless, the FDA not only reaffirmed its position that GMO foods need not be labeled but went further and voiced opposition to the use of the term *non-GMO* on food labels, currently the only useful selection information the consumer has. While GMO facts are debatable, there is no argument to be made that the FDA is not once again clearly ignoring the wishes of the people it is supposed to serve.

When the safety of the products it regulates is challenged, whether by concerned citizens, doctors, or scientists, the FDA's longstanding response has been to ignore the situation, often in violation of its own rules. A scathing GAO investigation found that less than 10 percent of the citizen's petitions filed in the past twelve years have been responded to, despite a policy requiring the FDA to do so within 180 days. Some have stretched out more than a quarter century without action. When a group of scientists were hired by the FDA itself to identify suspect ingredients, they recommended thirty-five specific items be pulled from our food supply for health concerns. Three decades later, not one has been banned, and over half of the suspects were never investigated any further. As the GAO noted, the FDA "could not readily explain why, even though almost 30 years had passed."

But there is no one place the FDA fails citizens more obviously than on seafood, a very substantial part of the U.S. food chain that has gone to hell on its watch. I understand at some level that the administration has manpower and budgetary constraints and can't check every bottle of olive oil, but that is different from letting

almost all of the seafood imported into this country go unques-
tioned, when it is widely known to be rife with problems. How can
the FDA be trusted to enforce the rule of law when it routinely
breaks the law? Federal regulations require (as in mandatory, not
optional) the FDA to inspect less than 2 percent of imported seafood, hardly a rigorous analysis. Still, in 2013, inspectors managed
to achieve barely a quarter of that incredibly low threshold—and
their poor performance has been getting shoddier annually, down
from the year before.

You may have noticed there is not a lot of comment from FDA
officials throughout this work, except from published documents,
and that is not an accident. Over the course of a year, my attempts
to interview or question specialists, scientists, and policy makers in
the numerous different areas the FDA oversees were almost completely rebuffed. The FDA's Office of Media Affairs lists fourteen
different people whose job it is to interact with media, and four
of these are specifically assigned to the following issues: labeling,
seafood, food safety, food, and color additives.

I requested interviews in all of the relevant areas in this book
and was repeatedly promised access to FDA staff. Promised and
promised and promised. But no amount of follow-up could make
those promises come true or make interviews actually happen. I
offered to fly to Washington at my own expense and come to their
offices to meet them. I offered to do it by telephone and gave
several-month-long windows. In the end, the FDA was willing to produce exactly one expert, who was willing to address only olive oil—
out of all these issues—and only anonymously as "an FDA source."
The person, who has given countless other similar interviews under his real name wouldn't do that this time. In addition, I had to
submit my questions in advance for vetting by email.

I've done plenty of other interviews over the past two decades,
and publicists at companies are often protective about what em-

ployees say and to whom. I get that. But what the FDA has forgotten is that it isn't a company. Its officials work for you and they work for me, and as a journalist, an American citizen, and a taxpayer, I find it offensive that they so completely ignore their obligation for transparency. It reflects a culture in which the FDA has forgotten its mission. Since it does not have enough money, and the folks in the Office of Media Affairs are not doing their jobs anyway, I think their wasted salaries would be much better spent on checking our seafood. But I don't expect anything to change and don't look to the FDA for any sort of Real Food salvation.

Still, it's worth all of us putting in our two cents when the FDA does open public comment sessions (though the window for "natural" closed a year ago). An even better strategy might be complaining loudly to whomever will listen, starting with your senator or U.S. representative. As more and more states are taking charge with their own regulations in areas where the FDA has failed, like higher olive oil standards in California and Connecticut, you might have better luck with your state representative and governor.

WHAT CAN YOU and I do to eat more Real Food and less Fake Food right now? The answer is twofold: shop better and cook more. You have more control over the final product if you make it than if you buy it made. For particular foods like olive oil and seafood, I've laid out specific shopping details at the end of each chapter. In general, I suggest shopping at better stores, whether it is Whole Foods, Trader Joe's, Costco, or the local fishmonger you trust.

Cooking is the easiest solution to eating more Real Food at home. Despite the extra labor and time, in many cases doing it yourself pays off. The single biggest shopping rule is to read ingredient labels carefully, and remember that any "ingredient" that is actually a category (e.g., artificial colors, natural flavors) rather than a specific thing is probably hiding something. The sheer number of components in heavily processed foods is a problem, as each can hide unsavory things, as well as where they came from. To me there is just something intrinsically wrong about eating a lot of unnecessary chemicals.

Between fast food and supermarkets, no item is more popular than pizza, and America's favorite topping is pepperoni, so let's consider the humble pepperoni pizza. Take Red Baron's classic crust pepperoni version. Not only does this frozen pie have at least fifty-two separate ingredients, but these include lots of things I don't want to eat, like butylated hydroxytoluene, which is banned in England and the FDA has said (for years) "should" be investigated owing to the possibility of turning other ingredients toxic or cancer causing. It also has butylated hydroxyanisole, a petroleum derived additive that has been "pending" FDA review of a citizen petition for a quarter century. I say "at least" fifty-two ingredients because several are categorized as "may contain one or more of the following," and there might be sixty, but even if you read the list closely you can't ever be sure what is actually in it, and that doesn't include all the potential antibiotics and steroids and artificial flavors, which are never listed at all.

In most frozen pizzas, the dough itself is likely is made with highly processed and bleached flour plus artificial flavors and colors not listed on the label. There is also the sauce, laced with potential residues of pesticides and chemical fertilizers, probably made from unripe tomatoes colored red with gas. Even if the manufacturer uses actual mozzarella cheese versus some cheese-like substance, it still almost certainly came from cows loaded with steroids, growth hormones, and antibiotics and that have been fed animal by-products. But it is the pepperoni that is most suspect.

Before I started researching this book, I didn't know that the

USDA had a lower grade of pork than "acceptable," the only grade consumers are allowed to buy. So who buys the not-acceptable pork if we can't? Processed food producers. And that's assuming the pepperoni on your pizza or the pork in it even came from the United States—it might well have been made in a factory in China, but by virtue of it being a processed food, you will never know. What you can know is that the pork, whether acceptable or not, Chinese or not, was almost certainly raised on antibiotics and an unnatural diet.

Now let's imagine making pizza at home. When I cook it, I cheat and take the shortcut of buying freshly made dough at my local market, cutting out the most laborious step. I usually opt for the whole wheat, but the regular white version, more comparable to the frozen or fast-food processed pizza, contains the following: flour, water, oil, yeast, and salt. At my natural-centric supermarket, even the particular flour used is indicated, unbleached from King Arthur, a renowned supplier of quality baking ingredients. A very good Neapolitan pizza sauce can be made by combining nothing but a can of tomatoes and a teaspoon of sea salt in a food processor. I buy Pomì, a widely available brand from Italy that many Italian chefs use. It contains nothing but 100% Italian tomatoes, actually picked after ripening. This makes it taste better. Pomì is also USDA Organic certified, has no preservatives or artificial flavors, or anything added at all, and if you care, it is also free of bisphenol A and GMOs. I buy actual fresh mozzarella cheese, and while I get one made locally, even a mass-market supermarket brand like BelGioioso from Wisconsin tastes much better than the frozen stuff, is made from milk that does not contain growth hormones, and has no other ingredients except enzymes and salt, which are in pretty much all cheese. That leaves the pepperoni: I buy mine from Vermont Smoke & Cure, which is available at gourmet stores nationwide and made from locally raised pigs where I live, but you can also buy similar products around the country, and one nationally available option is Applegate.

Nothing in my recipe needs to be cooked separately—just spread the ready-made dough, top, and go. Because it's not frozen, it actually cooks faster, and at the end of the day, it takes me maybe five minutes longer to make—at the most. It tastes so much more delicious that there is no comparison, but it is also Real Food. I know everything I need to know about my pizza, and including every component of the pepperoni, dough, and every other ingredient I used, there are twenty-three of them in my finished pie, none objectionable. I could splurge and add basil leaves, garlic, and grated Parmigiano-Reggiano and still have half as many ingredients as the at least fifty-two in the frozen pie.

My wife and I love pizza, and on a warm summer night, I make this very recipe but opt to cook it on my outdoor grill for variety, getting a little more crispiness and flecks of smoky char on the bottom that add to the homemade flavor. Because our garden is in full bloom, I throw on some just-picked peppery arugula leaves to add yet another flavor dimension. That's the great thing about pizza, it's a blank canvas, and you can add anything from potatoes to peanuts to Prosciutto di Parma, using whatever Real Food you have in your fridge or cupboard to make a delicious and wholesome meal.

This pizza is the cornerstone of a comforting dinner we eat on the porch, enjoying the fresh night air. Because I am going to add grated cheese anyway, I start the feast by breaking off a plateful of Parmigiano-Reggiano nuggets from the wedge we always have on hand, then drizzle some twelve-year-old balsamic vinegar and a few drops of Australian extra-virgin olive oil over them. We don't bother with utensils—this is all finger food—but we do bother with wine. I set out a couple of glasses and open a bottle of Colosi Nero d'Avola from Sicily, which uses a lesser known red varietal to produce a young and intense dark ruby full-bodied elixir that goes perfectly with our pizza. And like the pizza, it is very affordable culinary luxury, a thirteen-dollar bottle that gets scores of 88 to 90 from esteemed critics like Robert Parker and James Suckling, the same ratings as wines costing two to three times as much. This delicious dinner was cheap and easy to make, but that does not make it any less satisfying, and we savor the last glasses of wine long after the final bite of chewy crust has vanished.

It's worth the time to cook Real Foods. It is also worth the effort to shop for them and worthwhile to support the real people who make them. Keep it real.

**AOC:** France has the most elaborate system for grading the quality of place-based production of food and wine products. The Appellation d'Origine Contrôlée (Controlled Designation of Origin) indicates that products with this seal were made in places known for making it well, such as Roquefort cheese from Roquefort or Champagne from Champagne.

**AVAS:** American Viticultural Areas are regions legally designated as producing high-quality grapes in the United States, and wines made mostly of grapes from those regions can carry the AVA designation and the name of the particular AVA on their label. An example would be Pasa Robles, California.

**BAP:** The Global Aquaculture Alliance's Best Aquaculture Practices is considered the best national third-party certifying body for the quality of farmed fish.

**COOC CERTIFIED EXTRA VIRGIN:** The California Olive Oil Council offers use of this label to producers in the state using California grown olives and meeting higher testing standards for extra-virgin olive oil than those used by the United States and European Union.

**DOCG:** Denominazione di Origine Controllata e Garantita (Controlled Designation of Origin Guaranteed) is the highest of three grades given by the Italian government to its country's best-quality wines (many lesser wines receive no designation at all). It indicates that the wine was made under strict rules governing allowable grape varietals, aging, and so on and that the wine uses only grapes from a particular area whose vineyards have been designated as excellent. The next two grades are DOC (Denominazione di Origine Controllata, or Controlled Designation of Origin) and DO (Denominazione di Origine, or Designation of Origin).

**DOOR:** The Database of Origin and Registration is a searchable online database of all fourteen-hundred-plus products either awarded or under review for PDO, PGI, or TGI status. *See* GIs.

**EVA:** The Extra Virgin Alliance offers use of this label term to producers worldwide whose oils meet higher testing standards for extra-virgin olive oil than those used by the United States and European Union.

**EVOO:** Common shorthand for Extra Virgin Olive Oil, the higher of two grades for virgin olive oils.

**GIS:** Geographic indications is the catch-all term for foods from anywhere in the world whose very names include a specific place and assure a level of quality. An example would be Prosciutto di Parma, protected under both U.S. and EU law as a particular type of ham made under strict regulations and quality control only in Italy's Parma region. The European Union has adopted a three-tiered grading system for GIs from all around the world, not just Europe. These terms, each with a specific seal/logo, can appear on foods to designate higher quality:

**PDO:** Protected Designation of Origin is the highest grade and certifies that production of the food occurred in a particular place and with an exceptional level of quality.

**PGI:** Protected Geographic Indication is the second tier of the EU system for grading outstanding geographically indicated products. It guarantees the product was made in a particular place well known for producing that product in a notable way.

**TGI:** Traditional Specialties Guaranteed is the third tier of the EU system for grading outstanding geographically indicated products. It designates the food was made in a manner considered traditional, and must have been made and sold in this way for a minimum of 30 years.

**IOC:** The International Olive Council is the main regulatory body of olive oil in the world, setting the standards and definitions used in Europe, the United States, and most other places.

**MSC:** The Marine Stewardship Council is considered the best national third-party certifying body for the accuracy of wild-caught fish. Its logo on food labels is a blue fish in the shape of a check mark.

**OLIVE OIL GRADES:** All "virgin" olive oil must be entirely from the mechanical crushing or spinning of whole olives, nothing else. There are just two edible grades, extra virgin, which meets a number of laboratory and sensory testing standards, and virgin, which scores lower on these tests (though, in practice, both labels are widely misused). Below the virgin grades is simply olive oil, which has been chemically refined and/or distilled to remove impurities and may also contain oil from non-whole-olive by-products. While fit for human consumption, olive oil is considered inferior to virgin olive oils for purposes of both taste and health. Light olive oil falls under this category, as does most oil labeled as "premium," "super," "blend," or "pure."

**UNAPROL/100% QUALITA ITALIANA**: UNAPROL is a trade association of Italian olive growers who make oil from their own domestically grown olives (most olive oil from Italy is made with oils imported from other countries). Its label for extra-virgin olive oil, "100% Qualita Italiana," certifies that all the olives used were grown in Italy and that the grading standards are higher than those required under Italian law or those used by the United States or European Union.

**USDA BEEF GRADES**: All beef sold to consumers in the United States can carry one (or none) of three grading claims reflecting its quality. USDA inspectors inspect each carcass and assign it a grade. The highest is USDA Prime, followed by USDA Choice, then USDA Select, while some beef does not carry any grade designation. USDA Prime represents about 2 percent of the beef sold in the country. Ungraded beef is typically of lower quality than USDA Select, but some small farmers opt out of grading altogether because of the cost, while others may do so because for some styles of beef production, such as grass-fed or exotic breeds, USDA grading may not accurately reflect quality.

# NOTES

## Epigraph

viii *"There's nothing more fundamental"* Kelsey Timmerman, *Where Am I Eating? An Adventure through the Global Food Economy* (Hoboken, NJ: John Wiley, 2013), 54.

## Introduction

xi *"Food fraud, or"* Renée Johnson, "Food Fraud and 'Economically Motivated Adulteration' of Food and Food Ingredients," CRS Report R-43358, Congressional Research Service, Washington, DC, 2014, https://www.fas.org/sgp/crs/misc/R43358.pdf.

xii *Many fakes are* Denise Purcell, "The State of the Specialty Food Industry 2015," Specialty Food, April 7, 2015, https://www.specialtyfood.com/news/article/state-specialty-food-industry-2015/.

xv *The Grocery Manufacturers of America* Johnson, "Food Fraud."

xvi *Commonly sold fake* Jeffrey C. Moore, John Spink, and Markus Lipp, "Development and Application of a Database of Food Ingredient Fraud and Economically Motivated Adulteration from 1980 to 2010." *Journal of Food Science* 77, no. 4 (April 2012): R118–26.

xvi *One of the world's* Chris Elliott, *Meat Authentication: The European Horsemeat Scandal* (video), Global Food Fraud and Safety symposium, Queens's University, Belfast, Northern Ireland, 2014, http://www.selectscience.net/food fraud.aspx?videoID=6&utm_source=ASSET&utm_medium=video&utm_campaign =foodfraud2014.

xvii *Michigan State University's* Royal Society of Chemistry, "Fighting Food Fraud with Science," September 2007, http://www.rsc.org/chemistryworld/Issues/2007/September/FightingFoodFraudWithScience.asp.

xvii *In 2013, Great Britain* Claire Marshall, "Ministers Back Food Crime Unit Recommendation," BBC News, September 4, 2014, http://www.bbc.com/news/science-environment-29047911.

## 1. Real Food, Perfected: A Day in the Life of Parma

1   *"This is one of the most"*   John Fischer, *Cheese: Identification, Classification, Utilization* (Clifton Park, NY: Delmar, 2011), 112.

1   *"The Parmesan cheese you sprinkle"*   Lydia Mulvany, "The Parmesan Cheese You Sprinkle on Your Penne Could Be Wood," Bloomberg Business, February 16, 2016, http://www.bloomberg.com/news/articles/2016-02-16/the-parmesan-cheese-you-sprinkle-on-your-penne-could-be-wood.

22   *This may not be as far*   Clint Rainey, "FDA says 'Parmesan' Cheese Might Actually Be Cheddar or Wood Pulp," Grub Street, February 16, 2016, http://www.grubstreet.com/2016/02/parmesan-cheese-fraud.html.

22   *"all of which contained"*   Ibid.

22–23   *Neal Schuman, whose family-owned*   Mulvany, "The Parmesan Cheese."

25   *This first happened in 1921*   Carol A. Melton, "Generic Term or Trademark?: Confusing Legal Standards and Inadequate Protection," *American University Law Review* 29, no. 1 (1979): 109–33, https://www.wcl.american.edu/journal/lawrev/29/melton.pdf.

26   *Or as Franz Fischler*   Charlotte Denny, "Food Fight on the Menu for WTO Talks in Cancun," *Guardian*, August 28, 2003, http://www.theguardian.com/business/2003/aug/29/wto.internationalnews.

27   *But when the Codex*   "EU Parmesan Request Shunned," *Dairy Industries International* 69, no. 6 (June 2004): 10.

## 2. What Is Fake Food?

33   *"None of us likes"*   Bee Wilson, *Swindled: The Dark History of Food Fraud, from Poisoned Candy to Counterfeit Coffee* (Princeton, NJ: Princeton University Press, 2008), xi.

35   *A good example*   "Italian Police Raid Nets 30,000 Bottles of Fake Wine, ABC News, May 29, 2014, http://abcnews.go.com/blogs/lifestyle/2014/05/italian-police-raid-nets-30000-bottles-of-fake-wine/.

35   *The following month*   "Deluge of Fake Italian Wine May Hit Shop Shelves Worldwide," RT, May 29, 2014, http://rt.com/news/162324-fake-wine-seized-italy/.

36   *In 1986, Italian winemakers*   Wilson, *Swindled*, 63.

36   *The worst version*   Ibid., 32.

40   *The owners of the real*   Hugh Merwin, "Grimaldi's Shanghai Imposter Looks Pretty Horrible," Grub Street, October 22, 2014, http://www.grubstreet.com /2014/10/patsy-grimaldis-shanghai.html.

42   *During a court case*   Michael Tarm, "Sara Lee, Kraft Argue Wiener War in Federal Court," Bloomberg Business, August 15, 2011, http://www.business week.com/ap/financialnews/D9P4QQI02.htm.

## 3. Fishy Fish

44   *"Most seafood buyers"*   U.S. Government Accountability Office, "Seafood Fraud: FDA Program Changes and Better Collaboration among Key Federal Agencies Could Improve Detection and Prevention," GAO-09-258, March 20, 2009, http://www.gao.gov/products/GAO-09-258.

46   *Pulling no punches*   Elizabeth Weise, "Something Fishy? Counterfeit Foods Enter the U.S. Market," *USA Today*, January 23, 2009, http://usatoday30.usatoday .com/news/health/2009-01-19-fake-foods_N.htm.

47   *A study of New York City*   Kimberly Warner, Walker Timme, and Beth Lowell, "Widespread Seafood Fraud Found in New York City," Oceana, December 2012, http://oceana.org/reports/widespread-seafood-fraud-found-new-york-city.

47   *Consumers ordering*   Ibid.

48   *In the seafood industry*   Jenn Abelson and Beth Daley, "On the Menu, but Not on Your Plate," *Boston Globe*, October 23, 2011.

48   *It was effectively banned*   Marian Burros, "A Fish Puts Chefs in a Quandary," Eating Well, *New York Times*, March 10, 1999, http://www.nytimes.com /1999/03/10/dining/eating-well-a-fish-puts-chefs-in-a-quandary.html.

48   *When people get sick*   AnonymousEater, "The Pleasure and Pain of Escolar," *Food in Houston*, August 2, 2007, http://foodinhouston.blogspot.com/2007/08 /pleasure-and-pain-of-escolar.html.

48   *"You can probably go"*   Stephen Nohlgren and Terry Tomalin, "You Order Grouper; What Do You Get?," special report, *St. Petersburg Times*, August 6, 2006.

48   *Florida's economic*   Kim Severson, "Under Many Aliases, Mislabeled Foods Find Their Way to Dinner Tables," *New York Times*, December 15, 2012.

48   *One served an expensive*   Ibid.

51   *Other Florida grouper*   Nohlgren and Tomalin, "You Order Grouper."

52   *In the Oceana study*   Warner, Timme, and Lowell, "Widespread Seafood Fraud."

52   *"Your Red Snapper"*   Carol Vinzant, "Your Red Snapper Is Probably Fake," DailyFinance, August 25, 2008, http://www.dailyfinance.com/2008/08/25/your -red-snapper-is-probably-fake/.

53   *The most common fakes*   Warner, Timme, and Lowell, "Widespread Seafood Fraud."

53   *Better known to exotic diners*   "Tetraodontidae," *Wikipedia*, modified October 1, 2015, https://en.wikipedia.org/wiki/Tetraodontidae.

53   *but no one prepared*   U.S. Government Accountability Office, "Seafood Fraud."

53   *Domestic seafood industry*   Nohlgren and Tomalin, "You Order Grouper."

54   *Just as the* St. Petersburg   Abelson and Daley, "On the Menu."

54   *The study also demonstrated*   Ibid.

56   *Oceana took its study*   Kimberly Warner, Walker Timme, Beth Lowell, and Michael Hirshfield, "Oceana Study Reveals Seafood Fraud Nationwide," Oceana, February 2013, http://oceana.org/reports/oceana-study-reveals-seafood-fraud -nationwide.

60   *In addition*   Darryl Fears, "Seafood Study: Up to 32% Imported to the U.S. Is Caught Illegally," *Washington Post*, April 20, 2014.

61   *"roughly half of the seafood"*   Eric Schwaab, "Is Well-Managed Good Enough?" keynote speech presented to the Monterey Bay Aquarium Sustainable Food Institute's Cooking for Solutions conference, Monterey, CA, May 15, 2014.

61   *Adding insult to injury*   U.S. Department of Labor, Bureau of Labor Statistics, "Shrimp Disease in Asia Resulting in High U.S. Import Prices, *Beyond the Numbers* 3, no. 14 (June 2014), http://www.bls.gov/opub/btn/volume-3/shrimp -disease-in-asia-resulting-in-high-us-import-prices.htm.

61   *the State Department released*   Kim Severson, "Cooking with the Locals: Going Wild for American Shrimp," *New York Times*, August 5, 2014.

62   *A 2004 study*   David Schardt, "Fish for the Best," *Nutrition Action Healthletter*, April 2015, 9.

62   *As a result*   Weise, "Something Fishy."

62   *In 2014, the Department*   U.S. Department of Justice, U.S. Attorney's Office, Southern District of Florida, "Miami Seafood Firm Pleads Guilty and Is Sentenced for Imported Seafood Labeling Fraud," press release, August 5, 2014, http:// www.justice.gov/usao-sdfl/pr/miami-seafood-firm-pleads-guilty-and-sentenced -imported-seafood-labelling-fraud.

63   *When* Consumer Reports   Weise, "Something Fishy."

63   *Shrimp is the nation's*   U.S. Government Accountability Office, "Seafood Fraud."

67   *In 2007, the FDA*   U.S. Government Accountability Office, "Seafood Fraud."

67   *This incident came to light*   Ibid.

68   *Life often imitates*   Ibid.

68   *The FDA did all this*   Ibid.

68   *Nonetheless, a lawsuit*   "FDA Okays Name of Rubio's 'Langostino Lobster' Products," Restaurant News Resource, June 30, 2005, http://www.restaurantnews resource.com/article17305.html.

68   *This court decision*   "Fish Fraud: No Matter What You Call It, 'Squat' Isn't Lobster," *Wild Catch*, January–February 2007, 17, http://www.seagrant.umaine.edu /files/pdf-global/07CSlangWC.pdf.

68   *According to a 2016*   Lisa Guerrero (reporter), "A Third of Tested Restaurant Lobster Dishes Actually Contain Cheaper Seafood," February 8, 2016, http://www.insideedition.com/headlines/14518-a-third-of-tested-restaurant -lobster-dishes-actually-contain-cheaper-fish-meat-investigation-shows.

69   *But in his book*   Kelsey Timmerman, *Where Am I Eating? An Adventure through the Global Food Economy* (Hoboken, NJ: John Wiley, 2013), 169.

69   *Timmerman reports*   Ibid.

70   *Maine's lobster industry*   "Fish Fraud."

70   *Maine's U.S. senator*   Severson, "Under Many Aliases."

70   *When FDA officials collected*   U.S. Government Accountability Office, "Seafood Fraud."

71   *"Dealers often label"*   Gulf of Maine Research Institute, *Culinary Partners Program Newsletter*, June 2013.

71   *Further embellishing*   Ibid.

73   *A 2015 study*   Kimberly Warner, Beth Lowell, Carlos Disla, Kate Ortenzi, Jacqueline Savitz, and Michael Hirschfield, "Oceana Reveals Mislabeling of Iconic Chesapeake Blue Crab," Oceana, April 2015, https://usa.oceana.org/sites /default/files/crab_testing_report_final_3.27.15.pdf.

73   *One participating restaurant*   Shante Woodward, "12 Anne Arundel Restaurants stay 'True Blue' with Maryland Crabs," *Capital Gazette*, June 3, 2013.

74 *In practice* U.S. Government Accountability Office, "Seafood Fraud."

75 *where the average imported* Paul Greenberg, "Bring Local Seafood Back," editorial opinion, *Seattle Times*, July 8, 2014.

75 *Congressman Ed Markey* News Desk, "Rep. Markey Introduces SAFE Seafood Act to Combat Fish Fraud," Food Safety News, March 8, 2013, http://www.foodsafetynews.com/2013/03/rep-market-introduces-safe-seafood-act-to-combat-fish-fraud/#.U-PMi_ldXTo.

75 *But two years* Tyler Hayden, "The Bait and Switch of Seafood Fraud," *Santa Barbara Independent*, July 9, 2014.

76 *Alaska has the largest* Alaska Seafood Marketing Institute, "Salmon Buyer's Guide," brochure, 2009.

76 *none have been classified* National Oceanic and Atmospheric Administration Fisheries Service, "Status of Stocks: 2010 U.S. Fisheries Report to Congress," Silver Spring, MD, June 2011, http://www.nmfs.noaa.gov/sfa/fisheries_eco/status_of_fisheries/archive/2010/2010_status_of_fisheries.pdf.

78 *Real scallops* Gulf of Maine Research Institute, *Culinary Partners Program Newsletter*.

78 *Seventy percent* Ibid.

79 *Whole Foods also has* "Aquaculture, " Whole Foods, accessed February 28, 2016, http://www.wholefoodsmarket.com/mission-values/seafood-sustainability/aquaculture.

79 *In the* Boston Globe Abelson and Daley, "On the Menu."

80 *"When customers walk"* Brittni Furrow, "Changemakers: Accountability and Traceability in the Market," paper presented to the Monterey Bay Aquarium Sustainable Food Institute's Cooking for Solutions conference, Monterey, CA, May 15, 2014.

## 4. Spoiled Oils: Olive and "Truffle"

81 *"This is what"* Tom Mueller, *Extra Virginity: The Sublime and Scandalous World of Olive Oil* (New York: W. W. Norton, 2012), 5.

82 *Despite rapid growth* Selina Wang, Ben Moscatello, and Dan Flynn, "Survey: Consumer Attitudes toward Olive Oil," Olive Center, University of California, Davis, May 2013, http://olivecenter.ucdavis.edu/research/files/surveyfinal052913reduced.pdf.

83   *Nobody captures*   *The Fresh-Pressed Olive Oil Club* newsletter, Winter 2012.

85   *Despite being the world's*   U.S. International Trade Commission, *Olive Oil.*

86   *Yet studies*   U.S. International Trade Commission, *Olive Oil: Conditions of Competition between U.S. and Major Foreign Supplier Industries,* Investigation No. 332-537, USITC Pub. No. 4419, Washington, DC, August 2013, http://www.usitc.gov/publications/332/pub4419.pdf.

86   *"Once someone"*   Mueller, *Extra Virginity,* 35.

87   *approved by the FDA*   U.S. International Trade Commission, *Olive Oil.*

87   *Unlike vegetable oils*   Ibid.

87   *The subject*   Mueller, *Extra Virginity,* 104.

87   *Extra-virgin olive oil also contains*   "Made in Italy: A Journey with UNAPROL through the Values of Extra-Virgin Olive Oil," Italian Trade Commission press release, 2013.

88   *A more recently*   Mueller, *Extra Virginity,* 101–6.

88   *"Bad oil"*   Ibid., 7.

88   *This illegal adulteration*   Bee Wilson, *Swindled: The Dark History of Food Fraud, From Poisoned Candy to Counterfeit Coffee* (Princeton, NJ: Princeton University Press, 2008), 290.

89   *There is a long history*   U.S. International Trade Commission, *Olive Oil.*

89   *Consumer studies*   Wang, Moscatello, and Flynn, "Survey."

89   *and the industry's domestic*   "What the American Consumer Really Thinks about Olive Oil," report, North American Olive Oil Association, June 2014, http://c1.oliveoiltim.es/library/naooa-survey.pdf.

89   *by dollar volume*   "What the American Consumer Really Thinks."

90   *The "olive oil"*   Mueller, *Extra Virginity,* 110.

90   *where Italian investigators*   Ibid., 199.

91   *some experts put*   Ibid., 62.

91   *Worse, the vast majority*   Ibid., 114–15.

92   *"Wait even"*   Bill Marsano, "Find the Fake," panel, Fancy Food Show, New York, 2014.

94   *"The three biggest"*   Michele Bungaro, "Find the Fake," panel, Fancy Food Show, New York, 2014.

94–95    *"The enormous popularity"*    Mueller, *Extra Virginity*, 45.

95    *Just in Italy*    Branislav Pekic, "Italy to Introduce Extra Virgin Anti-Fraud Label," *European Supermarket Magazine*, February 15, 2016.

95    *bigger than Coca-Cola, Disney,* Fortune 500 list, *Fortune*, 2014.

95    *In 2010, the University*    E. N. Frankel, R. J. Mailer, C. F. Shoemaker, S. C. Wang, and J. D. Flynn, "Report: Tests Indicate That Imported "Extra Virgin" Olive Oil Often Fails International and USDA Standards," Olive Center, University of California, Davis, July 2010, http://olivecenter.ucdavis.edu/research/files/oliveoilfinal071410updated.pdf.

95    *Subsequent tests*    Selina Wang, Edwin Frankel, and Dan Flynn, "Report: Evaluation of Olive Oil Sold to Restaurants and Foodservice," Olive Center, University of California, Davis, September 2012, http://olivecenter.ucdavis.edu/research/files/RestaurantsandFoodservice.pdf.

95    *A follow-up supermarket*    Frankel, Mailer, Wang, et al., "Evaluation."

96    *In November 2015*    Nick Squires, "Italian Olive Oil Scandal: Seven Top Brands 'Sold Fake Extra-Virgin'" *Telegraph*, November 11, 2015.

96    *As recently as 2016*    Ibid.

96    Consumer Reports *magazine*    "How to Find the Best Extra-Virgin Olive Oil: Our Taste Tests Show That Some Oils Don't Make the Grade," *Consumer Reports*, September 2012.

96    *In Spain, an investigation*    Julie Butler, *Olive Oil Times*, December 5, 2011.

96    *The main governing body*    U.S. International Trade Commission, *Olive Oil.*

97    *There are three grades*    U.S. Department of Agriculture, "United States Standards for Olive Oil and Olive-Pomace Oil," Washington, DC, October 25, 2010, http://www.ams.usda.gov/sites/default/files/media/Olive_Oil_and_Olive-Pomace_Oil_Standard%5B1%5D.pdf.

98    *One of Mueller's*    Mueller, *Extra Virginity*, 62.

98    *Unlike all other*    Ibid. 19.

99    *"Both olive pomace"*    U.S. International Trade Commission, *Olive Oil.*

100    *the vast majority*    "What the American Consumer."

100    *In a consumer perception*    Ibid.

100    *When Australia enacted*    U.S. International Trade Commission, *Olive Oil.*

100   *After more than seven*   Mueller, *Extra Virginity*, 173–74.

101   *California Republican*   "US Olive Oil Pushing Government to Test Imported Oils, NorthJersey.com, February 18, 2014, http://www.northjersey.com/food-and-dining-news/us-olive-oil-pushing-government-to-test-imported-oils-1.675846#sthash.5xV2K3Hl.dpuf.

101   *After the Canadian*   U.S. International Trade Commission, *Olive Oil.*

104   *In 2007, acclaimed*   Daniel Patterson, "Hocus-Pocus, and a Beaker of Truffles," *New York Times*, May 16, 2007.

105   *Jean-Georges Vongerichten*   "In My Kitchen: Jean-Georges Vongerichten," interview by Jackie Cooperman, *Wall Street Journal*, January 22, 2011.

105   *Equally high-profile celebrity*   Rebe Lynch, "Chef Gordon Ramsay on the One Ingredient You Should Not Have in Your Pantry," *Los Angeles Times*, June 7, 2011.

105   *In a self-proclaimed*   J. Kenji López-Alt, "Rant: Enough with the Truffle Oil Already," Serious Eats, April 8, 2011, http://www.seriouseats.com/2011/04/rant-enough-with-the-truffle-oil-already.html.

109   *In early 2016*   Branislav Pekic, "Italy to Introduce Extra Virgin Anti-Fraud Label, *European Supermarket Magazine*, February 15, 2016.

110   *The impartial U.S.*   U.S. International Trade Commission, *Olive Oil.*

## 5. What's in a Name? Real Foods Come from Real Places

112   *"This can't be repeated"*   Arthur Schwartz, "Italian Food Labels," *The Food Maven Diary*, The Food Maven, June 24, 2002, http://www.thefoodmaven.com/diary.html?diary_start=320.

112   *Kō's website claims*   Kō, February 26, 2016, http://korestaurant.com/.

112   *"A recipe I like"*   Jen Russo, "Kō's Chef Tylun Pang's Ginger Steamed Kumu with Chinese Sausage," MauiTime, March 26, 2013, http://mauidish.com/maui-restaurant-reviews/kos-chef-tylun-pangs-ginger-steamed-kumu-with-chinese-sausage-fairmontkealani/.

115   *"Terroir has no direct"*   Justin Hughes, "Champagne, Feta, and Bourbon: The Spirited Debate about Geographical Indications," *Hastings Law Journal* 58 (2006): 299.

117   *In 1935, a special*   "Appellation d'Origine Contrôlée," *Wikipedia*, modified November 18, 2015, http://en.wikipedia.org/wiki/Appellation_d%27origine_contr%C3%B4l%C3%A9e.

117    *According to Professor Hughes*    Hughes, "Champagne, Feta, and Bourbon," 299.

117    *As Hughes notes*    Ibid.

119    *The pampered poultry*    "Bresse Chicken," *Wikipedia,* modified July 13, 2015, http://en.wikipedia.org/wiki/Bresse_chicken.

119    *The* Guardian *newspaper*    Jon Henley, "Top of the Pecking Order," *Guardian,* January 9, 2008.

119    *The European Union takes*    European Commission, "New Framework for Quality Schemes in Agriculture Enters into Force," Agriculture and Rural Development, modified April 22, 2015, http://ec.europa.eu/agriculture/newsroom /100_en.htm.

120    *The highest designation*    Regulation (EU) No. 1151/2012 of the European Parliament and of the Council, "On Quality Schemes for Agricultural Products and Foodstuffs," November 21, 2012, http://eur-lex.europa.eu/legal-content /EN/TXT/?uri=uriserv:OJ.L_.2012.343.01.0001.01.ENG.

120    *In 2007, the European*    "NVV Has Assumed the Duty of Preserving the Napa Valley Name for Those Who Have Earned the Right to Put It on Their Labels, Napa Name Protection," February 24, 2016, http://www.napavintners.com /about/napa_name_protection.asp.

121    *There are five*    Anna O. Perret and Erik Thevenod-Mottet, "The Florida Oranges Local Agro-Food System—Geographical Indication or Commodity?," paper presented at the European Association of Agricultural Economists, 116th Seminar, October 27–30, 2010, Parma Italy, http://purl.umn.edu/95215.

122    *For more than*    European Union Code 2081/92, Application for Registration: Article 17(1) National File No: PDO/00116, accessed February 24, 2016, http://ec.europa.eu/agriculture/quality/door/registeredName.html?denomi nationId=364.

123    *So unlike the vague*    Idaho Potato Commission, "Our Most Common Varieties," accessed February 24, 2016, https://idahopotato.com/directory/varieties.

123    *when someone buys*    European Union Code 2081/92.

123    *The San Marzano is an illuminating*    Regulations for the production and processing of PDO "Pomodoro San Marzano Agro-Nocerino Sarnese," "Register of Protected Designations of Origin and Protected Geographical Indications," *Official Gazette,* no. 257, November 5, 2001, within the meaning of Regulation (EC) 1263/96.

125   *In comparison*   Robin Abcarian, "Ever Heard of 'Pine Nut Syndrome'? Neither Had I, until I Got It," *Los Angeles Times*, July 22, 2014.

125   *As the* Telegraph   Alastair Jamieson, "Cheap Chinese Pine Nut Exports Blamed for Rare Condition," *Telegraph*, April 17, 2011.

126   *It calls wines*   "Napa Victory a Problem for Cheap Wine," *Box Wines*, June 20, 2007, http://www.boxwines.org/articles/napa-victory-a-problem-for-cheap-wine.htm.

## 6. Q: Where's the Kobe Beef? A: Not on Your Plate

128   *"Restaurants across America"*   Olivia Fleming, "$40 for a Burger and $100 for a Steak . . . But Is That Kobe Beef on Upscale Restaurant Menus Only 'Faux-Be' Meat?" *Daily Mail*, April 12, 2012.

129   *Early in his trip*   Mark Schatzker, *Steak: One Man's Search for the World's Tastiest Piece of Beef* (New York: Penguin, 2010), 149.

131   *"With so-called 'Kobe beef'"*   Katy McLaughlin, "Bring on the Fat, Bring on the Taste: Celebrity Chefs Join Burger Wars, Baste Beef Patties in Butter," *Wall Street Journal*, November 17, 2010, http://online.wsj.com/articles/SB100014240 52748704312504575618450888182376.

133   *"The USDA currently bans"*   Katy McLaughlin, "Eating Around," *Wall Street Journal*, February 6, 2003.

133   *New York's Old Homestead*   Jay Cheshes, "Knockoff Kobe: What's the Provenance of Prized Super-Fatty Beef in New York Restaurants? Probably Not Japan," *New York*, April 11, 2005, 18.

133   *Japanese beef became*   "What They Got for It . . . The $170 Cheeseburger," *Maclean's*, May 12, 2008, 61.

134   *As a reporter*   Fleming, "$40 for a Burger."

134   *"Kobe beef, it seems"*   Russ Parsons, "Truly, Madly Moonstruck: Chefs and Diners Are Paying a Fortune for Kobe Beef, the Marvelously Marbled Japanese-Style Delicacy. But Is It Worth the Price?" *Los Angeles Times*, October 12, 2005, http://articles.latimes.com/2005/oct/12/food/fo-wagyu12.

134   *As Olivia Fleming*   Fleming, "$40 for a Burger."

135   *As recently as 2010*   McLaughlin, "Bring on the Fat."

135   *For a Fake Food slap*   Arjun Kharpal, "Chef Creates 'Glamburger' for $1,770," CNBC, October 7, 2014, http://www.cnbc.com/id/102065328#.

135 *So many people* Michael Booth and Jennifer Brown, *Eating Dangerously: Why the Government Can't Keep Your Food Safe . . . and How You Can* (Lanham, MD: Bowman & Littlefield, 2014), 52.

139 *the* Los Angeles Times *estimated* Parsons, "Truly, Madly Moonstruck."

140 *This is a fundamental* Justin Hughes, "Champagne, Feta, and Bourbon: The Spirited Debate about Geographical Indications," *Hastings Law Journal* 58 (2006): 299.

141 *we reap what we sow* Patrick J. Kole, "Needs and Expectations of the GI Sector in the USA in Terms of Multilateral Trade Rules Affecting GIs," presentation, Idaho Potato Commission, Eagle, ID, February 24, http://www.origine.coop /IMG/pdf/2013/21%20MAI/21-33%20Kole%20Idaho%20IG%20USA.pdf.

142 *what is protected* Steakhouse Elite, "Football Tailgate Groups Partner with Steakhouse Elite to Deliver Better Beef, Burgers & Franks," press release, PerishableNews.com, September 19, 2013, http://www.perishablenews.com/index .php?article=0031806.

142 *"What's this 'American'"* Michael Atkins, "What's 'American Kobe Beef'?" *Seattle Trademark Lawyer,* July 6, 2011, http://seattletrademarklawyer.com/blog /2011/7/6/whats-american-kobe-beef.html.

143 *"Many a pork cutlet"* Kim Severson, "Under Many Aliases, Mislabeled Foods Find Their Way to Dinner Tables," *New York Times,* December 15, 2012.

143 *Tom Colicchio* Ibid.

144 *Attorneys representing* Anne Bucher, "McCormick & Schmick's Kobe Beef Class Action Settlement Approved," Top Class Actions, July 9, 2014, http://top classactions.com/lawsuit-settlements/lawsuit-news/33657-mccormick-schmicks -kobe-beef-class-action-settlement-approved/.

144 *Perhaps emboldened* Gillian Ferguson, "There's No Such Thing as a Kobe Slider: Kobe Fraud Is Rampant in the US," *Good Food,* KCRW, August 29, 2014, http://blogs.kcrw.com/goodfood/2014/08/theres-no-such-thing-as-a-kobe -slider-kobe-fraud-is-rampant-in-the-us/.

145 *But despite Shenkman's* Erin DeJesus, "SBE Group Settles Class-Action Kobe Beef Lawsuit," Eater, August 21, 2014, http://eater.com/archives/2014/08/21 /sbe-restaurant-group-settles-classaction-kobe-beef-lawsuit.php.

148 *the American Wagyu Association* Bill Daley, "Kobe Beef Explained: Ask for Proof of Origin when Ordering," The Daley Question, *Chicago Tribune,* August 27, 2013.

149 *The USDA disagrees* U.S. Department of Agriculture, Agricultural Marketing Service, "USDA Specification for Characteristics of Cattle Eligible for Approved Branded Beef Programs Claiming Wagyu Influence, February 13, 2014, http://www.ams.usda.gov/sites/default/files/media/GLW%20–%20Wagyu%20 Live%20Animal%20–%20021314.pdf.

152 *Shea Gallante* Jay Cheshes, "Knockoff Kobe."

152 In *Gourmet* Barry Estabrook, "Raising the Steaks," *Gourmet*, December 2007, 250.

152 *Florence Fabricant* Daley, "Kobe Beef Explained."

154 *In 2015, renowned* Ian Harrison, "Antonio Park Just Became the First Chef in Canada with a Kobe Beef License, Eater Montreal, April 13, 2015, http://montreal.eater.com/2015/4/13/8312653/antonio-park-lavanderia -montreal-restaurant-kobe-beef-first-in-canada.

## 7. Champagne and Scotch: The Sincerest Form of Flattery

170 *"The winery is the largest"* "History," Pleasant Valley Wine Company, February 24, http://www.pleasantvalleywine.com/.

171 *"California champagnes are made"* "California Champagnes," Korbel, February 24, 2016, http://www.korbel.com/toast-life/.

172 *In an interview* Shirley Skeel, reporter, "EU Agrees to Protect Napa Wines' Good Name, NPR, June 19, 2007, http://www.npr.org/templates/story/story .php?storyId=11193986.

172 *Acclaimed wine journalist* Lettie Teague, "California Sparkling Wine Sneaks Up on Champagne," *Wall Street Journal*, August 1, 2014.

172 *Eric Asimov succinctly* Eric Asimov, "Champagne: How Low Can You Go?" *New York Times*, December 14, 1005.

173 *Today, there are* Justin Hughes, "Champagne, Feta, and Bourbon: The Spirited Debate about Geographical Indications," *Hastings Law Journal* 58 (2006): 299.

173 *The agreement included* U.S. Department of the Treasury, Alcohol and Tobacco Tax and Trade Bureau, "Wine Appellations of Origin," TBB.gov, modified October 16, 2015, http://www.ttb.gov/appellation/index.shtml.

177 *The* Code Scotch Whisky Association, "SWA Legal Report 2013," February 24, http://www.scotch-whisky.org.uk/news-publications/news/swa-legal -report-2013/.

177   *Some play*   Ibid.

178   *"Consumers and Governments"*   Ibid.

178   *Single malts, made from*   "Scotch Whisky Regulations 2009," The National Archive, February 24, 2016, http://www.legislation.gov.uk/uksi/2009/2890/regulation/3/made.


## 8. Cheesy Cheeses

191   *The entire category*   U.S. Dairy Export Council, "Why U.S. Cheese," More Statistics, http://www.thinkusadairy.org/products/cheese/why-us-cheese.

192   *Nonetheless, the U.S. Patent*   Mark Anstoetter and Madeleine McDonough, "When Gruyère Cheese Is Not Made in Gruyère, Is It Still Gruyère Cheese?" Lexology, May 11, 2012, http://www.lexology.com/library/detail.aspx?g=59aae75f-2e16-47a1-98dc-a924cb34dc02.

192   *America, not Switzerland*   U.S. Dairy Export Council, "Why U.S. Cheese," World's Largest Cheese Producer, http://www.thinkusadairy.org/products/cheese/why-us-cheese.

195   *According to its producers'*   "P.D.O Manchego: The History of an Ancient Cheese," Denominación de Origen Queso Manchego, accessed January 7, 2015, http://www.quesomanchego.es/news/p.d.o-manchego-the-history-of-an-ancient-cheese?set_language=en.

196   *This is an international*   Jeffrey C. Moore, John Spink, and Markus Lipp, "Development and Application of a Database of Food Ingredient Fraud and Economically Motivated Adulteration from 1980 to 2010," *Journal of Food Science* 77, no. 4 (April 2012): R118–26.

196   *Twelve percent*   Dan Nosowitz, "British Goat Cheese Secretly Made from Non-Goat Milk," *Modern Farmer*, November 3, 2014, http://modernfarmer.com/2014/11/british-goat-cheese-secretly-made-non-goat-milk-watchdog-group-finds/?utm_source=feedly&utm_reader=feedly&utm_medium=rss&utm_campaign=british-goat-cheese-secretly-made-non-goat-milk-watchdog-group-finds.

196   *Elliott's researchers*   Chris Elliott, Global Food Fraud and Safety symposium, *The Geographical Origins of Cheese* (video), Queen's University, Belfast, Northern Ireland, 2014, http://www.selectscience.net/foodfraud.aspx?videoID=16&utm_source=ASSET&utm_medium=video&utm_campaign=%20Food-Fraud-2014.

197   *Canada, which has*   Nicole Potenza Denis, "Supporters Argue It's Good for the Industry and the Consumer, but the EU's proposal on Restricting Naming

Conventions for Cheeses Could Result in Consumer Confusion and Hardship among American Cheesemakers," Specialty Food Association, March 24, 2014, http://www.specialtyfood.com/news-trends/featured-articles/article/cheese-industry-embattled-over-eu-naming-proposal/.

197 *"I am a 12-year veteran"* Liz Thorpe, "Let Them Eat 'Feta': Why the EU Should Allow US Cheesemongers to Steal Names," *Guardian*, March 15, 2014, http://www.theguardian.com/commentisfree/2014/mar/15/eu-us-cheese-names-regulations

198 *The "Muenster" cheese* Latoya Dennis, "Europe Tells U.S. to Lay Off Brie and Get Its Own Cheese Names, *The Salt*, NPR, March 4, 2014, http://www.npr.org/blogs/thesalt/2014/03/04/280736997/europe-tells-u-s-to-lay-off-brie-and-get-its-own-cheese-names.

198 *U.S. senator* Associated Press, "Say Bye Bye to Parmesan, Muenster and Feta: Europe Wants Its Cheese Back," *Guardian*, March 11, 2014, http://www.theguardian.com/lifeandstyle/2014/mar/11/europe-trade-talks-cheese-back-parmesan-feta.

199 *Farr Hariri* Nicole Potenza Denis, "Cheese Industry Embattled over EU Naming Proposal," March 24, 2014, http://www.specialtyfood.com/news-trends/featured-articles/article/cheese-industry-embattled-over-eu-naming-proposal/.

200 *Shawna Morris* Dennis, "Europe Tells U.S."

200 *"Recently concluded"* "U.S., China Reach Agreement on Cheese Exports," Specialty Food, December 22, 2014, https://www.specialtyfood.com/news/news-center/article/us-china-reach-agreement-geographic-indicators-cheese-exports/.

201 *In 2014, leading* Daniel Gritzer, "Taste Test: Is Domestic Parmesan Cheese Worth Using?" Serious Eats, September 24, 2014, http://www.seriouseats.com/2014/09/domestic-parmesan-taste-test-parmigiano-reggiano.html.

## 9. Fine Wines and Not-So-Fine Wines

213 *"It was fifty"* "Gallo Family Vineyards Celebrates 50th Anniversary of Its Hearty Burgundy Wine," PR Newswire, January 21, 2014, http://www.prnewswire.com/news-releases/gallo-family-vineyards-celebrates-50th-anniversary-of-its-hearty-burgundy-wine-241298301.html.

213 *The press release* Ibid.

214 *From another company* "Gallo Family Vineyards Hearty Burgundy," fact sheet obtained by author in 2014, n.d.

214 *Specifically, the fourteen* 27 C.F.R. §4.21 (2012) and 27 C.F.R. §4.24(b) (2000).

215 *The TTB ostensibly* U.S. Department of the Treasury, Alcohol and Tobacco Tax and Trade Bureau, "TTB's Responsibilities—What We Do," October 29, 2015, http://www.ttb.gov/consumer/responsibilities.shtml.

215 *In California, some* Fred Tasker, "California Sangiovese Is Not Your Father's Chianti," *Chicago Tribune*, January 31, 1996, http://articles.chicagotribune.com/1996-01-31/entertainment/9601310182_1_sangiovese-marco-cappelli-california-winemakers.

216 *"Now, here's"* Ibid.

219 *According to the San* Tara Duggan, "A Jug Full of Tradition: Wine Country Vintners Serve Up Wines Straight from the Barrel," SFGate, July 4, 2008, http://www.sfgate.com/wine/article/A-JUG-FULL-OF-TRADITION-3278393.php.

219 *"Port wine"* "Port Wine," *Wikipedia*, modified December 10, 2015, https://en.wikipedia.org/wiki/Port_wine.

219 *Australia, long a major* Matt Paish, "Labelling Law Change: Australian 'Sherry' and 'Port' Forbidden," AFN, November 30, 2011, http://ausfoodnews.com.au/2011/11/30/labelling-law-change-australian-'sherry'-and-port'-forbidden.html.

219 *Canada stopped allowing* "Canadian Wineries Will Say Goodbye to "Port" and "Sherry" by December 31, 2013, Canadian Vintners Association, February 24, 2016, http://www.canadianvintners.com/?p=498].

223 *In its 2014* "*Wine Spectator* Announces Its 2014 Wine of the Year, *Wine Spectator*, November 14, 2014, http://www.winespectator.com/webfeature/show/id/50854.

226 *Ghengis Khan* Brotherhood, February 24, 2016, http://www.brotherhood-winery.com/winesSpecialty.html.

228 *the advantage to Napa* Elizabeth Barham, ed., "American Origin Products (AOPs): Protecting a Legacy." Organization for an International Geographical Indications Network, Geneva, Switzerland, http://www.aop-us.org/uploads/2/1/2/5/21255810/american_origin_products_protecting_a_legacy_final_23_02.pdf

229 *Patterned loosely* Crystal Blum and Mihaella Smith, "The Wine Trade Dispute between the United States and the European Union: An Interview with Richard Mendelson of Dickenson, Peatman & Fogarty, *Business Law Journal*, May 1, 2004, http://blj.ucdavis.edu/archives/vol-4-no-2/wine-trade-dispute.html.

229   *Likewise, vintage wines*   27 C.F.R. §4.27 (2012).

229   *Bronco Wines*   Associated Press, "How a $2 Bottle Transformed the Wine Industry," NBCNews.com, May 28, 2007, http://www.nbcnews.com/id/18868861/ns/business-us_business/t/how-bottle-transformed-wine-industry/#.Vs3dpPkrKUm.

230   *Wine production in China*   "China to Double Wine Production within Five Years," Wine-Searcher, November 22, 2013, http://www.wine-searcher.com/m/2013/11/china-to-double-wine-production-in-five-years.

230   *"Consumers worldwide"*   "Napa Valley Vintners Continues Fight to Prevent Consumer Deception," Napa Valley Vintners press release, August 27, 2013, http://www.napavintners.com/press/press_release_detail.asp?ID_News=400217.

## 10. The Other Red (and White) Meat?

234   *"Suddenly this hippie-food fad"*   Kimberly Lord Stewart, *Eating between the Lines: The Supermarket Shopper's Guide to the Truth behind Food Labels* (New York: St. Martin's, Griffin, 2007), xviii.

242   *save only the tiny*   "World Health Rankings," World Life Expectancy, May 2014, http://www.worldlifeexpectancy.com/cause-of-death/coronary-heart-disease/by-country/.

242   *Argentines, now in second*   Simon Romero, "Argentina Falls from Its Throne as King of Beef," *New York Times,* June 13, 2013.

245   *To me, there*   21 C.F.R. §589.2000 BSE (1997).

245   *95 percent*   Avinash Kar, health attorney, Natural Resource Defense Council, personal communication, April 10, 2015.

245   *The CDC*   Ibid.

246   *"Most people"*   Martin J. Blaser, *Missing Microbes How the Overuse of Antibiotics Is Fueling Our Modern Plagues* (New York: Picador, 2014), 84–85.

247   *It is not only legal*   21 C.F.R. §589.2000 BSE (1997).

247   *Here is the main way*   U.S. Department of Agriculture, Food Safety and Inspection Service, "Water in Meat and Poultry," May 2011, http://www.fsis.usda.gov/wps/wcm/connect/42a903e2-451d-40ea-897a-22dc74ef6e1c/Water_in_Meats.pdf?MOD=AJPERES.

248   *However, when Tyson*   Ruth Winter, *A Consumer's Dictionary of Food Additives,* 7th ed. (New York: Three Rivers Press, 2009), 16.

252 *Consumers Union tested* Stewart, *Eating between the Lines,* 35.

252 *The FDA received* U.S. Government Accountability Office, "Food Safety: FDA Should Strengthen Its Oversight of Food Ingredients Determined to Be Generally Recognized as Safe (GRAS)," GAO-10-246, February 2010, http://www.gao.gov/assets/310/300743.pdf.


## 11. Fakes, Fakes and More Fakes: What Else Is There?

254 *"One of the greatest"* Bea Parks, "Fighting Food Fraud with Science," Royal Society of Chemistry, February 24, 2016, http://www.rsc.org/chemistryworld/Issues/2007/September/FightingFoodFraudWithScience.asp.

255 *the FDA summarily* Petition Denial Response from FDA CFSAN to the American Beekeeping Federation Inc. et al. Macfarlane Ferguson and McMullen re: FDA Docket No. 2006 P 0207 0008, October 5, 2011, http://www.regulations.gov/#!documentDetail;D=FDA-2006-P-0207-0007.

256 *As the* Federal Register *Federal Register* 76, no. 2 (January 4, 2011): 251–53.

256 *"Two honeys could"* "USDA Honey Grading," Honey Traveler, February 24, 2016, http://www.honeytraveler.com/types-of-honey/grading-honey/.

257 *But the bottom line* Andrew Schneider, "Don't Let Claims on Honey Labels Dupe You," *Seattle Post-Intelligencer,* December 30, 2008, http://www.seattlepi.com/local/article/Don-t-let-claims-on-honey-labels-dupe-you-1296249.php.

258 *Reports of widespread* Bee Wilson, *Swindled: The Dark History of Food Fraud, from Poisoned Candy to Counterfeit Coffee* (Princeton, NJ: Princeton University Press, 2008), 177.

258 *A 2014 investigation* Harry Wallop, "Manuka Honey Fraud—What Else Is Fake in Our Food?" *Telegraph,* July 1, 2004, http://www.telegraph.co.uk/foodanddrink/10938108/Manuka-honey-fraud-what-else-is-fake-in-our-food.html.

258 *According to a comprehensive* Jeffrey C. Moore, John Spink, and Markus Lipp, "Development and Application of a Database of Food Ingredient Fraud and Economically Motivated Adulteration from 1980 to 2010," *Journal of Food Science* 77, no. 4 (April 2012): R118-26.

258 *And Americans buy* Susan Berfield, *Businessweek,* September 19, 2013.

258 *The FDA's honey guy* Elizabeth Weise, "Something Fishy? Counterfeit Foods Enter the U.S. Market," *USA Today,* January 23, 2009, http://usatoday30.usatoday.com/news/health/2009-01-19-fake-foods_N.htm.

259   *One German honey*   Gretchen Voss, "What Is Food Fraud?" *Women's Health*, October 15, 2012, http://www.womenshealthmag.com/food/food-safety.

259   *"Chinese honey was often"*   Susan Berfield, "The Honey Launderers: Uncovering the Largest Food Fraud in U.S. History," *Businessweek*, September 19, 2013, http://www.businessweek.com/printer/articles/153774-the-honey-launderers-uncovering-the-largest-food-fraud-in-u-dot-s-dot-history?src=longreads.

260   *Ground coffee*   Wilson, *Swindled*, 99.

260   *Coffee is the world's*   "Coffee FAQ," Global Exchange, February 24, 2016, http://www.globalexchange.org/fairtrade/coffee/faq.

260   *Contemporary researchers*   Mandy Oaklander, "11 Most Fraudulent Foods: Why Adulterants May Be Lurking in Foods You Eat Every Day," *Prevention*, January 25, 2013, http://www.prevention.com/food/healthy-eating-tips/food-fraud-11-most-common-cases?s=7.

260   *According to* Chemistry World   Emma Stoye, "Test Catches Fraudulent Coffee Ingredients," *Chemistry World*, August 12, 2014, http://www.scientificamerican.com/article/test-catches-fraudulent-coffee-ingredients/.

261   *In 1996, the owner*   Debra Barayugarr, "Cheap Coffee Had Been Repackaged as Expensive Kona Beans for Years," *Honolulu Star-Bulletin*, http://www.davislevin.com/in-the-news/class-actions-kone-coffee-farmers-win-fake-bean-suit/.

261   *If the product says*   Elizabeth Barham, ed., "American Origin Products (AOPs): Protecting a Legacy." Organization for an International Geographical Indications Network, Geneva, Switzerland, http://www.aop-us.org/uploads/2/1/2/5/21255810/american_origin_products_protecting_a_legacy_final_23_02.pdf.

262   *In its broad*   Renée Johnson, "Food Fraud and 'Economically Motivated Adulteration' of Food and Food Ingredients," CRS Report R-43358, Congressional Research Service, Washington, DC, 2014, https://www.fas.org/sgp/crs/misc/R43358.pdf.

262   *In 2008, two*   D. Radhakrishnan, "Adulterated Tea Destroyed in Nilgiris," *Hindu*, December 31, 2008, http://www.thehindu.com/todays-paper/tp-national/tp-tamilnadu/adulterated-tea-destroyed-in-nilgiris/article1405216.ece.

263   *Nonetheless, it is estimated*   Sutanuka Ghosal, "Hard Days Ahead for Fake Darjeeling Tea," July 15, 2006, http://articles.economictimes.indiatimes.com/2006-07-15/news/27433288_1_darjeeling-tea-association-organic-darjeeling-basudeb-banerjee.

263 *Spices, especially when* Dana Tyler, "Spiked Spices," CBS News Channel 2, New York, January 20, 2016, http://newyork.cbslocal.com/video/category /news/3348948-seen-at-11-spiked-spices/.

265 *"flavored juice blend"* "Organic Cranberry Blueberry," R.W. Knudsen Family, accessed July 2014, http://www.rwknudsenfamily.com/.

265 *According to Michael Roberts* Catherine Zuckerman, "Food Fraud: Labels on What We Eat Often Mislead," *National Geographic,* July 12, 2013.

266 *That's why Coca-Cola* Bruce Horovitz, "Honesty: New Ingredient in Food Labels," *USA Today,* June 12, 2014.

266 *The 2014 Congressional* Johnson, "Food Fraud."

267 *In her book* Wilson, *Swindled,* 291.

267 *Krueger Food* Dana A. Krueger, "Food Science and Economic Adulteration," Krueger Food laboratories, February 24, 2016, http://robertmondaviinstitute .ucdavis.edu/events/media/FoodScienceandEconomicAdulterationDanaKrueger .pdf.

268 *In the spring* U.S. Food and Drug Administration, "Import Alert 22-04," March 21, 2014, modified June 22, 2015, http://www.accessdata.fda.gov/cms _ia/importalert_1101.html.

274 *"Maple Brown Sugar"* product description for Nature Valley Granola Bars, Nature Valley, February 24, 2016, http://www.naturevalley.com/nv-products /maple-brown-sugar-crunchy-granola-bars/.

## 12. In Conclusion

276 *"How did we ever get"* Michael Pollan, *The Omnivore's Dilemma* (New York: Penguin Press, 2006), 1.

278 *have been coded ASP* U.S. Food and Drug Administration, "Everything Added to Food in the United States," updated April 23, 2013, http://www.access data.fda.gov/scripts/fcn/fcnNavigation.cfm?rpt=eafusListing&displayAll=false &page=4.

280 *As of 2015* Truman Lewis, Lawsuits May Force Feds to Define 'Natural' Foods: FDA, FTC, USDA Have All Dropped the Ball," Consumer Affairs, March 24, 2015, http://www.consumeraffairs.com/organic-and-natural-food-scams-and -lawsuits#lawsuits-may-force-feds-to-define-natural-foods.

280   *As a result*   U.S. Government Accountability Office, "Food Safety: FDA Should Strengthen Its Oversight of Food Ingredients Determined to Be Generally Recognized as Safe (GRAS)," GAO-10-246, February 2010, http://www.gao.gov/assets/310/300743.pdf.

280   *It is the first*   Mary Clare Jalonick, "Genetically Altered Salmon a 'Frankenfish,' Activists Say," Associated Press, November 20, 2015.

281   *research has shown*   Stephanie Strom, "F.D.A. Takes Issue with the Term 'Non-G.M.O.,' *New York Times*, November 20, 2015, http://www.nytimes.com/2015/11/21/business/fda-takes-issue-with-the-term-non-gmo.html.

281   *A scathing GAO*   U.S. Government Accountability Office, "Food Safety."

282   *Federal regulations*   Adam Minter, "Where Do You Think Those Fish Sticks Are From?" Bloomberg View, March 23, 2015, http://www.bloombergview.com/articles/2015-03-22/where-do-you-think-those-fish-sticks-are-from-.

284   *like butylated hydroxytoluene*   Ruth Winter, M.S., *A Consumer's Dictionary of Food Additives*, 7th ed. (New York: Three Rivers Press, 2009), 122.

# ACKNOWLEDGMENTS

You have to break a lot of eggs to make an omelet, or so the old saying goes. In my case, you have to eat a lot of food, Real and Fake, and visit a lot of places where foods are made, to write a book like this one. I certainly couldn't have done either alone, and there are so many people I have shared these meals with, traveled with, or spoken to that I am doubtless forgetting some and leaving them out in these next few paragraphs. But their contributions are still appreciated, and any such omissions are entirely my bad.

I'll start close to home with the obvious, my wife, and apologize for ruining so many meals for her. Like me, she now knows altogether too much about Real and Fake Food and can no longer countenance bogus sushi or drug-addled industrial beef. While this is a good thing, it makes it harder to eat out. Much harder. On the other hand, she did get to go with me to Parma, Japan, Argentina, Chile, Burgundy, and all sorts of other Real Food places, and to taste Real olive oils at the Culinary Institute of America (CIA) in Napa and Real manchego cheese in Spain, so I guess we are even.

I'd like to especially thank Alice Fixx for first introducing me to the very notion of geographic indications (GIs) and the inequities of our country's approach to them all those many years ago when we visited Parma and Modena together. We saw Parmigiano-Reggiano being made, hams being cured into Prosciutto di Parma, and barrels of grape juice slowly concentrating into balsamic vinegar, and we tasted them all in endless iterations.

This book would have been utterly impossible without the

many experts and artisans who took time out of their busy lives to speak with me: Tom Mueller, author of *Extra Virginity* and all-around olive oil sage; Steven Raichlen, the world's leading authority on cooking with fire, TV host, author many times over, and winner of so many awards I can't count; Leo Bertozzi, director of the Parmigiano-Reggiano Cheese Consortium, for taking so much time to answer my questions about trade, to arrange tastings and meetings with farmers, and for all his insights into the larger world of GIs for food; James Beard Award–winning author and cheese expert Laura Werlin; spirits journalist extraordinaire and *American Wino* author Dan Dunn for his informed insights into the Real and Fake of American winemaking; Bill Briwa, chef-instructor and olive oil expert at the CIA's Napa Valley campus; attorney Steven Kronenberg, who specializes in food fraud and normally gets lots of money per hour for chatting about the subject; Dr. Kimberly Warner, lead scientist at Oceana and the nation's seafood fraud guru; Dr. Mark Stoeckle, MD, DNA researcher, species analysis expert, and fellow golden retriever lover; Dr. David Kessler, former FDA commissioner and public health advocate; Ken Peterson of the Monterey Bay Aquarium, a leading expert on seafood sustainability and aquaculture; Chef Michael Mina, an early adapter of real Japanese beef who spoke to me at length about the subject; butcher extraordinaire George Faison of New York's DeBragga, who did the same; Chef Tom Colicchio, a fellow Real Food enthusiast, who serves only drug-free meats in his many excellent restaurants; Michael Preston, founder and owner of Frenchy's Rockaway Grill in Clearwater Beach, Florida, the ultimate lunch host and ambassador for serving fish caught by the restaurant itself, in his case fantastic grouper; Mike Bradley, founder of Veronica Foods, who not only spoke to me at length about olive and truffle oil but also changed the way American consumers can buy Real olive oil for the better—much better; Chef Troy Lee of the Oak Door steakhouse at the Grand Hyatt Tokyo, arguably the world's best place to sample great beef; Damian Newman, publicist for Japan's Agricultural Bureau for setting up my extensive trip to Kobe and all the facility tours and restaurants; Guillaume Hubert, my host for an insightful trip through France's Champagne region and lots of meetings with winemakers, big and small; Chef David Walzog of SW Steakhouse in the Wynn Las Vegas resort for guiding me through a Kobe and wagyu beef tasting; Thomas Schneller, head chef-instructor in the meat department for the CIA and author of the CIA's textbook *Meat*; Colorado rancher Leo Causland, who raises gorgeous Scottish Highland cattle; David Jessup of Sylvan Dale, a guest ranch serving its overnight guests real grass-fed/ finished beef; zealot Casey Cook, a former U.S. Army Special Forces soldier raising the purest imaginable grass-fed and -finished beef (and also thanks for your service!); Pete Eshelman, author and cattle farmer raising 100 percent genetically pure wagyu cattle the ethical way; media mogul Ted Turner and his ranches and Ted's Montana Grill chain for greatly expanding the profile of bison, one of the most Real Foods available to American consumers; Deborah Rodgers, olive oil maker at California's McEvoy Ranch for giving me the grand tour; and especially to T. J. Robinson for devoting years to sourcing and importing the world's finest Real extra-virgin olive oils through his Fresh-Pressed Olive Oil Club so that I am never without the finest example in my kitchen.

Back to the writing world, I need to thank Jane Lee, my editor at *Forbes*, for giving me the freedom to pursue my most widely read previous Fake Food work, my Fake Kobe beef exposé. Likewise, kudos to Veronica Stoddart, former travel editor at *USA Today* and Ben Abramson, my current editor at *USA Today*, for letting me write the Great American Bites column for the past five years, chasing down regional American foods of every ilk across the continent.

Movie directors leave a lot of good stuff on the cutting room floor, and the same is true for writers, especially when they have a subject as rich and varied as this one. To exacerbate the issue of too much material, I tend to write long, really long, and sometimes in too much detail. Though it has been a long and at times frustrating process, discarding favorite sentences, mind-boggling stats, and more disturbing studies than you could imagine, in the end this work is stronger for it. The thanks for that goes to Amy Gash, my talented Algonquin editor with a velvet-clad iron fist. There are a lot more people at Algonquin involved in what I hope is the success of this work, in marketing, publicity, production, and copy editing, some of whom I may never meet, but thanks to all of you! And thanks to my agent, Larry Weissman, for finding this project a home at Algonquin.

I really love the cover. I'm not a photo- or image-driven person and could not even have offered a suggestion or place to start, but nonetheless it came out exactly as I would have wanted if I had known what I wanted, and for that, the credit goes to Evan Gaffney, and the art department at Algonquin Books.

Closer to home, I need to thank my sister, Elizabeth, and her husband, Randy, who among many other charms, throw the best book parties you can imagine. It's been eight years, way too long, since my last hardcover release and their first soiree. They have filled the void with book parties for nonrelatives, but it is good to be back, especially since they've had practice!

Finally, to my many friends whom I have dragged to some odd places to eat in the pursuit of more food knowledge, especially Rob P., who has the good fortune to have a home in California wine country, which I used as a base for various olive oil and wine research, and Pat G., who has joined me in some legendary Real Food steak and seafood consumption, from New York to France, and Vegas to Alaska.

To all of you, I offer a toast of "Cheers" and raise a glass of Champagne. The one from France.

# THE REAL FOOD REVOLUTION:
## SIGNS OF HOPE

One big leap for a tomato producer, one small step for Real Foods. For years, a company called Simpson Brands has been selling cans of so-called San Marzano tomatoes in supermarkets all over the country. As readers of this book know, the vaunted San Marzano is considered the world's greatest sauce tomato. San Marzanos are strictly regulated for quality and authenticity. Rules govern how the seeds are bred, how closely together the plants can be grown, and how the tomatoes are picked (that is, by hand). The fruits must meet specific size and shape requirements and there are even guidelines for how they can be canned, jarred, processed, flavored, and sold. It is wonderful thing, and means that San Marzanos are a very Real Food.

In the United States, though, as with fake Kobe beef and ersatz Champagne, it has long been legal for producers to call pretty much anything they want San Marzano tomatoes. The mystique of the San Marzano is so giant that the *New York Times* ran an infographic slideshow just about this issue, noting that the sales of the falsely labeled tomatoes hurt the farmers who grow San Marzanos. The Simpson cans were particularly misleading to consumers, with Italianate, homespun-looking labels that clearly—and repeatedly—read San Marzano in prominent type. The cans also read, though not so clearly and in much smaller letters, "Grown domestically in the U.S.A."

All of this came to a crashing halt right around the time this book was released in hardcover. In a surprise move the company voluntarily changed the name of its product to San Merican tomatoes. I applaud this move by Simpson, and consider it a small victory for American consumers—and it is not the only one. Despite all that I have learned about the often-deceptive world of food production, marketing, and distribution, I remain an optimist at heart. Although fakery remains everywhere, two areas in which I have seen significant and encouraging changes are olive oil and seafood.

As I've noted in these pages, after decades of testing extra-virgin olive oil and finding plenty of fakes, the FDA simply decided to stop trying. But in 2016, the U.S. Congress ordered the FDA to resume testing imported extra-virgin olive oil for adulteration and misbranding. Their specific concern was the safety threat to Americans allergic to soy and/or peanuts—the congressional committee's report cited the presence of seed oils in so-called olive oil as a "serious health threat to consumers." This is hardly new news, but I'm glad something is finally being done about it.

At roughly the same time, Italy announced plans to use sophisticated counterfeit techniques on olive oil and create a new high-tech, tamper-proof certification for bottles of real extra-virgin olive oil. It has not happened yet, but it's another step in the right direction. And just this spring, one of the world's largest olive oil brands, Salov North America Corp., owner of the Filippo Berio brand, agreed to settle a class action lawsuit over its labeling practices. The suit alleged that the company's olive oil products were deceptively labeled as "Imported from Italy."

The gist of the lawsuit was that the phrase implied the olives and oil in question were *originally* from Italy, which is more desirable to American consumers, and thus led shoppers to pay a higher price than they would have had they been aware that the contents included olives and oil from other countries. Although other mislabeling still remains, the elimination of the "Imported from Italy" loophole is another small win for consumers.

The bottom line is that it is quickly becoming easier for consumers to select and buy high quality real extra-virgin olive oil, and as consumer awareness grows and demand rises more good players step in to meet the need. Governments are also taking a more active role in policing oil, both in the United States and abroad. But there is still a long way to go. Tests in Germany in 2016 found that about half of all retail oil sold as EVOO failed to meet legal standards. And in 2015, the Italian newspaper *La Stampa* tested twenty leading brands and found 45 percent of them fake. That same year, in "Operation Mama Mia," Italian police seized two thousand tons of fake EVOO, worth nearly $15 million. Just two months later, they seized another twenty-two tons of counterfeit oil in Tuscany. That's no simple labeling error or small-scale, mom-and-pop fraud. These kinds of EVOO scandals are worldwide, taking place as far afield as Ghana and Taiwan.

When it comes to seafood the progress is similar: two steps forward, one step back. Sushi in particular remains a nightmare scenario for Fake Food, with study after study confirming the slim chance of ever getting the real thing. *The Dr. Oz Show*, *The Doctors*, *20/20*, and *Inside Edition*, as well as local news stations and newspapers around the country, all conducted their own independent investigations using DNA testing, and they all found extremely high levels of fraud. A four-year study of Los Angeles sushi restaurants conducted by UCLA from 2012 to 2015 found just under half (47 percent) of all sushi mislabeled. Notable substitution rates ranged from "just" 13 percent (one in seven) for salmon to 100 percent for both halibut and red snapper. These were never real! For four years! In the nation's second-biggest city!

So where's the good news? Not at your local sushi bar, that's for sure. But several bigger-picture events have conspired that taken together dangle hope on the horizon, maybe in the not-so-distant future.

In this book I mention the scathing report by the Government Accountability Office on the FDA's oversight of imported seafood. It noted that the administration routinely failed to come remotely close to meeting its congressional mandate to inspect 2 percent of imported seafood. After the report, the FDA began implementing a new project called Seafood Compliance and Labeling Enforcement (SCALE). It compares samples to a genetic database. Early tests were encouraging, flagging at least a dozen producers and importers for violations and earning them temporary bans. SCALE also immediately began generating important data, including one study revealing that 85 percent of inspected seafood was correctly labeled at the last point of wholesale distribution. This suggests that, contrary to conventional wisdom, it's not the Byzantine food supply chain—i.e., importers and distributors—that is to blame for most fraud; instead, restaurants and retailers are pulling most of the bait-and-switches. This knowledge, in turn, should make Fake Food easier to police.

Another immediate payoff from SCALE? The number of shipments of imported shrimp turned away at our borders by the FDA jumped 74 percent from 2014 to 2015, mainly because they finally started testing them. In 80 percent of the cases, the reason for refusal was the detection of illegal or banned antibiotics in the shrimp. The bad news here is that this has been going on forever. The good news is that we are finally doing something about it. However, while the groundwork for SCALE was completed in 2014, the training of investigators and setup of interagency cooperation remain officially "on hold" indefinitely—which means, so does widespread implementation.

More progress occurred in 2014 when President Obama used an executive memorandum to create the Presidential Task Force on Combatting Illegal, Unreported, and Unregulated (IUU) Fishing and Seafood Fraud. And in 2016, the United Nations also jumped on board with an Agreement on Port State Measures to Prevent, Deter, and Eliminate Illegal, Unreported, and Unregulated Fishing. Familiarly known as the Port State Agreement, it requires participating countries to verify the origin of the catch of any fishing boat arriving in their ports, which is a very strong tool for enforcement. The agreement was approved way back in 2009, but it required twenty-five national signatories to take effect, and that just occurred last June. This is a sea change, and American consumers will be among those it benefits.

Nonprofits, NGOs, and even individual chefs have also become much more involved in fighting the good seafood fight. The Monterey Bay Aquarium has continued providing consumers with educational resources and buying guides. The Freshwater Institute, another nonprofit, built the nation's first and only closed-tank salmon farm in rural West Virginia. I toured it, and this drug-free, low-impact method may well be the future of sustainable aquaculture. Global Fishing Watch is a new collaboration between Google, an environmental nonprofit called Oceana, and Skytruth, an organization that uses cutting-edge technology, data mining, and predictive algorithms, along with aerial and satellite imaging and on-board transponders, to watch boat behavior, predict and detect illegal fishing, and notify police.

Activist chefs like Rick Moonen and Kerry Heffernan are using their platforms to push consumption of more sustainable species. I think these "underutilized species" are one of the most promising frontiers for Real Food progress, and I joined Chef Heffernan to talk about them on *The Dr. Oz Show*. Because they are less commercially desirable and valuable, underutilized species are less counterfeited, far less expensive for consumers, often taste better, and are better for Mother Nature. They're a promising answer to the question I am asked most often: "How can I eat Real Food on a normal budget?" Next time you get scared by the antibiotics in shrimp, consider sautéing some squid, which has a similar taste profile but is drug-free. Pacific rockfish is up to ten times cheaper than similar red snapper, yet many chefs think it tastes even better, and unlike with snapper, you will actually get it when you buy it. Ninety percent of the fish Americans eat comes from just ten species, but there are more than five hundred commercially available options. So skip the red snapper, but next time you see porgy or dogfish on a menu, order it.

Seafood is likely the most complicated of all the topics raised in *Real Food/Fake Food*, and there is no easy one-size-fits-all solution to all of its problems. But what I find encouraging is a rising tide of action at so many different levels, coupled with increasing consumer awareness. With such widespread movement, we are starting to see real change. The same is true in varying degrees for many of the other problem sectors herein. Especially now, I remain hopeful that we are on the cusp of a Real Food revolution.